About the Author

Jeremy Hardy became a stand-up comedian in January 1984, and went on to win the Perrier Comedy Award at the Edinburgh Festival Fringe in 1988. A regular on BBC Radio 4, Jeremy was best known for his appearances on panel shows *The News Quiz* and *I'm Sorry I Haven't a Clue*, as well as for *Jeremy Hardy Speaks to the Nation* – which ran for ten series – and *Jeremy Hardy Feels It*.

Jeremy died on 1 February 2019. He is survived by his wife, Katie Barlow, and his daughter, Elizabeth. This collection is edited by Katie, and Jeremy's long-time producer, David Tyler.

Jeremy was posthumously awarded the Comedians' Comedian Award for Outstanding Achievement in 2020.

Jeremy Hardy
Speaks Volumes

words, wit, wisdom, one-liners and rants

Edited by Katie Barlow and David Tyler

First published in Great Britain in 2020 by Two Roads
An Imprint of John Murray Press
An Hachette UK company

This paperback edition published in 2020

1

A CIP catalogue record for this title is available from the British Library

Paperback ISBN 978 1 529 30036 9
eBook ISBN 978 1 529 30037 6

Typeset in Simoncini Garamond by Palimpsest Book Production Ltd.,
Falkirk, Stirlingshire

Printed and bound in Great Britain by Clays Ltd, Elcograf S.p.A.

Two Roads policy is to use papers that are natural, renewable
and recyclable products and made from wood grown in sustainable forests.
The logging and manufacturing processes are expected to conform to
the environmental regulations of the country of origin.

Two Roads
Carmelite House
50 Victoria Embankment
London EC4Y 0DZ

www.tworoadsbooks.com

Dedicated to all Jeremy loved and all who loved him

Contents

A Few Words from Jack Dee

Jeremy Hardy was one of the stand-ups I saw when I visited The Comedy Store for the very first time one September evening in 1986. Here was this peculiar man in a (not deliberately) appalling cardigan who seemed, effortlessly, to resist all convention. Was he twenty-five or fifty-five? Subversive misfit or the indignant member of a caravaners club who had somehow teleported onto a West End stage? Part of Jeremy's appeal was that he had the air of not quite belonging to the newly emerged UK comedy scene whilst simultaneously defining the very best of it. Like everybody else in the audience, I realised that I was watching an outstandingly funny, original and charismatic performer. But I can also pinpoint that evening as a turning point in my life, and the catalytic moment that resulted in me approaching the MC and putting my name down for the open mic spot. It was my stand-up debut and the start of my career as a comic. (When I got to know Jeremy and told him this, by way of a tribute he responded with his characteristic, 'Ah, bless'.)

A few years later, Jeremy and I made Jack and Jeremy's Real Lives *for Channel 4. You might even remember the first episode. If you remember episodes two to six then you were probably an insomniac in the 90s or you were working nights with access to a television because, after the critical mauling it received, we were mercilessly dumped from our 10 p.m. slot to something approaching dawn. This felt like a career-ending disaster at the time but, as an experience, it had two redeeming elements. One was that if I was going to crash and burn, who better to do it with than the person I most admired in comedy? The second was that, throughout our subsequent friendship, one of my favourite ruses when chatting with Jeremy on those long car journeys to* I'm Sorry I Haven't A Clue *recordings and live shows was to mention* Real Lives *and then sit back and enjoy the tirade of abuse that he still held in reserve for those critics, TV executives and even several crew members who had, in his view, conspired to thwart our budding double-act. There was something majestic about his genius for not letting go, for not forgetting and not moving on. It just got increasingly hilarious each time he listed the perpetrators, what they had said or done and, more importantly, what rightly should happen to them if this was a fair world in which karmic justice could be relied upon to deliver retribution. It was as if Jeremy needed his resentments not in order to exercise any real malice, but to add vivid colour to his comedic palette – and for the sheer wicked joy of being utterly unreasonable.*

Certainly, much of his stand-up material is steeped in the unfinished business of long-held and knowingly petty grudges. Even when he was gravely ill towards the end of 2018 he insisted on listing for me all the things that would be rubbish about his memorial and the various people from his past that it would annoy him to see there. By then, I suppose, he was whistling in the dark, enjoying at least an audience of one, having been forced to step down from his planned tour. (In fact, his memorial was an extraordinary celebration of Jeremy's life in a packed Battersea Arts Centre, attended by family and friends from the worlds of comedy, music, politics and the media. There were so many contributors who wanted to speak or sing that it lasted for more than six hours and I don't think any of us wanted it to end.)

To focus on the casual and mischievous misanthropy that underpinned so much of his wit is, however, a mistake and does Jeremy no justice. Jeremy was a master of silliness. He was informed and profound, but these were really only ever back notes to his wild, comic exaggerations and ludicrous rants. I remember him saying to me once that our job, as comedians, was to never lose sight of our own ridiculousness. He never did.

As a political comedian he was peerless. Even at his most acerbic he remained disarmingly funny, like a child savant reducing the grown-ups to hysterics with his atrocious outbursts. But his political rhetoric was no hollow piece of stagecraft. Jeremy's life was inextricably bound to the causes that he cared so much about. It is no idle claim to say that he impacted hundreds of people's lives in the most positive way. He campaigned tirelessly for some of the most demonised figures in our society without ever evangelising or seeking credit, other than positive results, for his activism.

One of my favourite things was Jeremy's knack for remastering clichés for comic effect. Who could fail to love a comedian who starts a show with 'Thank you for joining me at this difficult time'? Or who greets a friend at the front door with 'Ah Doctor, thank goodness you've come'. Climbing out of the car after I'd driven him back from North Wales he said 'Give my love to Jane' (my wife), adding 'She'll know what I mean'. I still remember him snorting with laughter as he walked away – rightfully delighted with his quip. In comedy, everything Jeremy said was struck through with real mirth and an unstoppable sense of the absurd. There was never any self-importance or preachiness that can so easily contaminate topical comic routines.

I don't know a single stand-up comedian (including, or perhaps especially, Jeremy) who would enjoy seeing their material in print. It is an ungenerous medium for such a nuanced and idiosyncratic artform. Reading song lyrics cannot be a substitute for hearing the singer, but it can enrich that experience and give us insights that might otherwise be missed. So too with Jeremy's material. As I suspect you'll agree as you read on, it thoroughly deserves to be archived and preserved in this format. The book has been compiled with great care and obvious pride by David and Katie and stands as a fitting tribute to one of the great comic talents of our generation. For those that followed Jeremy as a comedian it provides a fine and rather touching reminder of his brilliance; but for future readers, I hope it will serve as an introduction – who knows, perhaps even a study guide – to a comedian who should not be forgotten.

And a Few More by Mark Steel

Jeremy Hardy made us laugh.

For example, at the memorial on the Kent coast for our close friend, Linda Smith, a fairly pompous celebrant asked us each to 'take a flower, and cast it into the sea, taking the moment, as we do so, to pause. And as we pause, I want you to think of Linda.' Jeremy was sat next to me and said, 'Thanks for that advice, as I was going to take that moment to think of General Franco.' I got the giggles, and this made him laugh, until we were both howling so much it disrupted the rest of her monologue.

It was the sort of reaction you expected from Jeremy, whose comedy seemed to be driven by a unique cocktail of social outrage and infantile mischief. I was at a dinner party in his flat, with my son who was about eleven, and several people were sat formally as the meal was being dished up. One guest politely asked Jeremy if he could pass the salad, and he immediately replied, 'Get it yourself you lazy wanker'. My son thought it was the funniest thing ever and laughed for an hour. Because what children understand at that age is that to be funny, you have to be naughty.

Jeremy's ability to combine masterfully crafted comedic

social commentary with brazen cheekiness, meant you had no idea what would come next. One week on The News Quiz *he answered a question about refugees who, according to the government, were older than they were claiming to be. He responded with a powerful improvised routine, in which he suggested certain activities, such as escaping from war-torn lands on a dinghy, could make you look older than you actually were. Then he turned to the presenter Miles Jupp and said, 'Or another example is Miles, who has five children. That's why he's only forty but looks like Margaret Rutherford in her later years'. Somehow he'd gone from the plight of people fleeing Syria, to naughty schoolboy, while giving maximum respect to both conditions.*

Maybe he was helped by a speed of thought that allowed him to find the perfect phrase, as quick as he could say it. In one News Quiz *routine he pretended to be a member of the gentry in Cornwall, beginning, 'This very morning I had been playing the harpsichord to my falcon'. Most of us would spend hours trying to find such a fitting combination, but Jeremy found it with instant instinct.*

Of the generation of stand-ups who circulated around the new comedy clubs of the nineteen-eighties, Jeremy was one of the first to attract his own following, and within five years of his first gigs he was winning national awards and attracting the attention of TV executives. But he never seemed to be comfortable in this world, and the further he travelled from celebrity, the more contented he appeared to be.

So he found his home on radio, and in countless shows in

theatres across Britain. He described the moments in his dressing room before a show, when he would peruse his notes in solitude, as his most contented of times. Even then, he relished some of the low-key points, such as the evening at an old theatre in Wales, in which he was disturbed in the dressing room by a passing rat. Telling this story, Jeremy said 'The duty manager came in to ask if I needed anything, so I told him about the rat. And he just said, "oh he's back again is he" and left'.

Eventually Jeremy became so distant from the world of TV and celebrity, he rang me to say he'd been asked to go on a peculiar TV show he'd never heard of. I asked what it was called and he tried to explain, until I said 'Is it Pointless'? *'Yes, that's it', he said. 'Have you heard of it'? As a result, he must have been the only person to appear on the show who had never seen it.*

And yet his consistency on the radio and in his live shows resulted in him attracting a bigger following than most people regarded as famous. Year after year he packed theatres in which regulars from TV could only bring half that number. Maybe there was another reason why his shows and radio appearances were so powerful. In any pompous debate about comedy, someone will ask the question 'Is war / violence / climate change a suitable subject for comedy?' This assumes laughing can only be frivolous, that you can make jokes about things that don't matter, but to be funny about anything important trivialises the subject. It's an infuriating suggestion, and Jeremy is the possibly the finest retort. Because he was so funny about serious subjects, not because he didn't care about them, but in part because he cared about them so much.

As if to make that unarguable, Jeremy dedicated himself to an array of magnificently unfashionable causes, such as campaigning for the wrongly imprisoned, often becoming a key figure in the campaign, rather than simply turning up to perform at a benefit or two. Occasionally he pondered whether he should have been a human rights lawyer rather than a comic, but that would probably have been a disastrous idea, as he'd have told the judge 'no you stand up you lazy wanker' and got himself and his client banged up in Guantanamo Bay.

One of the many reasons Jeremy was funny was because he meant it. He wasn't funny despite being a social commentator. Nor he was political for a few minutes, then funny for a few minutes. He was magnificently poignant and outrageously impish, all at once.

A few hours after he'd left us, a journalist from a broadsheet newspaper called me because he was writing an obituary. It became clear this man had no idea who Jeremy was, and he asked 'Would you say Jeremy had any interest in politics? And did he follow sport?' I wish I'd had the presence of mind to say 'He was a member of the East Surrey Conservative Association. And he played Rugby League to a very high standard. And he never missed an episode of Pointless*'.*

A Note on the Text

This book is, by a happy coincidence, exactly what the cover suggests – the words, wit, wisdom, one-liners and rants of Jeremy Hardy – and is the result of an extensive trawl through Jeremy's stand-up sets, newspaper columns and every show he wrote or took part in; pretty much everything apart from some bits which will have to remain forever locked in the bowels of his laptop, a device with which Jeremy had a love-hate-dataloss relationship. Or as Jeremy himself said, 'We were better off when the computer was a big thing with spools which filled a whole warehouse and was operated by a treadle'.

So, we've included material which ranges from the profoundest political satire through to jokes about aubergines, from passionate disquisitions on the plight of refugees to the glorious off-kilter punning of *I'm Sorry I Haven't A Clue*'s 'Uxbridge English Dictionary', 'Midwifery: partway through breaking wind'. And what we re-remembered, while going though all his words, every benefit gig, column, *News Quiz* and all fifty-three(!) of his own BBC Radio 4 shows, was that Jeremy was first and foremost a comedian. He never pandered to his audience, but he never forgot to be howlingly, cryingly *beautifully* funny. His depth of thought was extraordinary but his insight into political realities equally so. Or, as Jeremy said, 'For thousands of years the rallying cry of the Left has been, "I thought *you* were bringing the leaflets".'

Apart from the wonderful reflections by just some of the people who knew and loved him, every word from here on in is written by Jeremy – which includes all the sketches and indeed the conversational bits with the guests actors from *Jeremy Hardy Speaks To The Nation*. Jeremy would delight in putting words into the mouths of the likes of Miranda Richardson, Juliet Stevenson or Father Ted's Pauline McLynn – so whenever there's dialogue, that's all Jeremy's mischievous work.

We've also included extracts from the 'Ask Mr Hardy' parts of his radio shows where he took genuine unprepared questions from the studio audience in a sort of Q & A session or, as Jeremy called it, 'karaoke for the middle classes'.

We hope you enjoy it. Some of it might take your breath away – like the radio critic who said that his show '. . . made me drop the kettle in shock' – but then Jeremy knew you could never please everybody. As he said, 'You know what people who listen to the radio are like. They all sit there naked with balaclavas on, waiting for something to phone in and complain about.'

Jeremy would often begin a show by saying to the audience, 'Thank you for joining me at this difficult time'. For those who knew and loved him, this will always be a difficult time. But knowing that the reader will pick up this book, get that wonderful swooping 'rambling nasal drone' in their head and start to laugh is a comfort. So welcome to, in Jeremy's own words, 'a free and frank exchange of my entrenched views'.

Jeremy Hardy Speaks Volumes

Jeremy Hardy Speaks About . . .

Childhood

'There are lots of funny things children say that charm us, like, "Why is the sky blue?" and "If Grandma lives with Jesus, where does she sleep?" and "I hate you and I wish you were dead".'

My Childhood

Early Stand-up Set, The Cabaret Upstairs, 1985

I suppose 'Jeremy Hardy' is not much of a name for an alternative comedian, but there you go, that's the cross I have to bear. I'm not ashamed of it, I'm in no way embarrassed about being middle class. My father is actually a self-made man, he got himself in kit form originally. I don't know if you know the Airfix range of historical figures? My dad looks a bit like HMS *Victory*.

The only real problem about being middle class is the great shortage of material for comedy. (PAUSE) umm . . . (PAUSE) goodnight.

* * *

Jeremy Hardy Speaks to the Nation, 1993

I come from a place called Mytchett in Surrey, which is a small suburb of the M3. I was born on a council estate but once I'd been called Jeremy, we had to move. My parents bought a little bungalow in suburban Surrey, a county not generally associated with social deprivation. My father had come from a poor family and was fiercely proud to be a homeowner for the first time. He kept inviting people in to use the toilet just because it was indoors. And we were the only Labour family in the street. Because Surrey is something of a Conservative stronghold. In fact, I can remember Methodists still being hunted for sport right into the 1960s.

I suppose that at that time, we were what was described as lower middle class, but this is not a term I like to use, as the lower middle class form the backbone of fascism. This might sound a bit harsh, but it is historically accurate. The shock troops of fascism, its most visible face, are those tattooed and lively young men who have a flair for violence but difficulty in using a spoon. But these are not the ideas men, they just passionately and sincerely believe what they're told. The people behind the scenes doing the telling are always lower-middle-class fascists; people who've worked all their lives to own an ailing small business and some patio doors which no left-handed, pot-smoking asylum seeker is going to be allowed to take away from them.

So who are the lower middle class? Well, they can always be found at Neighbourhood Watch meetings – which I'm not knocking necessarily. If you want to learn German, it's as quick a way as any.

* * *

Early Stand-up Set, The Cabaret Upstairs, 1985

I come from a very large family indeed – mammals as a matter of fact. And my mum was a classic matriarchal figure. She'd say things like, 'Jeremy, you're playing football on the Shabbos? You want to break your mother's heart? Saturday, you should be in shul!' And I'd say, 'Mother, we're Church of England.' Dad was adopted, and obsessed with finding out who his real children were. I was the youngest, I was actually wanted but my mother was thirty-seven, and the doctors said that it would be unwise for her to have another baby – so she had me when I was already four, which meant that I was a bit precocious really, a bit disorientated, mal-adjusted about the whole thing; I couldn't get on with other children. I didn't even have an imaginary friend. I had an imaginary nodding acquaintance. Mum would sometimes lay an extra place for him at dinner time and I'd say, 'Well – I don't really know Colin that well, Mum.'

* * *

Early Stand-up Set, The Cabaret Upstairs, 1986

My father was a very active father, he wanted to teach me things. He was a very keen cyclist for example, and when I was about seven he took me over to the recreation ground and he sat me on my sister's bike. And he held on to the back to steady me while I pedalled along. And I was going up this path at about fifteen miles an hour, and I didn't realise, of course, what he'd done, as all people's dads do at that moment, is let go at the back. I had no idea. I thought he was *deliberately* scraping my knee along the tarmac.

When it came to swimming, though, my parents were picking up at that time in the early sixties on theories that all babies are born with an ability to swim. So, I was a few months old when they took me over to the Aldershot Lido for the very first time. And they lowered me, very gently, into the water and immediately I woke up, realised my nappy was soaking and cried to be changed. But then something took over in me, something I still can't explain to this day, something animal, something inborn – I think really an instinct took over in me. I began to fly south for winter.

* * *

I'm Sorry I Haven't A Clue, 2005

HUMPH (LYTTELTON): Jeremy, I'd like you to suggest some updated nursery rhymes.

JEREMY: Jack and Jill went up the hill
>To fetch a pail of water
>Jack fell down and broke his crown
>And phoned Clumsy Direct, the accident helpline for the greedy and accident-prone

>Jack Sprat could eat no fat
>His wife could eat no lean
>So she ate in McDonald's
>And he in the school canteen

* * *

Jeremy Hardy Feels It, 2017

My parents were born in the 1920s and had no sense of entitlement to constant improvement in their circumstances. They'd lived through the Depression and the war. Known hunger and fear and terrible sadness. They were cautious and worried. They saved and hoarded. My mum had drawers full of used wrapping paper with the Sellotape picked off. In the fridge, she'd keep a single roast potato, housed in a yoghurt carton sealed with cling film – because you never know.

My dad dug for victory. He spent all weekend growing vegetables, and my mum spent all weekend cooking them. There was no *al dente* in those days. We hadn't beaten Mussolini for nothing. A pan stayed on the hob so long, you didn't know if Mum was boiling carrots in it or melting it down to make a Spitfire.

The whole house was stuffed with food and kept at refrigeration temperatures to preserve it. I will probably live till I'm a hundred because I spent my first eighteen years in cryogenic suspension. My date of birth should be the day I left home. My parents didn't need to make a choice between heating and eating, but they did, and they came down firmly on the side of eating, cos you don't need radiators when you've got food. You can just put on another layer, of fat.

* * *

Jeremy Hardy Speaks to the Nation, 2003

We used to have mini-holidays, days out, picnics. We went in for Sunday motoring, which meant eating those hard-boiled eggs with grey yolks you don't see any more, parked in a lay-by on the A3. We had an enormous black Thermos flask with a handle, that looked as though it should contain radioactive isotopes or frozen sperm. In the summer, it held very dilute orange squash and ice cubes. In the winter, it held lukewarm vegetable soup that slipped down easily, and slipped back up just as readily and completely unchanged.

* * *

Early Stand-up Set, The Cabaret Upstairs, 1987

I think like so many of us today, I went to school when I was five years old. A feature of my school was its proximity to the Broadmoor Hospital for the Criminally Insane – this is true, in Camberley there – and the thing about the Broadmoor Hospital was the siren which was tested on Monday mornings at 10 a.m., and local people familiarised themselves with the sound of the siren cos we knew if we heard it at any other time than ten o'clock Monday morning when it was tested, it meant there'd been an escape. Somebody, possibly a dangerous psychotic, was on the loose and then local people and the police would be on their guard.

So at ten o'clock every Monday morning, 500 dangerous psychotics would escape and not be rounded up until Thursday afternoon – by which time they'd have successfully infiltrated the local Rotary Club and the local battalion of the Territorial Army.

I should explain, if anyone's unfamiliar with the Territorials, they're a group of paramilitary insurance salesmen – called 'Territorial' cos, like dogs, they mark out territory by urinating everywhere they go.

* * *

Sometimes I regret the fact that I never had a Gap Year and did the backpacking thing. But, then, 'going travelling' is only a self-important way of going on holiday. Well done, free spirit, you camped out for three nights with the Tuaregs. Did it ever occur to you that you might be imposing? You might feel an incredible affinity with desert people, but perhaps they don't feel the same way about Cotswold people. Do you really think they need the stress of an entitled, arrhythmic games designer wanting to join in their drum circle?

* * *

So, is education a waste of time? As for myself, I applied to the University of Life but couldn't get in so I had to go to Southampton.

* * *

I chose not to go to Cambridge. The reason I chose not to go there is that they chose not to offer me a place and there was no way I was going to humiliate myself by just turning up and starting to unpack my things. And the reason they chose not to give me a place was not that I had the wrong accent or background, but because I wasn't clever enough. That doesn't mean they were right not to give me a place, I wouldn't have been any bother. I wouldn't have got in the way. I mightn't have understood everything but I'd have appreciated it in my own way. And it would have given me a head start in the arts. Definitely. People deny it. My Cambridge friends say, 'If anything, I think it was a disadvantage.' No, bless them, they're wrong. Having any sort of advantage is always an advantage. Saying a Cambridge background is a disadvantage is like saying –

PERSON: If anything, basketball is *harder* for tall people because everyone expects more from you and they resent you, and what they don't realise about tall people is that we're so painfully shy.

* * *

Jeremy Hardy Speaks to the Nation, 2010

In terms of social class, if you want to be in a particular one, your best bet is to grow up in it, because we are not a socially mobile country.

Class is a particularly emotional subject for me because I grew up lower middle class, which is neither one thing nor the other. I get upset by social deprivation, but also by people holding their knife like a pen. If I were *properly* middle class, I wouldn't know anybody who holds their knife like a pen. But I do, and I don't look down on them, I want to protect them. To tell them, 'Listen to me, don't let posh people see you do that, they will think less of you. I don't; I'm on your side. Trust me, I'm your only hope. They're going to despise you anyway. But be hated because you are strong and defiant, not because you are common – I mean downtrodden.'

And the reason I hold fast to my knowledge about knives is that that is the limit of my grasp of etiquette. Knife not like pen, pudding not dessert, 'may I use the lavatory?' not 'can I have a dump?'

I'm just middle class enough to worry about not being middle class enough. I'm jealous of people from a clearly defined background. I hate snobbery and I also hate it when people flaunt their humble origins to impress. They say,

COMMON PERSON: (REGIONAL) Well, Jeremy, speaking as someone from a traditional working-class background . . .

And I say, 'Could you just tell me how much is in my current account, please?' It annoys me because if I were from a working-class background, that's what I'd do, but I can't. I'm also envious of my friends who went to Cambridge, especially the ones from working-class backgrounds because they get to be privileged *and* bitter. How cool would that be?

* * *

Jeremy Hardy Speaks to the Nation, 2014

Am I drawn to people who come from exactly the same substratum of the lower-to-middle middle class as I do? Well, it would be interesting if I could find one. We ate salad cream, but my dad made his own mayonnaise for special occasions. No other family in the world has that.

And we were of different classes within our *own* family. We climbed socially so I was the poshest of five. And then I moved to south London aged twenty-one, and now the rest of Surrey's come to find me. And being lower middle class, I suffer from sympathetic accent syndrome, the subconscious urge to blend that makes people involuntarily lapse into the accent of whoever they're speaking to. My mum did it. We had cousins come to stay from Holland, and my mum would say, 'Vud u like sem brekfist?' and I'd say, 'Mum that's not even Dutch, that's just talking funny. In Holland, Dutch people speak Dutch; they don't speak English in a foreign accent as though they were in a war film.'

And *I* do what my mum did. If I'm talking to John who fixes my car and he says, 'Yer head gasket's gone, Jeremy,' instead of saying, as I should, 'My darling man, I have absolutely no idea what you're saying,' – instead of that I'm like, 'Az it? Me ed geskit? Blardy ell! Yeravinalarfincha? Cam ere, ed geskit, I'll av you, yer lil bleeder.'

And then, if I'm speaking to someone who's upper middle class, I become fantastically RP and say fewer all the time, even when it's wrong. 'Are you going to the Henry Moore exhibition?' 'I think you mean the Henry *Fewer* exhibition.'

Reaching Adulthood

Jeremy Hardy Speaks to the Nation, 2014

All nicknames are to be grown out of. I can't abide meeting people who say, 'My real name is Penelope, but when I was younger, my little brother couldn't pronounce it and called me Ploppy and so everyone calls me that', and I think, you're thirty-eight and you're representing me in court.

* * *

Jeremy Hardy Speaks to the Nation, 2010

Some people will tell me that's all very well my being comfortable with immigration when I live in trendy cosmopolitan London. What about people in smaller, monocultural communities, they ask. It's harder for them to adjust and accept newcomers.

Well . . . I grew up on the borders of Hampshire and Surrey in the 1960s. You could not have got more monocultural than that, and I couldn't wait to get out of it. My mum tells me that the first time I saw a black man in the street, I thought he was a man made of chocolate. I don't believe that story. I think it much more likely that it *was* a man made of chocolate than a black person in Mytchett in 1965.

But in 1982 I moved to London and immediately my eyes were opened to a whole new world. What's that smell, I wondered? That's jerk chicken. What's jerk chicken? It's Caribbean and really spicy. And there was real Indian curry, not the spicy trifle white people made. There is every kind of restaurant in London: Malaysian, Lebanese, Peruvian. There are Ethiopian restaurants. You think what happens in there, does the food fall out of a plane? But it's like Eritrean food with that pancakey thing.

But this isn't just about food. I'm not just being a pig. What I mean is that every part of the world is represented in London. And now I've lived in London for more than half my life and I can honestly say that I can be the only white person on the bus and not notice. Conversely, if I'm on the bus and everybody's white, I think, 'Blimey, there really *are* a lot of Polish people in the country.'

Because there are, but so what? There are a lot of Polish people. Some days it feels a bit strange, but so what? It's just a feeling. It's my problem and I should deal with it. Not develop it into an Action Plan. There are days when I'm at the bus stop and I hear people speak and I think, 'What's happening? Everyone's Polish.' But then I see someone who's black and I think, 'Well, he's obviously not Polish or he's unlikely to be . . . and she looks South American, and I know him, he's my neighbour and he's Muslim so he's probably not Polish even though quite a lot of people are Polish, but it's not really a problem. I mean, in Poland, *loads* of people are Polish and they seem to manage. If anything, they'd like *more* Polish people in Poland because so many have left but a lot are going back so it'll be all right.'

Because it *will* be all right. It always evens out. Every few years there's a big panic about immigration and then it all calms down, because we do cope and people do fit in and come to belong here.

Now I'm not saying you're evil if you feel the occasional little spasm of prejudice. Feelings are involuntary. Human beings have all kinds of weird feelings. Morals come into play when we decide whether or not to *indulge* those feelings. You might feel you want to hug the other commuters on the railway platform, you might feel you want to grab their private parts. Most likely you'll feel you want to push them in front of the oncoming train. What's important is that you know that none of those actions is appropriate and at least two are an invasion of personal space.

* * *

Jeremy Hardy Speaks to the Nation, 2014

I moved to London from Surrey, which is a journey of only forty miles but I was forced to leave Surrey because I was at risk of suicide. And as so many migrants do, I now resent new migrants moving to what I now consider my patch. Other middle-class, media people making the same journey and diluting the authentic Afro-Caribbean character of the Brixton area. Nip out to buy a plantain and find a pop-up locally sourced restaurant where a Caribbean veg shop used to be. I look around me thinking, 'Dis area seen some changes, you could be in downtown Guildford.'

* * *

Musicport, 2016

I am white British of British descent. I am one of the whitest people I know. I've done my family tree. I thought, this will be interesting. It really wasn't. I thought I had to be *something*; a bit Jewish. I was born in Hampshire. I went back 200 years of family history, the furthest I could get from Hampshire was Norfolk, which is a blind alley in terms of diversity – a family tree turns into a poplar once you get up there.

So, I am probably the most Englishist person that I know, apart from my siblings. But I don't care. It doesn't make me have any more claim to this soil than anybody else. I'm a migrant because I moved from Hampshire to Surrey, and then I moved from Surrey to London and that means I'm a migrant. People move. Most of you are probably migrants. You probably don't live where you were born because that was a hospital and they'd be getting pissed off with you by now. They need the beds.

The Uxbridge English Dictionary

HUMPH: Jeremy, I'd like you to supply examples of words in English that have acquired new definitions:

5-A-Side / To kill a boy band

Asking / King of the Bottoms

Brothel / A place you go to buy illicit soup

Circumspect / Point of view of a Rabbi

Cogitate / Pensioners' art gallery

Copulate / The time it takes the police to show up in an emergency

Deferral / A bikini wax

Dermatology / The study of Irish names

Dictator / A humorously shaped root vegetable

Dignitas / Donkey sanctuary with a difference

Dissuade / To insult Hush Puppies

Jeremy by Rory Bremner

When I try to sum up Jeremy, the trouble is that he got there first, so it's always his lines that I hear in my head. 'My name's Jeremy Hardy. I'm going to make you laugh. Going to make you cry. Play your cards right, I'll make you breakfast.' That is the first line I remember.

On my first ever tour, visiting small theatres and student unions in 1984, Jeremy was my support act. It should have been the other way round. 'Middle-class, uninteresting, unethnic comedian from Surrey' was how the poster described him, quoting some underwhelming review. But that was Jeremy's style. He wore it like the cardigans he would wear on stage, always unfussy and unshowy but funnier than all the rest of us put together. 'People say I'm self-deprecating,' he'd say, 'but I don't think I'm very good at that'. Of his short stature, he'd say, 'I'm not that small. Compared to my genitals, I'm huge'.

I met Jeremy on the circuit around 1984. He'd come to London a couple of years before and was living in a squat behind King's Cross Station. Being Jeremy, he'd applied to the Thatcher government for a business grant as a stand-up comedian and got a £40-a-week small business development allowance. He was writing for radio light entertainment shows like Week Ending *and* The News Huddlines *and doing stand-up in the evenings in the clubs along with people*

19

like Paul Merton, Julian Clary, Jenny Éclair and Mark Steel. What was brilliant about Jeremy was that he arrived fully-formed, the finished article. If you see pieces from him in 1986, 1987, 1988 and compare them to his later work, it's the same delivery, the same rhythm, the same confidence. He'd shuffle almost shyly onto the stage and deliver brilliant self-deprecating one-liners, each one better than the last. He didn't have to sell them, they were so good already and if one didn't go perfectly, he had plenty more. Fellow comics would watch and wonder at his ability to charm and defuse audiences with the sheer quality and originality of his material. It's no exaggeration to say his downbeat, deadpan style inspired a whole generation of stand-ups on the 1980s cabaret circuit.

For Jeremy it was never about fame and fortune, but about people and causes that he took on and supported all his life. There were benefits for the miners, for the Birmingham Six, for refugees. And one where, for the first time, I saw him actually heckled. At a benefit, for heaven's sake! He didn't break rhythm, he just said, 'I don't do put downs, I just have people followed home and their houses burnt down'. A great line, but possibly not that evening, when we were raising money for the victims of the Bradford fire disaster.

Around that time, I was living in my brother's house in Fulham and Jeremy moved in. He later said to Jack Dee, 'I lived in Rory's attic. That's why he looks so young'. I was always off doing gigs, just coming back and shoving my clothes in the washing machine, 'You don't have clothes Rory do you? You've just got washing'. He'd take the piss out of me trying to cook, 'Those flavours don't belong together, that's like making a fish trifle. Look everyone, Rory's making a liver meringue pie'. When I got my first BBC series in 1986 it was like a gang show, with acts from the circuit – Jim Sweeney and Steve Steen, the Flaming Hamsters, John Dowie – and Jeremy. We had to find a way of incorporating his individual style so Marcus Mortimer, the director, came up with the idea of him being the boom operator, a wry BBC staffer who could share his view of the world. They certainly got that. Never afraid to bite the hand that fed him, he ended his very first appearance with 'At the BBC, you have to start at the bottom. And kiss it'.

He always enjoyed and parodied that peculiar Englishness of the old black and white films (his favourite self-image was as Wilfrid Hyde-Whyte, being wheeled round the ward in his pyjamas, saying 'Everyone's been very kind'). But his distaste for the twee and complacent attitudes and the cant of the privileged middle classes found an outlet in the inspired, brilliant and peerlessly funny 'rants' that marked his radio appearances from Jeremy Hardy Speaks to the Nation to The News Quiz. No subject was spared his originality and irreverence: politics, social attitudes, even the crucifixion. ('People blame the Jews. But I've got lots of Jewish friends and they're all hopeless at DIY. They could never get a cross to stand up like that, not for three days.') Apparently spontaneous, his flights of imagination were in fact brilliantly conceived, fuelled by genuine rage or exasperation, and unfailingly, show-stoppingly funny, often featuring voices and accents for which he had a remarkably good ear. Particularly remarkable, consid-

ering his appalling singing, which became a highlight of his appearances on Radio 4's I'm Sorry I Haven't a Clue.

There was so much to love about Jeremy, his humour, his intelligence, the fact that his material and his politics always worked together which, as every comedian knows, is really hard to do without being mawkish or pious or preachy. If people did applaud him when he made a point, he'd say, 'Don't clap, that means you agree but it's not very funny'.

Jeremy by Paul Bassett Davies

*I met Jeremy about thirty-five years ago, when we were both writing bitingly satirical sketches fo*r Week Ending *on BBC Radio 4. Those sketches were so scathingly powerful that the Thatcher government collapsed a mere seven years later.*

I was also present at Jeremy's first ever gig as a stand-up. There were about thirty people there, at least two of whom were aspiring stand-ups themselves, and after Jeremy's set, when they discovered it was his first one, they promptly gave up. I'm not saying Jeremy didn't put in years of hard work to develop his craft, it's just that everything was there from the beginning, especially his extraordinary imagination.

We've all experienced the unique pleasure of hearing Jeremy go off on one of his extended tirades, and the breathtaking inventiveness of those unstoppable flights of fancy, when you didn't even want to laugh because you were so intent on hearing every word of what he was saying and where he was going with it. For me, that was a kind of inspired, sublime playfulness and, of all Jeremy's gifts, I loved that gift for play most of all.

Play is not the same as frivolity. You've only got to see small children playing, to watch the commitment they bring to it, to know that. And I think Jeremy's gift for play was part of his political activism; it's all about imagination and conviction. And what else was Jeremy's courageous commitment to justice and equality if not a supreme act of imagination? He imagined a better world and put his whole heart into making it happen. I see that as the very highest kind of play.

Of course, Jeremy was also capable of the very lowest kind of play. The most fun I've ever had was when we worked together, especially on our own radio sitcom. The ways we distracted ourselves from working – working that was more like playing in any case – were invariably puerile and often disgusting. But sometimes we laughed until we cried, and I value the memory of that laughter more than almost anything in my life.

I loved spending time with Jeremy. I'll never stop missing him, and I feel very lucky to have been his friend. I was with him for a couple of hours a few days before he died and after we'd said goodbye, just as I was walking out of the door, he looked up and said, 'Don't worry.' And those were the last words he ever said to me. I'll always remember it as his final message to me, and all of us. Don't worry.

2

Jeremy Hardy Speaks About . . .

Settling Down

*'My daughter wanted a new pair
of trainers. I told her, "You're eleven,
make your own!"'*

Love and Marriage

Aspects of the Fringe, 1986

I could tell you a bit about my sex life – since you ask. I used to do a lot of casual sex. I did it in a safari suit, actually.

No, it's not true, I've never had much of a sex life, but I have always had lots of very close friends who 'don't think about me in that way' and I think that's very supportive of them, really. In particular, I met a woman about eighteen months ago, and we became very close friends and for a while it was a very intense sort of close friendship, but there was no sex because she said that it would 'spoil things'. Spoil her sex life, I suppose. She said that she just 'wanted to be like a sister to me'. So she breaks things and then blames me for it. I told her that I used to have baths with my sisters, but she wasn't impressed by that, oddly.

I've always been very unlucky in love; when I was twenty-one I caught a Platonically Transmitted Disease. Got glandular fever from sucking somebody else's security blanket.

And to tell you the honest truth, I used to have a lot of trouble, personally, in bed, in bringing . . . somebody

27

else . . . to the point . . . of sexual ecstasy. Cos I was always alone.

* * *

The News Quiz, 2010

JEREMY: The Tories have to make a big deal about marriage, because for Tories marriage is a hallowed and sacred institution, so sacred that it's worth bribing people to do it. And you think there's already plenty of incentive for people to get married, because they reach thirty and they think, 'Well, I've already slept with everybody I was considering so I may as well keep this one', and so they get married and then they write to everybody that they know and everybody's forced to give them a present. This was based on a time when people had nothing; they were still living with their parents, they'd never seen each other's pudenda inside a building and they had no belongings, they were starting out in life and they needed everything, but when people have been cohabiting for five years they've *got* eggcups. So what do they do? They do a John Lewis thing where you're forced to spend forty quid buying them a quince spoon stand made of Waterford crystal. 'Oh,' they say, 'Oh actually, we've already got everything, so a gift of money would be most welcome.' I don't mind the charity thing where they say, 'Could you buy an owl for this village in Burkina Faso where we met when we were trekking and everyone was so smiling and poor but unhappy in their simple way . . .'

SANDI: You see, up until then, I was really pleased with the owl you gave me . . .

Fertility

Jeremy Hardy Speaks to the Nation, 1994

Man's sex drive is believed to be sublimated by other activities. American social anthropologist Myra Belsinger, in her book *Is the Erection an Extension of the Penis?*, argues, for example, that aggressive driving is a typically male displacement activity. 'The automobile,' she writes, 'is merely a substitute phallus.' But if this were so, you wouldn't drive too fast. You'd just back in and out of the garage – or maybe just polish the car a lot.

* * *

Jeremy Hardy Speaks to the Nation, 1994

I'm joined by an expert in fertility, and TV personality, Dr Alistair Handsome. Alistair, what steps can a man take to maximise the likelihood of fertilisation?

ALISTAIR: Oh, well, a man's sperm count can be
adversely affected by heat, caffeine and alcohol, so try
to avoid soaking your plums in Irish coffee before sex.

Diet is also very important. A healthy diet will contain a
balance of foods to provide all the nutrients you need but
will make you very depressed because there won't be any
sweeties or crisps in it. Worrying certainly isn't going to help
matters, but if it makes you feel better, you may as well keep
doing it for the sake of your peace of mind.

Timing too is key. Many women can tell if they are ovulating
by the texture of their mucus, so blow your nose before sex
and have a look. If this doesn't work, which it won't, try
using a thermometer, although a penis is usually more effec-
tive. A woman may be able to calculate when her ovulations
should take place by looking at her diary or calendar. If she
finds a date when she has an important job interview, that
will be the day when her period starts and she can work it
out from there. It's important not to waste your goes by
doing it on the wrong days because then you'll just start
enjoying yourselves and forget what you're supposed to be
doing it for.

But are we trying too hard to have babies? Fertility treatment is an increasingly controversial subject. For most men,
it is hard to accept the fact that there could ever be anything
wrong with their sperm other than the fact that it's very
hard to clean off a suede jacket. But if you suspect you might
have a problem, 'DON'T PANIC!' Get your GP or someone

who knows a bit about medicine to refer you to a fertility clinic and arrange to have your semen analysed. You will be given a small plastic flask. This has the word 'sterile' on it which isn't very encouraging. It also has a childproof lid which I'm sure is considered a great joke in fertility clinics. You will also be given an instruction manual – 'manual' being the operative word. The instructions will tell you not to have an ejaculation for four days before producing your sample. That is because, after four days without an ejaculation, you will quite fancy the small plastic flask.

But what are the experts looking for? In a word: sperms. The analyst will conduct a sperm count. To do this he has to catch and ring the sperms. This is quite painless and the sperms often see it as a game. (All the vegetarians are worried now. There'll be animal rights activists breaking into sperm labs and setting them free in the countryside. 'Swim, Tarka, swim!') Anyway, when the total number is added up, the clinic will be able to tell you your sperm count. If your count is low or non-existent, you have a fertility problem. This is not the same thing as being impotent. It does not affect your ability to perform sexually but it does mean that you've spent two years leaping off the wardrobe onto your partner holding a stopwatch and a wall-planner for no very good reason.

And the worst thing about finding out that you can't have children is that the person you will probably find out from will be a hospital receptionist, or 'border guard' as they are now called. In my view, hospital receptionists should not be given the job of imparting delicate information to people, because they do not have interpersonal skills. They should be working underground, without light or air. There may be no preparatory phone call from them, no appointment with your consultant, they'll probably just shout your results from an open window when you're walking past one day.

This all sounds very bleak, but the battle isn't lost yet. It is unlikely that you have *no* sperms. You probably just don't have very many, or it may be that your sperms are non-swimmers. In this case, you may be looking for a donor. Many people carry a semen donor card. In the event of their having an accident, their sperm can be used to help someone who needs it. Alternatively, you can go to your nearest sperm bank and ask to see the small business adviser.

What to Expect When You're Expecting

Jeremy Hardy Speaks to the Nation, 1994

For women, you probably won't feel like sex when you first become pregnant because you'll have done it so much in the last two years. Men must also bear in mind that all the nausea and vomiting will leave her feeling quite unsexy, so it's best to lay off the drink for a while if you do want her to do it with you. You may also be nervous that sex with your partner might damage the baby in some way. In this case, you should talk to your GP, who will examine you and either set your mind at rest or suggest you enter a competition.

Some men feel unattractive during pregnancy but only if they were unattractive beforehand. But your partner may need some reassurance. Try telling her that you find the gravid turn of her belly and heavy, blue-veined breasts very sexy, although she'll probably think you're weird.

In any case, as the time of the birth approaches, it is wise to abstain from coital sex, particularly if you are in an ambulance.

* * *

Jeremy Hardy Speaks to the Nation, 1994

As well as choosing a name, you may also want to choose a sex for your child. Clinics offering gender selection now have a success rate of up to 50 per cent. The male and female gametes are separated thus. Semen is put into a tube of water. The male sperms separate from the females by swimming faster, because the females are all doing breaststroke so as not to get their faces in the water.

But trying to predetermine the sex of an infant is controversial. You should remember that babies are born sightless and covered in fur, and do not develop a gender until they are seven or eight years old. It is vital that you let the child determine her own sex at her own pace.

Conditioning is very influential so clothes will affect the outcome. In the past, parents disappointed by the sex of their offspring have sometimes dressed children in the clothes of the sex they wanted. I was the fifth child and what my parents really wanted was a holiday, so they dressed me as a caravan until I was eleven.

* * *

Jeremy Hardy Speaks to the Nation, 1994

One thing which faces all prospective fathers is vastly increased expenditure. And there is such a bewildering array of goods on the market that you can be quite perplexed about what to buy for a new baby. In general, it is best to choose small things. Babies are not very big and tend to be rather dwarfed by a double bed or size thirteen Dr. Martens. You can waste an awful lot of time and money if you're not absolutely clear what you will actually need. Here is a checklist which I hope is a useful guide. One: Clothes, Two: Bottles. Three: Nappies and that. Four: Other stuff. You will also need to go to classes and keep lots of towels boiling.

The other thing you can usefully do is to choose a name. Jeremy is probably the best name for a boy – Jeremella for a girl. The origin is biblical, deriving from the prophet Jeremiah. Biblical names are always favourites, although Herod, Judas and Sodom are to be avoided. Also try to avoid a name which has been made temporarily fashionable by a film or TV series. If you've ever met a man called Spartacus, you'll know what I mean.

* * *

Although attitudes to adoption have improved, many people have a prejudice about it they aren't even aware of. I've heard parents described as having one child of their own and one adopted one, as if it's the difference between an actual child and one made of plastic. The prejudice multiplies when you adopt from abroad. Journalists have a field day with this subject. When a journalist writes 'Childless couples' you can interpret it as meaning 'broken desperate lizard people who will stop at nothing to get a baby from somewhere'. And people who've read about your story in the paper will catch sight of you in the supermarket and wheel their tots away from you in case you grab them and try to pay for them at the checkout. Even quite close friends will dumbfound you with questions like these,

DEBBIE: So how do you go about it then? Do you just phone their Embassy and they send one round?

GORDON: So, how much did it cost to have the real parents murdered?

DEBBIE: Inter-country adoption? Is that when they buy a Turkish man's kidneys, transplant them into your sperm and you give birth on behalf of an American couple?

GORDON: Will she have an accent?

People who are rather more socially aware may well ask you what efforts you are making to teach her about her own culture, to which a useful reply is, 'Probably more than you

– I don't see your little Jack doing much morris-dancing in his Flintstones shell-suit.' All my parents taught me about English culture is that a picnic is something you do in a parked car by a busy main road. Try to ignore people who ask you about genetics and think that because a child is Romanian, for example, she's suddenly going to start doing gymnastics in a job interview. Imagine that you yourself had been adopted from Britain as a baby by a foreign couple, and spent all your life in a peasant village, working the land, and speaking the language of that country. Then, ask yourself whether you think it likely that at the age of thirty you would suddenly find yourself saying, 'Very mild today, isn't it?' Having said that, if you adopt from abroad do be positive about the child's origins. It is very negative and destructive for a child to grow up with the idea that she comes from a country which is cruel and uncivilised and where people don't like children, so you can happily remind her that she wasn't born in Britain.

Babies

Jeremy Hardy Speaks to the Nation, 1994

Perhaps we all want a little replica of ourselves and a baby is a faster route to this than becoming a major historical figure in order to be included in the Airfix range.

And is it a bad thing to want to create a new person who looks a bit like you? Well, that depends on what you look like. Phil Collins would be best left as a one-off. However, to see some slight reflection of yourself in the face of an infant can be warmly reassuring, especially if you are not entirely convinced that you are the child's father. But what a man seeks from a child is not so much a copy of himself but a continuation of his existence. We want to be immortal. We want to know that, even after we are gone, there will still be a little piece of us, somewhere on the Earth, who hates our guts.

* * *

Jeremy Hardy Speaks to the Nation, 2013

Many of us seem to think you need to do different voices for different people. For old people it's shouting. For babies and children, it's that horrible, creepy, singy-songy CBeebies voice. Why talk to children like that? There's nothing wrong with them. Just because they're small and they don't know much. It's not their fault; they're picking stuff up as quickly as they can. They learn pretty fast. When you think how long it's taken you to learn half a dozen words of Spanish, and a toddler has nailed one, maybe two languages by the age of three just by listening. And you're not helping them to learn by talking to them as though you've just been hit by a car.

I reckon babies would learn much faster if their early interaction with fellow humans was not huge, strange, smelly faces looming in front of them making weird goo-goo noises. Why can't we all just speak calmly and sensibly to them?

DOCTOR: Good morning, you must be Emily. Delighted you could join us. We've been expecting you for some time.

* * *

Jeremy Hardy Speaks to the Nation, 1994

At some stage, even the most avid breastfeeder will accept that it is starting to affect their child's career. Getting a child onto solid food is a matter of experiment. A lot of very good advice books about kids and food have been produced by people with nannies, and by the parents' pressure group Bored Celebrity Housewives Against Food Additives. These books advise against packets and jars and tell you instead to simply 'purée some of what you're having'. The trouble is that Pizza Hut don't purée, not unless the lad on the moped goes under a bus. In general, it is extremely reckless to purée some of what you're having and give it to a baby – chicken tikka and half a bottle of Jameson's at two o'clock in the morning can sit very heavily on a tiny stomach.

Commercial baby foods are a mixture of good and bad. Don't be duped into thinking that the ones called things like 'Winter Vegetable Julienne with Braised Breast of Spring Chicken Mornay' will be any less foul-tasting than the rest.

Look at the labels and avoid the ones whose lists of ingredients read –

Water, dextrose, viscose, partially adulterated vegetable fat, chlorine, salt, liver-shaped pieces, lard extract, vegetable look-a-likes, shit.

When children are a bit older, you may like to experiment with foods that contain stabilisers, as this will stop them falling off their bikes. But do be careful with additives. I gave my niece a chemistry set one Christmas, and by Easter she was extracting the E-numbers from chewing gum and snorting them. Hi-tech food and hi-tech children are a dangerous combination. If you give most seven-year-olds a Pot Noodle, a home computer and some string, they can rustle up a tactical nuclear weapon in two or three days. But the food industry is very scrupulous in ensuring that anything which might harm infants is safely exported to developing countries.

When Baby is on to 'finger foods', there are many old-favourite ruses for enticing them. Here are some ideas from the popular daytime TV chef and former actress whose name escapes me.

Fun shapes are a good idea: try carving little pieces of cheese into the shape of ink pens or toilet brushes. Fill an icing bag with mashed avocado or swede and spell out the words 'Keep out of the reach of children' or

'Warning: contains hydrochloric acid' on a sheet of greaseproof paper. If you have the time, decorate your child's mouth as if it were the cassette compartment of your video recorder and sit her in front of a mirror with a plate of sandwiches.

And you can buy Nanette Newman's book, *Cooking for Jane Asher*, if your toddler sticks it in the shopping trolley when you're not looking.

Raising Children

Early Stand-up Set, The Cabaret Upstairs, 1987

As an adult, I find myself wanting to be stern and disciplinarian with young children. I want to say things like, 'I'll have none of your lip! You watch your step, young feller-me-lad, or I'll fetch you a clip round the ear! You can wipe that smile off your face or I'll come down on you like a ton of bricks! *I can hear you in the Staff Room!*' And the kids say, 'D'you want a lolly stick up your bum?'

* * *

Jeremy Hardy Speaks to the Nation, 1993

Children might talk rubbish, but it's passionate exuberant rubbish about games and food and telly and gravel-related injuries. Children don't say 'basically' or 'how goes it?' or 'I kid you not'. They don't invoice you, they say, 'Can I have money for sweets?' and if you say, 'How much do you want', they don't say, 'I wouldn't like to put a figure on it. I'll see how I get on and then give you a bell later on this afternoon', and if you won't give them money, they don't send you a court summons, they just go round all the neighbours saying, 'Will you sponsor me?'

* * *

I'm Sorry I Haven't A Clue, 2005

JACK: Jeremy, can you assist this anxious correspondent? What is snot?

JEREMY: One of your kid's five a day.

* * *

Jeremy Hardy Speaks to the Nation, 1997

Teachers are increasingly aware that religious education may not be fully backed up at home, so they're doing their best to turn the nativity into a kind of half-modernised, accessible story of everyday folk in bizarre circumstances.

JOSEPH: (CHILD ACTING) Mary, you look surprised. Has something happened?

MARY: (CHILD ACTING) Yes, Joseph, an angel has told me I'm going to have a baby. He will be the son of God.

JOSEPH: That is wonderful news.

FX: OUT-OF-TUNE PIANO.

TAPE: TRIANGLES AND RECORDERS PLAY THE TUNE AS LITTLE SCHOOL ORCHESTRA. 1-2-3-4 -

MARY: (SINGING) Why is it us?

Why have we been chosen?

I am a virgin.

You've never had your sperm frozen.

* * *

Jeremy Hardy Speaks to the Nation, 1994

Fatherhood Through the Ages – A Brief History:

Historically, the nuclear family is quite a recent phenomenon. In pre-industrial Britain, most of the population lived quite communally. Luckily, they were also illiterate and so couldn't leave terse notes to each other about whose turn it was to buy toilet paper. Fathers and mothers both worked the land and it was left to grandparents to stitch the children into hessian sacks and bury them in clay pits until they were fourteen. The start of the industrial revolution was signalled by the discovery of penicillin by Spinning Jenny, the inventor of steam.

Progressively, the largely rural population was driven off the land by rambling societies and began to settle in new towns like Harlow and Welwyn Garden City. From this time on, children didn't need to be babysat because they had jobs. Of course, the wealthy father did not need to put his children to work. But neither did he spend much quality time with them. He would employ a wicked governess, to scare the children and their frail, sickly mother, who would die of embroidery at the age of thirty. The father would go on to have various illegitimate children by a succession of scullery maids, each of whom he would cast out in turn. Shunned and shamed, his former servants would die of melodrama in a rude shack. But one of the children would survive and run away to sea to work his passage on the coffin ships to Belgium. Years later, he would return to his father's estate to claim his rightful share of the inheritance, and have to fight a duel on Salisbury Plain with his cruel half-brother – Brot – who would cheat and fire before he had taken ten paces, thus accidentally shooting himself in the head. Meanwhile, their father had died in the madhouse for tax reasons and left no will, but a kindly old gentleman recognised our hero – who was about to hang mistakenly for the shooting of his half-brother – as the bastard son and rightful heir to the old squire's estate, but by now a car park had been built on it so they hanged him anyway.

All this changed with the First World War. A profound social shift occurred as women were drawn into heavy industry by the need for munitions. The war also altered once and for all the attitudes of men to their roles as fathers, because they were all killed.

By the time a new generation had become fathers, it was the Depression and they were all unemployed so that was no good either but at least they were around more and could play with the kids. Then it was the Second World

War, then post-war austerity and then the fifties. The economic boom of the fifties and early sixties saw a dramatic growth in car ownership. The motor car caused a huge change in the paternal role. One Sunday a month, the whole family would rise at six so that Father could take them on an outing. By noon he would have finished packing the hard-boiled eggs into the boot of the Wolseley and would arrange his children inside after weighing and numbering them. This was in the days before safety belts and gaps between the front seats, so five or six children could be seated uncomfortably next to their father in the front. Mother would travel in the back and navigate while trying to subdue Grandma, who would be scaring the children with stories of a car accident she witnessed in 1936 and how the doctors couldn't tell which bits were the passengers and which bits were the knacker's horse. The children would take it in turns to get stung by wasps, be carsick and wet themselves but Father would refuse to stop until he reached the picnic site, a lay-by on a new stretch of dual carriageway. The picnic was eaten in the car to avoid the litter bin full of angry hornets but the children were allowed out of the car to collect something for the school nature table. Father told them, 'If you're not back in five minutes, I'm leaving without you.' He was not serious, but would nonetheless drive off leaving one child behind. By the time the child was retrieved two hours later, he was hysterical and needed to be consoled, so the rest of the day was spent looking for an ice-cream van. It was after dark by the time Father delivered his brood safely home, tired but unhappy.

* * *

The News Quiz, 1999

The thing is, having a lustrous head of hair is a problem because, when you're a dad, you think, 'Well, life's not going so badly, the daughter's safe, she's growing up, she's nine years old, you know, she's at primary school, she's doing all right, reasonably happy.' And then you think, 'I'm thirty-eight years old and I've got bleeding nits.' I'll be sitting in a meeting with some arse of a producer from somewhere – and I'll be sitting there scratching, and they'll say 'Ooh, is anything wrong, Jeremy?' and I'll say 'Oh Good Lord no, no, no, there's nothing wrong, just headlice'. And you can't catch them, they're tiny wee divvils, otherwise, you know, if you could trap them, you could collect up a lot and throw them over the walls of private schools.

* * *

Jeremy Hardy Speaks to the Nation, 2001

Now that my daughter is eleven, I find myself observing people with their babies and toddlers and thinking, 'Oh God, I wasn't like that, was I?' Coming back to London on a train recently, I was struck by the loudness of middle-class parents. This father opposite bellowed,

FATHER: Would you like some juice?

and –

FATHER: Did you know 'buffet' is a French word? We went camping in France, do you remember? And what's the French for camping? It's 'comping', isn't it, Giles?

And I realised it was being said not for the benefit of the child but the benefit of the other passengers.

And there was I, sitting alongside my eleven-year-old, who was quietly staring out of the window, stifling her boredom into a tight little ball of resentment that will explode in later years. And I wondered why this new parent imagined I'd be even slightly impressed that he had done two years of this.

I remember the production you get to put on as a new parent. The baby-care aisle of the chemist or supermarket is your props department and your chance to show how much you care. It matters to you that your baby stays fresh and dry. It doesn't occur to you that adolescent girls are a lot more worried about absorbency than is your carefree, stinky charge. You're impressed that he can projectile-vomit, but forget that a teenage girl can do that while turning her head 360 degrees. You know that sometimes he cries just because he's tired or disoriented. But you forget that he will start doing it again in his late thirties.

* * *

Jeremy Hardy Speaks to the Nation, 1997

Children learn best when they're relaxed and don't realise they're being educated. Unfortunately, this means many parents find it impossible to have any fun with kids without trying to teach them something at the same time. They can't even take them to McDonald's without trying to explain the Scottish clan system. Children are content with the fact that dinosaurs are bloody great big scary-looking monsters; they don't give a toss that they were actually extinct before the evolution of The Flintstones. And although kids can learn a lot through play, they soon see through the subterfuge; you can't entice a spotty sullen sixteen-year-old away from her Walkman by saying, 'I know, let's play the sedimentary rocks game again.' Sixteen's a dysfunctional age anyway, too young to vote and too old for a modelling career.

But structured education is starting earlier and earlier. It is interesting that the word 'nursery' means not only childcare but garden centre. This may be because we regard children as young growing things who need to be nurtured. Or it may be that, since a garden centre is our idea of a fun day out, we assume children feel the same way. The Germans also employ horticultural imagery in the term 'kindergarten', which translates as 'children garden', but unfortunately sounds like something to do with the Third Reich. That's just a problem with the German language as a whole. I don't want to give them a hard time, but I think they're going to have to learn to speak something else if they're ever going to live it down.

But I digress. Different kinds of nursery have different

emphases; some exist primarily to enable working-class women to scrape a living; some exist to enable middle-class women to block whole streets by double-parking huge Volvos with all the doors open during the rush hour.

* * *

The News Quiz, 2013

SANDI: Jeremy, who says that children are better off with a 'little buddha discipline'?

JEREMY: The leader of the Association of Teachers & Lecherers – which is, randy teachers – says that middle-class children are pampered little buddhas. (Was the buddha pampered? I thought that he was quite ascetic. I thought he went around saying, 'oh no more for me thanks, I'm the buddha'.)

We know that middle-class parents indulge their children. They say, (POSH VOICE) 'My children are so bright. They're very, very bright. That's why they're doing so badly at school, because they're so very bright. The teachers don't understand their answers, you see. The reason they misbehave is that they're bored in the classroom, because they're so bright. They're not being stretched. And Hermione's *so* bright. That's why she misbehaves because she's so much brighter than the other children. That's why she sets fire to them I think.'

Because the press concentrate on the children of the poor, (POSH VOICE) 'oh these terrible chav children, oh it's terrible. They're all gypsies and they park their caravans in the classroom, with their evil, violent dogs and they're all footpads and highwaymen and it's terrible. And these days your child daren't go to a state school because they'll be instantly impregnated by some awful, beastly costermonger's child.'

It turns out that the worst, most badly behaved, lazy and indulged children are the children of the middle classes. But it's the industrious, hard-working children – barefoot children from those parts of the country where the fish mines have closed – who are much maligned. The salt-of-the-earth children with stupid made-up names like Hosepipe and Ottawa.

And so the middle-class parents who can afford it put their children in private schools, where they make the children wear preposterous uniforms. And you think, 'that's a stone-magnet is that blazer'. By making them wear a vermillion trouser suit – you know the kind of Norman French falconer's gauntlet – you've just made your child into a pebble-target.

SANDI: (LAUGHING) Jeremy you have to stop because I'm going to die.

* * *

Jeremy Hardy Speaks to the Nation, 1997

The very concept of intelligence is flimsy and ill-defined. A person can be very bright in one way and very dim in another, brilliant at maths, and yet unable to understand how un-appealing dandruff is.

The IQ, or Intelligence Quotient, was invented in order that people with no other redeeming features could have something to feel proud of. In order to get into Mensa you have to complete some silly puzzles and be the sort of person who will never be asked to babysit. The only possible aim of the organisation must be to breed a master race of physically unattractive crossword enthusiasts.

* * *

Jeremy Hardy Speaks to the Nation, 2010

The monarchy and the aristocracy don't do parenting as such. Diana, God rest her, was a terrible mother. I doubt she ever met those boys from school, and they only needed picking up three times a year. What kind of environment is life in a boarding school? Kennelling for the children of the privileged.

* * *

Jeremy Hardy Speaks to the Nation, 2001

There is now a backlash to the effect that we've all become overprotective. For the last few years, there has been a movement to make us less careful about our children, led by one-man organisations called things like The Institute of Letter-Headed Paper who supply pundits for *Woman's Hour* and *Any Questions*.

Debbie, I believe you've been reading some childcare advice from this school of thought?

DEBBIE: That's right. I've just read *They've Got to Learn Somehow* by Freddie Franco who is Professor of Made-Up-ology at the University of His House. His view is that children who are not allowed to play with knives or take business cards from Thai modelling agencies are being hopelessly coddled. He says you should leave toddlers alone in cars, initially for short periods of an hour or so, building up as they get used to it, to the point where you can park overnight on a slope with the handbrake off and they'll be fine.

Some people wax lyrical about the days when they played out for hours on end on hills and in streams, coming home for a glass of barley water and then heading off again to look for tadpoles in bomb craters, but I think those people need to face the fact that their parents didn't care about them. A generation ago, people had huge families, on the expectation that two or three kids would die of diphtheria, one would get lost, one they'd just forget to feed, another they couldn't afford to feed so would send to live with someone who was believed to be an aunt although no one was sure; and the three survivors would provide grandchildren, which was their only function anyway. Police officers would go to schools to warn kids not to get into strange cars. A squirrel or a big man in tights would tell them not to throw themselves under strange cars. A nurse checked for nits. We were told not to swing on our chairs. And that was it. Children who told their parents they'd been molested would be told things like 'Nonsense, dear, he's a man of the church', and 'Well, it's only during term-time; you can come home at Easter'.

*   *   *

Guardian, 2001

Well, my little girl's pushing eleven now so I suppose it's high time I was choosing her career. I can't decide whether she has a special aptitude for computers or whether Virtual Springfield falls into the category of what used to be called 'fun'. She's very good at getting money out of me but I'm not sure she'd enjoy Business Studies, which is about taking money from strangers, something I've told her not to do. In fact, she lends me more than I give her, and at zero interest, so I don't think she's equipped for the Greed GNVQ.

She very much enjoys the performing arts and I think she excels in them. The trouble is that all parents think their child is the most magical, special and beautiful child in the world, which is clearly irrational, because *my* child is the most magical, special and beautiful child in the world. In any event, the nearest Performing Arts school has the good sense not to open their doors to children under fourteen, realising perhaps that children who are too young to know that *Hollyoaks* is unrelenting bollocks shouldn't be planning their working lives just yet.

It occurs to me that I haven't even chosen a religion for my daughter, but perhaps it's a bit late for that. Being an unbeliever, I tried to choose secular education, but it's not available, so I've put up with the obligatory religiosity of the nearest state primary. I've always figured that religion should come as the result of a blinding light, a nervous breakdown or a prison sentence, rather than being something that goes on a blazer or a blackboard.

The faith communities, however, seem to see scripture as something that needs to be injected into the child not long after the MMR vaccine. Once children are old enough to suss that 'Because I said so' is not a reasoned argument, they are susceptible to all kinds of questioning impulses. That is why faith declines the more freely people think. We don't yet know whether the government wants failing religions to be taken over by those with improving attendance figures, or simply handed over to the private sector and converted into academies of consumer fetishism, or luxury belfry apartments.

Those who want children to be segregated according to their parents' real or professed creeds claim that religious schools teach pupils to respect other religions. But, I am slightly sceptical about the idea that the best way to promote understanding is for children never to meet one another. 'Equal but different' has never been a happy prescription. No society that is serious about equality promotes segregation. Still, they get very good exam results in Northern Ireland. It's a shame about the bitter sectarian hatred but you can't have everything. And at least in the rest of the United Kingdom we have greater diversity of faith. Parents can choose from a rich variety of possible ways to isolate their children from others.

Perhaps the coming increase in religious schools will be the model for all specialisation and selection. In schools which, under the sponsorship and control of industry, concentrate on science and technology, pupils will learn about the existence of other ways of making a living, without really giving them serious consideration. Perhaps they will learn to respect the arts, while knowing that Information Technology is the one true vocation.

Specialist schools will say they do very well over a range of subjects. If true, it might have something to do with the fact that they get more money and resources, and the better they do, the more money and resources they get. They also practise selection, something that this government has done more than eighteen years of Thatcherism to promote. It's impossible to believe that its great vision for education is not about sorting the managers from the underlings as early as possible. Selection is always at the expense of someone. It means choice for the few, pot luck for the many.

You might argue that, if a child shows great aptitude for languages, she should go to a specialist school. But if her local specialist school happens to be St Nike's Academy For Keeping Troublesome Youths Shagged Out By Running, how exactly is her linguistic genius going to be fostered? What if, being Nigerian, she has an interest in her ancestral homeland, and her local centre of excellence is the Shell College of Short Memory?

What if you just want your child to go to an inclusive, free, well-resourced nearby school, with a range of abilities, a balanced curriculum and a policy of keeping children's options as wide as possible for as long as possible? But then, I'm talking about enriching children's lives with the joy of learning. I'm not thinking about the short-term needs of New Labour's business partners. Sorry, kids, it's time for a word from our sponsors.

* * *

40 Years of The News Quiz, 2017

SIMON (HOGGART): Jeremy, why shouldn't Mum and Dad 'let there be light'?

JEREMY: Oh, this is all these people who try and tell you you're messing up your kids' lives, as if we didn't know . . . Apparently, everything we do is wrong; every couple of years they bring out a survey saying 'Ooh, you mustn't give children bottled milk because their pelvis will explode when they're thirty . . .' And first they tell us that they're supposed to sleep on their back, then they say no, they're supposed to sleep face down in their own vomit. Then they tell you they're supposed to sleep upside-down in the wardrobe and *now* they say that they're better off screaming in terror and clawing at the bedroom door with their tiny little nails than having a little tiny cute nightlight on to give them some sort of comfort in this miserable dispiriting world. And we're all such evil parents that there is a minor risk that our children might be short-sighted because they sleep with the light on. And who *doesn't* go to bed in lurking terror, let's be honest. And besides, this is all irrelevant, because most children sleep with their mum and dad until they go to university. Who are these people who do these surveys? It's all done on mice anyway; they put a mouse to bed and then they shine a little Pifco torch in its eyes . . . and then they put a couple of cocktail sticks under its eyes and then they say, 'Oh! This mouse betrayed bizarre symptoms of running around chewing sideboards and running around in a big wheel and therefore all parents are wrong' as if we didn't know. I mean, as if we didn't have enough pressure; we're doing our best to screw our kids' heads up, we haven't got time to mess up their eyesight, let's be honest . . .

* * *

Jeremy Hardy Speaks to the Nation, 2004

Despite the fact that I understand that capitalism alienates people from their work by expropriating surplus value, I do cleave to the old-fashioned view that we should try to make a go of whatever we do for a living. It's like my daughter's homework; it's got to be done, so I might as well do it to the best of my ability.

* * *

Jeremy Hardy Speaks to the Nation, 2010

As well as being good for our health, mixing with other kids as we grow up is an important part of our education, because we learn that not everybody is exactly the same as us, if, that is, we go to a school where not everybody is exactly the same as us. All too often parents panic that the local state primary isn't going to stretch Hermione academically, so they lose the plot and transfer her to a private school, but they feel guilty and then try to convince you there's a really nice mix, by which they mean there's one mixed-race child, whose father is an architect and whose mother does that lovely thing with her hair. And *Tabitha*'s dad's a plumber, although he's actually one of those well-spoken plumbers people like to hire because, although they don't know how to make water go through pipes, they did study photography until their trust fund ran out.

The local state primary is fine, Hermione will be happy there, and she'll have a friend called Yusuf. In fact, I'm sick of property programmes where they say,

PRESENTER: Jonathan and Fiona need to move out of London because their children are about to start school.

Hold on there, Kirsty, you stuck-up Tory cow, back up and justify that sentence. All right, I accept that Jonathan and Fiona can't hack London because they're weedy milk-sops from Gloucestershire who just came to London to take our jobs but ultimately hope to move back nearer to where they grew up because actually they didn't grow up. But why subject their children to life in a village – I've seen *Straw Dogs* and it was a documentary – when their kids could grow up in London, one of the great cities of the world? What do they think is going to happen to their kids at a London primary school? They're not going to get leprosy or be recruited as child soldiers. Yes, the school might celebrate Eid but it doesn't involve female circumcision or explosions. And they say,

WOMAN: I'm not being funny but some of those people keep themselves to themselves.

What, you mean like avoiding contact with other cultures because of assumptions you make about them?

The great thing about young children is they have no preconceptions about one another. They don't think about race or class. The fact that other children come in different colours means nothing when you have a purple dinosaur. Your kids will think it's great where Jade lives because you get to go up in a lift, and there's no mayonnaise but they have salad cream which is really nice. And Jade will appreciate your garden, because she doesn't have one. She won't steal it. She won't organise an illegal rave. She won't drink from the dog bowl because she was raised by wolves. She won't pierce Hermione's nipples with a staple gun. She's a nice kid, and so's yours because you haven't yet been able to fill her head with your values, but God help her because you will.

* * *

Jeremy Hardy Feels It, 2017

A parent is whoever raises a child: birth parent, adoptive parent, step-parent, aunt, uncle, Slovakian au pair, or the wonderful little woman from the village whose husband does all your odd jobs round the house.

In fact, it's said that it takes a village to raise the child, but that depends on being accepted by the village, which takes about forty years, and it being an actual village, rather than an urban area that estate agents are keen to gentrify. This kind of rebranding happens all the time, especially in London. Tower Hamlets is now West Glyndebourne, and the area between Wandsworth and Brixton, formerly Clapham, is now 'Twixt the Prisons. Brixton is obviously the Ziggy Stardust Marina.

* * *

I'm Sorry I Haven't A Clue, 1999

Posh versions of TV shows

The Bill becomes *L'Addition S'il Vous Plaît*

Casualty becomes *I'm Sorry, This Is A Private Hospital. We Can't Handle Emergencies*

Home & Away at Our Other Home

Animal Hospital becomes *Animal Feng Shui Consultancy*

Chat-up Lines . . .

. . . for ornithologists

Fancy going down The Feathers later on?

Oh please – put it on my bill.

Don't let a little thrush put you off.

. . . for motor mechanics

I'll just roll you up onto the pavement and then we won't be in anybody's way.

I'll give you a jump-start and that should get you going in no time.

This looks like a tow job to me.

I'm gonna have to get underneath.

. . . for fishermen

Could you give me a hand? I seem to have got my fly tangled.

Don't worry, my dear, I've done this loads of times and I've never caught anything.

Jeremy by Jon Naismith

I first saw Jeremy Hardy in 1987 at a gig in Cambridge while I was a student there. My single abiding memory of his set was the amount of time he spent berating the audience for our unwarranted privilege, telling us he'd only accepted the gig due to the strong likelihood that at least one of us would be a future employer.

I first employed Jeremy in 1990 when working as a comedy researcher on a TV show called Jools Holland's Happening. *The show had started on BSB, one of the first UK satellite channels, but when I joined, BSB had just merged with Rupert Murdoch's Sky, much to the disapproval of the left-leaning alternative comedy circuit. So, I was surprised when Jeremy accepted my invitation to appear. The first Gulf War had just broken out and there was an injunction from the channel that no stand-ups were to do Gulf War material in case there was any significant loss of life. I explained this to Jeremy and he obligingly gave me a detailed précis of his set, which I took down verbatim and passed to the director. On the night of the recording, as I waited in the wings clutching the can of ice-cold lager he'd requested for afters, I listened in considerable dismay as he proceeded to do a fifteen-minute set comprised entirely of material about the Gulf War.*

In the early 90s, as a young producer of I'm Sorry I Haven't

A Clue, *Jeremy wrote me a letter asking if I'd have him on the show. In the twenty-seven years I've been producing the show, he's the only comic ever to have done this. It was a slightly graceless letter I remember – he opened by saying that as it was becoming clear to him that a television career was looking increasingly unlikely, he felt that radio was going to be his home. And he thought he'd be good on* I'm Sorry I Haven't A Clue. *He made his first appearance on the show at a recording in Harrogate in 1995. That recording was probably the most memorable of any in the fifty-plus series I've produced and marked a new era for the programme. It was the first I'd experienced where rounds other than 'Mornington Crescent' were cheered by the audience and it appeared for the first time that the show had acquired the cult status of its predecessor* I'm Sorry I'll Read That Again. *And it was the first show on which Jeremy's unique singing voice was revealed to an unsuspecting nation. As he brought 'Kung Fu Fighting' to the tune of 'Scarborough Fair' to a stunning, tuneless close, I remember there being a brief moment of almost silence on the part of the audience, until Willie Rushton pronounced ironically 'I smell points' and they erupted into applause.*

Years later, at a benefit performance at the Royal Albert Hall, Jeremy sang the words of 'Teenage Kicks' to the tune of 'Jerusalem' accompanied by a full seventy-piece orchestra – many of whom, it was clear at the afternoon rehearsal, were completely unaware of his limitations as a singer. After their soaring orchestral intro so familiar to Proms-goers had faded into the Albert Hall's distinctive acoustic ceiling 'mushrooms',

I shall never forget the bewildered looks on some of their faces as their latest soloist began to sing. I think it was one of Jeremy's proudest moments.

In his early days on ISIHAC it was frequently an effort for Jeremy not to swear. I remember during his first appearance on the show how, on fluffing a line, he just managed to stop himself from uttering a frustrated expletive. The audience, who had come to expect nothing ruder than a graphic (but swear-word free) double entendre, caught their breath. 'Oops', declared Jeremy, 'I nearly said the fuck W'. Our audiences were a good generation or two older than Jeremy, and he'd delight in pointing this out. 'As a show', he'd tell them, 'we have a very fragile demographic. One harsh winter and we're fucked'.

Though there are few in the world of comedy that won't at one stage or other have been the subject of Jeremy's withering scorn, there are many that have benefitted from his passionate and selfless loyalty. He was always loyal to ISIHAC and I'd often ask his advice when it came to finding a new panellist or round idea. Just looking back through my text messages, I found this very typical exchange with him:

Friday 29th June, 2018.

Me, 10.15 a. m.: Hi Jez. I've been toying with a round where you're asked to suggest expressions that might be heard in both the kitchen and the bedroom. Things like 'Would you like stuffing?', 'Stop talking with your mouth full' and 'I'm just going to pop it in for another 20 minutes'. What do you reckon?

Jeremy, 10.20: Dirty bastard aren't you?

10.21: That's it – beat it till it stiffens.

10.22: Always remember to grease the bottom.

Me, 10.23: Excellent.

Jeremy, 10.24: Are you sure you've washed this?

10.25: Blimey, what's this attachment for?

10.26: I can't be bothered with the table, shall we just have it in front of the telly?

10.27: Urgh, too salty

13.57: I promise you, by the morning it will have risen

13.58: Just whip it lightly or it'll go everywhere

13.59: If you toss too hard it'll hit the ceiling

Nothing Jeremy uttered on a stage was bland, complacent, easy or second rate. His speed of thought was breath-taking. Of his generation I think it's fair to say there's been no one who's enriched British radio comedy to the extent he has.

Jeremy was the youngest of five children and was for many years the youngest of five on ISIHAC. Lately I've wondered at the extent his being a youngest child might have shaped Jeremy's character: his fearlessness, his impudence, his ferocious righteous indignation, his unashamed juvenility and his uncompromising willingness to speak truth to power whatever the consequences. Whatever it was, we've lost a truly stunning talent, a loyal friend and one of the greatest radio comedians of our age.

Jeremy by Graeme Garden

Jeremy: a sharp and hilarious comic, a thoughtful and generous friend, and a singer.

A lot has been made of Jeremy's singing technique. I remember the first time he appeared on I'm Sorry I Haven't a Clue, *and what a revelation he was. At the time, of course, we didn't realise that Jeremy couldn't sing. The thing was – neither did he.*

Actually, he could sing, just not in tune. Like everything else he did, he sang with commitment and confidence. He sang his heart out. And he sang it his way.

However, there is another aspect of his musicality that sticks with me. On tour with Clue *we would play a game called Karaoke-Cokey. In this game every member of the audience would be given a kazoo, and then they'd be asked to perform a tune for us to recognise. A thousand kazoos, all playing together, in a thousand different keys, unaccompanied. But it was Jeremy who almost always got in first to name the tune. It was uncanny. But that was Jeremy. Through the chaos and the noise and the rubbish he could always hear the right tune.*

3

Jeremy Hardy Speaks About . . .

Politics

'I think what I really believe in is a truly benevolent dictatorship. But utterly benevolent mark you. Totally benign tyranny. Kindly despotism. The kind of society in which you're on your way to work and a van forces your car off the road and hooded men drag you out of your car, bundle you into the back of the van, drive you home and put you back to bed for a couple of hours.'

My Politics

Jeremy Hardy Speaks to the Nation, 1993

As I get older, although I haven't yet become a liberal myself, I have more and more respect for liberals. Not the Lib Dems particularly, but passionate, decent, old-fashioned liberals. Because, when liberals hear about some abuse of power, they are outraged that such things can go on, determined that something must be done and moved to put pen to paper. Sometimes they even put pen to placard. They turned out for the miners with their own personal, home-made banners saying things like, 'Please, Mr Heseltine, think about what you are doing and reconsider.' Which is a bugger of a chant to get behind. Whereas the left are so used to expecting the worst that it's much more of an effort for us to do anything about it. We have marches every week and the main reason I go on them is that you can get through London in half the time it takes by car. Nowadays, my militancy consists of sitting in front of the news saying 'bastards' periodically.

* * *

Jeremy Hardy Speaks to the Nation, 2003

Part of the reason some people get more right-wing as they age is fear. As we feel less strong and more mortal it's easy for us to be manipulated into fear of the Bogeyman and I'm not even going to make a mucus joke because this is a complicated point and these days I find I lose my thread very easily if I go off at too many tangents.

The target readership of the *Daily Mail* Leader column, or 'Führer column' as it was called in the thirties, is people who are afraid their way of life is being undermined, even though their way of life doesn't actually consist of very much. If you unplugged their telly, they'd have precious little to undermine. But they think of asylum seekers and they are afraid, afraid that foreigners are coming to clean their office buildings in an exotic way or open shops that sell funny-shaped veg and don't run out of bread by noon. Afraid that foreign-looking men will 'stand around' in the village, in that standing-around way that they have. Now, of course, people claim they are worried that asylum is a cover for terrorists. They've just heard of ricin, and they think, 'Well, everything foreign's got rice in.'

* * *

Jeremy Hardy Speaks to the Nation, 2004

I'm fascinated by the term 'nanny state'. In my day, your nanny was your dad's mum, who not only let you do more or less anything but also fuelled you with Quality Street and Tizer to ensure that you would. Today, of course, a nanny is an under-paid non-Anglophone babysitter who weeps for her war-torn country and does the ironing as well. But I think the image we're supposed to have in our minds is that of the starched and stern governess in Edwardian children's stories. The kind of person who appears in the Tories' worst nightmares and fetish parlours. And the implication of the accusation of a nanny state is that we are being treated as children.

But sometimes I wouldn't mind being treated as a child. Because I don't know what to do, I'm not very good at feeding myself and I'm not always able to hit the toilet.

* * *

Jeremy Hardy Speaks to the Nation, 2010

In politics, you get bags of credit if you used to be something else, if you came from a different belief system.

Years ago, I did a really dreary gig in a really dreary pub in Brixton for the now defunct Socialist Alliance. There was me and the Brixton Street Slam Poets Collective – the sort of thing you have to pretend to like on the left because the fact that they're no good means there's something really fresh and vibrant about them. Poetry is something that's hard to do well but terrifyingly easy to do badly. There are always poets who are available at short notice, but that's not a recommendation. If poets, plumbers and children's entertainers aren't booked up months in advance, for the love of God don't hire them. And as I was waiting to go on, one of the poets was hovering, and he was a large white man in his mid-thirties with a shaven head and various piercings and this buzz started about him. 'See that poet there. He used to be a Nazi.'

And people were really excited about this and seemingly impressed. And I was thinking, 'Well, excuse me but I've never been a Nazi. Isn't that somehow quite a lot better than having *been* a Nazi?' And I've given up my Saturday night and missed my friend Henry's fiftieth birthday and he's not only Jewish but also an authority on Primo Levi, which makes him really, *really* not a Nazi. And I've missed his party to do this when frankly I can actually get paid gigs unlike your recovering stormtrooper and his mates.

Maybe you won't like me so much because I've never been a Nazi. Maybe I should have been. It's not like I couldn't; I'm white, I'm Anglo Saxon, I'm lower middle class, and let's not forget that it's the petit bourgeoisie who are actually the most fertile soil for fascism despite the popular myth that the urban proletariat can barely contain themselves from sliding into the arms of the extreme right if poetry collectives don't get to them in time. Yes, maybe I should have been a Nazi, then I could stop being one and I'd get all this credit for not being something I shouldn't have been in the first place. You see, I'm like my house. Am what I always have been. Didn't have to be converted. But that's the great thing about Nazis, they have such potential for improvement.

Of course what people probably should have said about the ex-fascist poet was not that he used to be a Nazi but that a chain of circumstances and problems in his life led to him getting entangled with people on the far right but he never completely lost his humanity so he was able to see through their lies and come out the other side and have his swastika tattoo turned into a rather attractive windmill.

* * *

Red Pepper, 2010

I recently read a story in the *Guardian* that reported in all seriousness that scientists have discovered a liberal gene. This would mean that certain people are hard-wired to hold certain beliefs because of a propensity encoded in their DNA. It would mean they have innate liberal values because of a gene . . . a gene, presumably, that disappears when they are offered power.

Could there be a more illiberal view than the notion that political opinions are in the blood? In reality, the left can safely stand by our traditional, rational view that environment is usually the determining factor in how we turn out and what we believe. Science is not revealing that human behaviour is governed by genes; people are just choosing to interpret science that way. In reality, whatever we do inherit is subject to environmental influence immediately.

True, there are all those stories about twins separated at birth, but the ones who are completely dissimilar don't get much press, just as no one ever answers the phone and says, 'That's weird, I wasn't thinking about you just now.' The behaviour of the people around us has a huge influence on us even before we are born. Little about the human personality can be identified as innate because it's impossible to have a personality immune from human contact – unless that's what causes estate agents.

My point is that what happens to us as we grow up, and the circumstances in which we grow up, are the things that shape our outlook. That is why we oppose faith schools and the religious indoctrination of children. Children will believe anything, and it's not fair to exploit that. Let the god who made them make them with innate belief, and let their educational environment be secular.

* * *

Jeremy Hardy Speaks to the Nation, 2013

You'd think that, with everything that's happened in the last few years, everyone would realise that the private sector is just incompetence combined with greed. At least the public sector is well-meaning incompetence. Human beings are fundamentally incompetent. It's only our motivation that varies. Of course, the BBC is run by idiots; *everything* is run by idiots. Who do you know who's any good at their job? I mean, there are some things the private sector does better. Coffee, coffee is done better by the private sector. When the railways were properly nationalised, there was one jar of Mellow Birds for the entire network, invariably stranded at Crewe. Today if you turn up at a train station, there's a fighting chance you can buy a real cup of coffee made from real coffee beans. Sometimes even on the trains. On the InterCity ones, if the machine's working. So if that's your main reason for taking a train, you'll be happy. Seems an elaborate and expensive alternative to a cafetière, but if that's your motivation, you'll be thrilled by the bracing power of market forces. If, however, your main concern is that the train should stay on the long metal things that run along the ground, you'll lean towards renationalisation.

If you turn up at a hospital, dying for a cup of coffee,

you'll be delighted to find Costa in the atrium. If you turn up at a hospital just dying, you'll hope it's an NHS hospital, because private hospitals don't have A&E. Try turning up at a private hospital complaining of severe chest pains; all they can do is give you some breasts, one or two depending on your credit rating. And all those who don't want state regulation of the food industry, say 'Neigh'.

* * *

Jeremy Hardy Speaks to the Nation, 2013

Conservatives love a row with Brussels, because upsetting foreigners is second only to killing them in stimulating the pleasure centres of the Tory Party. But liberals love Europe more than anything, oh they love anything continental. The voting systems, the cheeses. Their whole inspiration stems from the vast superiority of French campsites. I'm not referring to old-fashioned, radical liberals, who are happy with a good cheddar, a Thermos and a wet walking holiday, reading a biography of Jo Grimond. And in fairness to liberals, all liberals like democracy a lot. We on the left are ambivalent about it. We pay lip service to it but privately can't help suspecting that people are too stupid to realise the very high regard we have for them.

* * *

Jeremy Hardy Speaks to the Nation, 2013

By now, of course, many listeners will have switched off, deciding that the last half-hour has been typical of everything they hate about the BBC. There is an angry constituency who believe that power in our society has shifted in favour of what they call the Liberal Elite, because in their minds the world is run not by politicians and businessmen, but by a conspiracy of creative progressives, the Illuminartyfarty, who operate the levers of power through the medium of performance poetry. Well, if the military–industrial complex were dependent on lottery funding, they might have a point, but the only area in which arty liberals wield any power is the arts, where in fairness there are quite a lot of them. And in all honesty, they do look kindly upon those of us who are on the left. So it might be fair to say we're rather numerous in the arts, but we have very little influence because we're not very popular. Bless those of you who are listening, but you're hardly representative. Well, we could talk for ever about power, in fact we do, and that's why we haven't got any.

* * *

Jeremy Hardy Speaks to the Nation, 2013

I'm still trying to learn the skill of polite disagreement. In the summer, I accidentally went to a Royal Jubilee party. My friend Sandi Toksvig lives on a houseboat on the River Thames and, as part of the jubilee celebrations, there was to be this huge flotilla down the river. She decided to have a party and invited me. And I said, 'Sandi, you're not a royalist,' and she said, 'No, but I love boats and there's going to be thousands of them going past my front room. I should have a party, will you come?' So I said yes.

Now her neighbour on the river is a wealthy theatre director with a much bigger boat and she went round to invite him but he said, 'Oh, I was just on my way round to invite you. Let's have a joint party and you can invite all your guests to mine.' Meanwhile, bear with me, Sandi had also been asked to be a commentator but figured she could do a bit of that and then get back and enjoy the party, but got stuck miles down the river and didn't make it back for hours, so there was this rather strange party involving some very well-to-do theatre people and a group of hardcore lesbians of whom I was one.

And I imagined it would all be tongue-in-cheek but quite a lot of people were serious monarchists. And at one point I went up on deck to watch some of the boats, and the rain was pouring down, but on both sides of the river were thousands of people cheering and waving flags and it was all in black and white and I was trying to make small talk with a lady who was very posh and is probably someone very important in the theatre but I didn't know who she was, but anyway. She suddenly said, 'Doesn't it make you proud? Only in Britain could you get a turnout like this.' And I said, 'Well, I think North Korea could pull it off.' And she said, 'Yes, but those poor devils don't have any choice.' And I thought, 'Well, that makes *us* the pillocks then, doesn't it?'

* * *

Musicport, 2016

I do hate floating voters, those people who just don't know and make up their mind at the last minute. 'Well last time I voted Lib Dem, but this time I'm thinking of giving Golden Dawn a try.' Just have some opinions and stick to them until I tell you they're wrong, will you?

* * *

Jeremy Hardy Feels It, 2017

Now, you've probably got some idea of my political views and I'm not expecting all of you to agree with me 100 per cent. Some of you will be wrong. But we might agree on more than you think we do. You might say, (TORY VOICE) 'I'm not a socialist, I believe in free enterprise.' Because that's how you talk, people who don't agree with me.

But the trouble with badging ourselves as socialists or free marketeers is that, in reality, hardly anyone thinks that *everything* should be in the public sector or that *nothing* should be in the public sector. We're mostly somewhere on a scale. A majority of Conservative voters support the NHS, which is socialism, and also think the railways should be renationalised. And no one wants the fire brigade to be privatised, taken over by Richard Branson and relaunched as Virgin Inferno.

So I win and you all agree with me. Good.

The Law, the Police and Protesting

Jeremy Hardy Speaks to the Nation, 1993

So, freedom. Of course, the only reason that I am able to discuss this issue at all is that in our country we have absolute freedom of expression. Up to a point. But even here, even here speaking to you audience members and listeners tonight, there are things I can't say: I can't say I've ever read any of Melvyn Bragg's books, for example. And there are legal restraints on my freedom of speech. For example, the police could prosecute me if I were to say something which is an incitement to racial hatred, although it's much more likely that they'd write it down and use it later.

* * *

Jeremy Hardy Speaks to the Nation, 1994

Let's talk about the challenge faced by the police at the end of the twentieth century. To some it seems anachronistic that there are still some police officers who don't carry guns. But some unarmed officers have been remarkably inventive in killing people with whatever else comes to hand. And whenever police marksmen are called in, someone gets shot, even if he's just some loser who's taken himself hostage with a water pistol. But many of the police themselves don't want to be armed because while you can give a suspect a good kicking without marking his face, bullet holes are a dead giveaway. Even the most sympathetic judge will have a hard time with the idea that the accused fell onto several live cartridges during the course of an interrogation.

But the police are keen to try the new LA-style baton. Presumably, LA-style means there's a black motorist on the end. I think they should have a Hawaiian-style one, with pineapple rings all the way down it. I also like the sound of pepper sprays. Arming the police with condiments would do more to bring us into line with our European partners.

But public sympathy for the police seems to have increased. When police officers are violent, their defence is that they reacted as any normal person would. But they are certainly not *paid* to be normal people. As I understand it, they are paid to contain, defuse and prevent violence, not do it. We don't pay surgeons to be normal people, and throw up during major bowel surgery. We don't pay train drivers to be normal people and take a little short cut they know through a housing estate. And we don't pay a plumber to say, 'Ooooh, I think we'd better get a plumber in.'

* * *

Jeremy Hardy Speaks to the Nation, 1997

Let us compare ourselves to our European neighbours on the matter of public protest. If a British person is apoplectic with rage about something, he writes to the local paper. If a Frenchman is even mildly vexed he hurls burning squirrels into the Bourse or blocks the Champs-Élysées with rotting crème brûlée.

* * *

Jeremy Hardy Speaks to the Nation, 2001

We have a very indulgent attitude to the forces of oppression in this country. Despite the fact that as a people we are very bad at seeing things through others' eyes, we are keen to see the point of view of the police. People say, 'Well of course they lose their temper – they're normal people.' The police are not normal people. Who do you know rides a horse round a shopping centre? I dare say that, in the country, a horse is an elegant beast, kitted out in the same kind of tackle that is proudly displayed in traditional country pubs, alongside the gaming machine and the blackboard advertising home-microwaved Country Fare, the country being Iceland. How many of these countryside marchers have seen a real horse, in all its cruel crowd-control equipment? How many of them have seen a miner or a photographer flattened by a mounted officer playing head-polo with a three-foot baton?

In fact, whenever a demonstration is seen as left-wing, involving industrial workers, students or anti-capitalists, there is every likelihood of it being attacked by the police. And I'm at the age when the prospect of trouble frightens me, which means being careful who you stand with. Try to find someone who doesn't look like they'll get hit. Vicars are a good bet. Best not to stand by someone who's clearly an anarchist because they're bound to get hit. Crusties are an obvious target. And I don't want to lack solidarity. I think, 'Fair play to you, mate, but you've got a dog on a string and I've got an eleven-year-old who's got a violin lesson in two hours.' Liberals are good to stand with. You sometimes see them on demos. You can tell them because they've made their own placard, from a piece of card, with a liberal slogan in big marker pen, saying, 'Please stop this madness now, if at all possible'.

*   *   *

Jeremy Hardy Speaks to the Nation, 2001

National boundaries have a huge impact on how we see ourselves and how others see us.

One summer, when I was on holiday in Ireland, my friend Deirdre from the Lower Ormeau Road in Belfast rang to invite me up for her birthday. The Lower Ormeau Road is a contentious marching route, a Catholic area through which the Apprentice Boys like to march, in celebration of the defeat of the Catholic armies of King James by William of Orange in 1690. It was actually a battle for the English throne, in which William had the blessing of the pope and used Catholic regiments, but King Billy has gone down in loyalist mythology as the saviour of Protestantism, and also as looking like Laurence Llewelyn-Bowen, which he almost certainly didn't, although he was by all accounts fairly camp and would trash your house if given the chance.

Some people in Britain see Orange marches as daft more than menacing. But the march down the Lower Ormeau

Road has been particularly unpopular since 1992, when it stopped outside the betting shop in which five Catholics had been murdered, so that marchers could dance and hold up five fingers, in celebration of another of Ulster's traditions.

In any event, Deirdre asked if I wanted to come up on the Friday night for her birthday, and in the morning block the road. And I thought, that sounds like a good weekend all round. So on the Friday I fetched up to Belfast with a bottle of Jameson's in time for the party, only to find out there was to be no party because it had been decided that in order for the community to be in control when the police moved in in the morning, there would be no carousing that night. And I thought, surely the best way to face this is with a hangover. We're all going to be sitting in the gutter anyway, feeling as if someone is beating us in the head with a stick, and they really will be. Surely it's best if we're confused about whether it's really happening or not. Plus, I thought, if we got really tanked up, we could block the road with sick, and show the Apprentice Boys what British culture is really all about.

Anyhow, at 5 a.m. the RUC arrived, I was woken, and we all went to sit on the road. I left all my valuables in Deirdre's house, but brought my press card in case of emergencies. That is, in case of an emergency happening to me, not so that I could push to the front of an emergency and demand to see. But interestingly, as the police moved in and the truncheons began to flail, it was the women who were struck first. The logic of this tactic is, apparently, to so affront the men by battering their dainty lady-folk that the men would leap to their feet, put their dukes up and be arrested for affray. It seems odd that after all these years the Royal Ulster Constabulary have so little knowledge of working-class Belfast Catholic women, because no sooner did the Land Rovers start to drive toward the huddled bodies on the road than the women all piped up, 'Come and get me, ye wee peeler bastards! Come and have a go if you think you're hard enough! I'll have ye, so I will, ye wee shite, ye. Come on, ye bastard, ye!' While all the men were going, 'Jesus Christ, Bridie, there's no need to swear . . .'

And sure enough, this RUC man started battering the woman sitting next to me. And all I could think to do was pull out my press card and say, 'Leave her alone.' And all of a sudden I felt like the archest, campest, most English person sitting on a road anywhere in the world. It was as though I'd said, 'Stop it at once, you fools! Can't you see you'll never get away with this?' (HUMS *DICK BARTON* THEME)

But then it was *my* turn to be taken off the road, and they didn't hurt me because Sky News cameras turned onto me. I don't know if you saw it but I think I was quite good. Don't know if we'll go to series, but fingers crossed. Anyhow, they lifted me off the floor. It's quite nice this, I don't know if you've ever done it but it's like flying. Then I was carried head-high by five burly men. I felt like Eartha Kitt making an entrance.

And then they chucked us all into the backstreets and penned us in while the Apprentice Boys came down the road. Now, the Boys had reached an accommodation with the Parades Commission, whereby their bands would fall silent but they would march to the beat of a single drum. And the reason they needed that single drum, they said, was it enabled them to march in time. And I thought maybe these people are British, because they have so little sense of rhythm they can't walk down the bloody street without someone tapping out the beat for them.

* * *

Jeremy Hardy Speaks to the Nation, 2014

It's interesting that the police have fallen out of favour with the Conservative Party, partly I suspect because they're public servants doing a difficult job, ripe for undervaluing – I don't mean financially undervaluing in the run-up to a sell-off; I haven't got inside dirt on a bid from G4S or Virgin Oppression – but partly because libertarian Tories also get worried by the police spying on us and beating us up.

The mantra of those who seek ever to extend state surveillance is that those with nothing to hide have nothing to fear. Then why do they close the door behind them when they go to the lavatory, except when they're in a long-term relationship in which respect has fallen by the wayside as companionship triumphs over adoration? We all want privacy. Of course we do. The security services are angry because we've found out what they know about us and they wanted it to be a secret. Well, if they're doing nothing wrong, they've got nothing to worry about.

Britishness

Jeremy Hardy Speaks to the Nation, 2007

The Union Jack I'm still squeamish about. I'm not sure I want to reclaim it from the right because they've got muck all over it. But should we blame a flag because it's flown over some terrible things in the past? I've flown over Swindon but I can't be blamed for that.

* * *

Jeremy Hardy Speaks to the Nation, 1993

The fashionable view is that we are all now middle class. I was arguing with someone about this recently and he said, 'Well, we're all middle class now', and I said, 'Well, what about the nurses, they're working class surely?' And he said, 'Well, not necessarily, no, because I know some nurses from middle-class backgrounds.' But what have backgrounds got to do with it? Backgrounds. When you're up to your elbows in giblets and blood and poo and pus, it's probably small consolation that you once rode in a gymkhana. If you're in hospital and you say, 'Ooh, Nurse, I think I'm haemorrhaging,' she doesn't say, 'I'd like to help you, but do you know I've just been reclassified into a different socio-economic bracket. *C'est la vie.*'

Or sewage workers; how could you call sewage workers

anything but working class? If they were upwardly mobile professionals, they wouldn't go trudging through collapsing Victorian tunnels full of excrement and super-rats; they would hold consultancy sessions and advise people on alternative ways of recycling their own excrement, and making tofu out of it.

One of the reasons why some people think that the British working class is a spent force politically is the declining power of the unions. But it might be argued that the unions would have more influence if they actually did something and stopped worrying about alienating public opinion. For example, twenty years ago union leaders called strikes. It was brilliant. You never had to go to school. The trains weren't running, or there were power cuts, or no diesel supplies so no buses, and if you did get to school there was a general election on and it was a polling station so you went home again. Now they call one-day strikes so as to cause the minimum inconvenience. What use is a one-day strike? How can you have a class struggle on flexitime? It's like waging the Second World War on alternate Thursdays so as not to alienate Switzerland. And the aim of every dispute nowadays is to bring management to the table. Why not bring them to their knees, never mind the table?

But perhaps I'm being very old-fashioned. Actually, no I'm not because the anger over the pit closures should have forced a retreat by Heseltine and saved the coal industry, instead of which all the pits are closing and all the support for the miners has gone to waste. And why? Moderation.

The TUC spends eighteen grand placing an advert on page seven of the *Guardian* when they could just bring the government down and get page one for nothing.

* * *

Jeremy Hardy Speaks to the Nation, 1993

In fact, Britain is a more unequal society than it has been in a hundred years. It is becoming increasingly apparent that there are people who have slipped out of mainstream society. Witness the blank-faced youths with nothing to do, roaming huge estates high on heroin. I'm talking about the aristocracy. Left behind by the rest of society, the upper classes are out of control.

The British upper class still exhibit some of the most bizarre extremes of human behaviour. Take foxhunting, something which is appalling to most of us. But as custodians of the British countryside, the nobility are dedicated to ridding it of all wildlife.

Most of us would say that foxhunting is barbaric. In response, the hunters say, 'Barbaric? Have you seen what a fox does in a chicken run?' Well, I can't say I have, but have you seen what a pensioner does in a jumble sale? Or come to that, have you seen what a human being does in a chicken run for that matter. We're not exactly noted for our benevolence towards chickens. I mean, we eat their embryos, force-feed them fishmeal, cut their heads off, put their entrails into plastic bags and force them up their bottoms. Which can't be construed as charity.

And yet, for some reason foxes are expected to be vegetarians. You can hardly blame a fox for being a carnivore; they're cunning beasts but they haven't got the wherewithal to rustle up a chickpea lasagne. But how the hunting fraternity justify their vendetta against foxes is by complaining that when a fox gets into a chicken run, he doesn't just kill one chicken; what he does is to slaughter every single bird, it's a total and horrifying carnage on a horrifying scale. But he's just shopping for the week. I mean, if you successfully broke into Tesco one night, you wouldn't think, 'Ooh, tin of Smedley's peas should do me nicely.' But having shown the ingenuity and persistence to tunnel into a chicken run, people expect foxes to say, 'Is it all right if I just make myself an omelette?'

* * *

Jeremy Hardy Speaks to the Nation, 1997

The UK has jurisdiction over Northern Ireland, even though it is not part of Britain but part of Ireland, as is plainly visible from an aerial photograph.

* * *

Jeremy Hardy Speaks to the Nation, 2001

After the war there was a sudden change in attitude to immigration. Let's listen to this World Service Broadcast to the colonies –

STATESMAN: (AS IF HEARD THROUGH A CRACKLY OLD RADIO) Good evening, loyal brown subjects of His Majesty, King George. Many of you will be tired having fought for the Empire against the Narzee and his yellow ally. And to reward your battle service, we the government invite you to come with lovely teeth and small guitars to do some of the worst-paid but most rewarding jobs in Britain.

Not just you, but your lovely wives. What could be better while you conduct your bus than knowing that your good lady is washing the bottoms of your kindly but less tolerant older hosts in one of our modern hospitals? But hurry, the post-war boom won't last forever, and once the vacancies run out, so does the invitation . . . !

* * *

Jeremy Hardy Speaks to the Nation, 2007

As a post-industrial country with falling trade union membership and little collective sense of oppression except about speed cameras, we have really lost much of our folk tradition. And we haven't found a way of celebrating our national identity that isn't right-wing. Some people, including Billy Bragg, say we need to feel a new kind of progressive patriotism. Billy is a splendid man, but you only have to hear him sing 'Jerusalem' to know that 'extraordinary rendition' means torture.

* * *

Jeremy Hardy Speaks to the Nation, 2010

I am actually very fond of our land and its people. But I believe that patriotism, like religion and flatulence, should be private. My relationship to my country is my own, and the reasons I love it are possibly completely different from yours. I love it when we're chipper in defeat. That is the Dunkirk spirit. I do think there was a wonderful Britishness about the way people kept their spirits up in the darkest hours of the war. People like my mum. My mum is the most risk-averse person I've ever known. She thought anything would have your eye out. 'Put that down, you'll have someone's eye out', 'Don't speak with your mouth full, you'll have someone's eye out', 'Don't swing on your chair, you'll have someone's eye out'. There must have been something deficient in the diet in 1920s Portsmouth that left a generation with very weak eye sockets, so if you burped a baby overzealously its eye popped out over your shoulder. And yet, at the age of seventeen, Mum became an ARP Warden during the Blitz. She had to go out after the bombers had passed, looking for fires and injured people and unexploded bombs and possibly German airmen, and she coped with all that, despite the fact if a Jerry had crept up on her with a snowball, she'd have panicked because there could be some grit in there and that'll have your eye out. That's Britishness.

* * *

Jeremy Hardy Speaks to the Nation, 2014

Now it's one thing to abide by a country's laws, but when did it become compulsory to *love* where you live? I don't even like our road if I'm honest. I hate our road. I like our flat and our area, but I hate our road. It's a rat-run, gridlocked day and night. Why we moved there, I don't know. Well I do know, because we were misled. When we came to view it with the estate agent, it wasn't like that. We thought, 'Ooh, this is a nice quiet residential street.' We didn't know it had been cordoned off because of a shooting. We thought, 'Oh, lovely – pavement artists are doing chalk drawings of the human form.'

No one loves everything about a country. There are things I hate about Britain, and things I love. I love the train across the Pennines and would never want it speeded up, or driven underground, where it would only become more dangerous and harder for trainspotters to keep under surveillance. I love pubs and tea, and *The Morecambe and Wise Show*. I love the NHS, but I don't even love everything about that. I don't love A&E at 5 a.m. I'm not proud of our nation to see the hapless, nocturnal hedonists who've had such a good night they passed their kidneys peeing on a bus shelter, but don't remember because they blacked out after getting into a fight with their own sick. But that's the wonderful thing about the Health Service; it makes no judgement. It asks for no bank details nor ID. Are we bad citizens if we over-burden it through our self-destructive indulgences? Yes, and it tries to nudge us onto a path of righteousness, but won't abandon us. If it refused to treat drunks and smokers alto-gether, it would have to start shunning potholers and motorcyclists, and people who operate heavy machinery after taking antihistamines. What kind of hospital dramas would we have if no one ever climbed a rickety ladder to try and destroy a wasp nest with a surface-to-air missile in the vicinity of an airport?

* * *

Jeremy Hardy Speaks to the Nation, 2014

But we British are, I think, quite well-placed to shake off the hubris of nationhood; we're better than that. Because one of our strengths is an indefatigable and good-natured sense of our own uselessness. Travel around the world and you'll find people crowded round battered tellies with precarious aerials in makeshift bars cheering on Man United and Chelsea. And yet millions of British people knowingly and determinedly support football teams that are rubbish. And they take their sons and daughters along to watch rubbish football teams to teach them that there is something heroic about blinkered loyalty to a doomed enterprise. Perhaps even deeper in our national psyche than all the glory of Empire is a humbling lesson learned from our illustrious past. We might have had a foothold in every continent and a navy that ruled the seas, but were we happy? Weren't there days when we wished we could be Finland? There must have been times when Britannia thought,

BRITANNIA: Well, I've got here, but what's it all been for?

JEREMY: – like Obama does every day.

* * *

We're probably one of the most successfully integrated multiracial societies in the world. That's a significant feature of our identity. And yet people complain that Britishness is under threat, while giving no suggestions as to what Britishness means. How many of us know anything about our history and culture? How many of us could pass a citizenship test? Only immigrants can pass that because they've done the revision. They've learned the names of all the characters in *Emmerdale*, which house plants you can take cuttings from, and what this country still manufactures apart from Kendal Mint Cake and instruments of torture. The average Briton knows nothing about this country. One bloke I saw interviewed on some programme about white people said,

MAN: This country used to be Great Britain. Now, it's the United Kingdom.

Now, we have been the United Kingdom of Great Britain and Northern Ireland since Ireland was partitioned in 1921, before which we had been the United Kingdom of Great Britain and Ireland since 1800. I don't expect everyone to know the ins and outs of the Act of Union but if you claim to love your country, find out what it's flipping called.

And UKIP are a funny lot. The United Kingdom Independence Party. Their name doesn't even work as four words together. United Kingdom Independence Party. It's like British Empire Liberation Organisation. They're not out-and-out Nazis but they're barbecue Falangists, *Daily Mail* readers, Tim Henman fans. They're fanatically hostile to immigration but adamant that they're not racist. 'This isn't about race, it's about space. Britain is just full.' But I travel the length and breadth of this country and I'm telling you: it's largely empty. The bottom right-hand corner is full, mostly with people from other parts of Britain. Go down to Cornwall: no bugger lives there and wages are still terrible.

Labour and the Tories

The News Quiz, 2002

Margaret Thatcher was usually there at every disaster, wasn't she – she was there consoling the bereaved. Sometimes fractionally before it had happened.

* * *

Jeremy Hardy Speaks to the Nation, 2007

Sometimes I'd love to be a Tory. A *proper* Tory. And I wouldn't just want to be some middle-class, middle-England Pinot Grigio Conservative. Not some nouveau riche Rotarian, who's got a bit of an accent and a bit too much of a tummy to play tennis convincingly. I'd want to be a proper, willowy, aristocratic Tory. Someone perfectly slim who never exercises. Perfectly English but with a French mother. With a perfect side parting but hair that doesn't flop about. Not louche, fey or fascistic hair. Proper hair. I'd like to be asked to join the establishment. I'd like to be approached outside an umbrella shop by two very polite henchmen in trilbies who coax me into the back of a Bentley, where I meet a Wilfrid Hyde-White sort of character only not quite so jolly, who says –

(WILFRID HYDE-WHITE VOICE) 'Ah, Mr Hardy. We've been following your career with interest for some time.'

He then explains convincingly and with no cynicism or self-regard why socialism is understandable but wrong. And then pulls his head off to reveal that he's an alien and says that everything is going to be all right when the mothership arrives.

* * *

Jeremy Hardy Speaks to the Nation, 2010

And look at our last two Prime Ministers. Lady Thatcher began as a humble grocer's daughter who rose to the highest office in the land after marrying a millionaire. That's a bit cynical actually. She might not have married Denis for his money; it might have been his looks, his charisma or his intelligence. And John Major, a self-made man – he looks like he got himself in kit form, doesn't he? Couldn't quite follow the instructions properly.

* * *

Red Pepper, May 2011

Something weird is going on. People don't hate the Tories as much as they should. They do hate the Liberal Democrats, or rather Nick Clegg. The only other contemporary Lib Dem most would recognise is Vince Cable, and people are, at the time of writing, suspending judgement on him. We still don't know what he might do. He could just go nuts with a chainsaw, so no one wants to write him off quite yet.

Generally, the Liberal Democrats have become a stab-vest for the Tories. This fact alone, however, can't fully explain the fact that the Conservatives are not more widely loathed. Maybe people have fallen for the newness. The Tories have taken on human form, which is when they're at their most dangerous.

Even some progressive commentators are toying with the idea that they might be on some kind of journey. John Harris in the *Guardian* suggested that the 'Big Society' should not be dismissed too readily by 'the tired old left'. I don't consider either of those adjectives to be an insult, by the way.

Of course, Conservatives are actually human and, aside from a fear of the unwashed and a simpleton's optimism about markets, they're not always rigidly ideological. They might easily smile on the odd co-op if they thought it an amusing wheeze.

David Cameron and chums seem to be in politics mostly for their own entertainment. It's no wonder Dave gets on so well with Prince William. They both treat Britain as their plaything, and perhaps Britain has mistaken their cavalier attitude to it as a refreshing informality that humanises serious men who have a profound sense of duty and a poshness that's almost a burden. I fear Britain has not shaken off a deference that borders on masochism, and which helped to keep Thatcher in power for a very long time.

* * *

The News Quiz, 2013

On the day of Margaret Thatcher's funeral, David Cameron was interviewed and he said, 'Well, today is the day for setting aside politics and really to remember to vote Conservative at the next general election.' And that funeral reminded you what horrible friends Thatcher had. I was thinking blimey, she didn't half know some horrible people, didn't she? I mean there's Netanyahu, Tony Blair, Henry Kissinger. I mean, I'll be lucky to get half-a-dozen people, but at least they won't be mass murderers and Andrew Lloyd Webber. 'Oh, look, there's F. W. de Klerk! There's Jeffrey Archer! Oh, there's Kelvin MacKenzie!' I haven't seen so many scary white men in one place since I was at Wimbledon dog track.

* * *

Jeremy Hardy Speaks to the Nation, 2013

Cameron doesn't really believe in anything apart from himself, he just likes Obama because he's always wanted to have a friend who's black. And that was the only way he was ever going to get one; become a world leader and do it that way round.

* * *

Jeremy Hardy Speaks to the Nation, 2010

You shouldn't condemn someone for their upbringing. There's no point damning David Cameron for his background. The most damning thing you can say about a member of the Conservative Party is that they're a member of the Conservative Party. If people know that and are still prepared to vote for them, I'm at a loss frankly.

* * *

Musicport, 2016

Cameron has never met an ordinary person. He was sent to boarding school at six, picked up at twenty-one. He's lived in a blissful dream-world all of this time. That's why Cameron talks about ordinary things as though we're not going to spot that he's a fake. He'll say, 'Oh I love soccer, I'm a huge fan of Leicester Wednesday United. But why don't they pick up the ball and run with it? Is it something to do with social housing?' And he talks about music and you think, oh shut up, now you're really going to piss us off. If you claim to like The Jam again, we are going to fuck you up, Cameron. Because you can destroy our public services, but don't talk about the punk years. You know nothing about music of any description. You think Van Morrison is poor people's Ocado.

* * *

The News Quiz, 2017

MILES: Imagine looking at David Davis – in any walk of life – and thinking, 'Yeah, you're the man to do this.' It's hard to think what 'this' could be in any situation.

JEREMY: Retrieving a piece of Lego from some stinging nettles.

* * *

The News Quiz, 2016

The Conservative Party has a really elaborate way of choosing a new leader. You start with the basis of disloyalty towards the current leader, and then you call a referendum into Britain's membership of the European Union, in which one of the main contenders blatantly lies about the benefits of Brexit, and in fact carries on using the same lie into the future. And then that side wins a referendum and there's a kind of weird sort of Mexican standoff where everyone is dead. Finally, Theresa May pops up unscathed from behind a bullet-strewn counter.

But then Theresa May did a really weird thing. Boris Johnson had been executed for her by Michael Gove, but then she gave Boris the job of Foreign Secretary. I mean, why would you? You know there's going to be problems.

The strange thing about Theresa May is that she is incredibly ambitious and scheming and calculating, but she's really bad at it. She's like a homeopathic poisoner. So now she's got the problem that Boris is just humiliating her at every turn. She's like the woman at the beginning of a horror film who's looking for the dog and the dog has run away and then there's a weird yelping sound and the dog goes silent and she decides to go looking for the dog. And it's three minutes into the horror film and you're just thinking, 'Bye-bye, Theresa'.

* * *

The News Quiz, 2017

What I find most disturbing about Jacob Rees-Mogg is that he's got six children and he says he's never changed a nappy. That house must stink.

Scotland and the Union

Red Pepper, 2014

If Scotland leaves the UK, it will be the Tories' fault. Not that they'll grieve uncontrollably; hardly any of them live there. A Scottish Tory with political ambition generally heads south. Gove represents Surrey Heath, and Liam Fox found sanctuary in a Somerset hamlet called Little-Bigot-on-the-Necks-of-the-Poor. So some Scots ask, 'Why should we live under bastards we don't vote for?' Labour's mistake has been to join forces with said bastards, instead of urging Scots to stay in the fight against them.

It is tempting to ask Scottish socialists voting 'Yes' how they feel about a party with National in the title, but they retort that this is not about nationalism but self-determination. It's always an intellectual fudge for the left, whereby folksy, blood-and-soil nonsense is inspiring up until the moment of independence but no further. We haven't heard too much of that stuff from the Yes camp, but the 'we are better governing ourselves' line is rather tainted by UKIP. Who are 'ourselves' and when do we stop drawing lines on maps? And the principle of self-governance offers the moral argument for unregulated markets, private schools, gun ownership and brutal immigration policies.

But the SNP's appeal is more about its leftish policies than its depiction of other Britons as alien. Alex Salmond may see the English as effete reactionaries, but for most Scots that idea is no more serious than the English thinking Scots all choke to death on battered sausages aged thirty. And left-wing support for independence goes way beyond the Nats. It's about the Tories – and New Labour.

But if Scotland goes, the rest of us will have to cope, combating the maudlin introspection that will follow. Our place in the world will diminish, but that will be good for us.

* * *

Jeremy Hardy Speaks to the Nation, 2014

Everyone was pleased by the high turnout in Scotland, although it was partly explained by the extension of the franchise to sixteen-year-olds, the first time single malt whiskies have voted.

* * *

Laugh for Freedom, 2017

Bloody Scotland saved Theresa May. It was the re-emergence of the Scottish Tories, however that happened. Twenty years ago, Scottish Tories were virtually extinct. Weird people used to hunt their eggs. And then what happened was that some mad scientists in the Glens started to breed Tories in captivity, and some of them escaped and mated with mink, who'd escaped from fur farms, to create a new breed of cuddly Tory with a nasty bite.

* * *

Glastonbury Cabaret, 2017

I mean, people get really excited by Nicola Sturgeon. There's a lot about Nicola Sturgeon that I like. I quite like the SNP in lots of ways, but they put nationalism first and that's what's wrong about them. But the thing is their audience, they love her. I watched the SNP conference and they were completely Pavlovian. If you don't know what that means it refers to this Russian ballerina who used to make a kind of meringue out of dog saliva. But I watched Nicola Sturgeon, it wasn't what she was saying, it was the fact that she put emphasis on the right word and she smiled in the right place, and she frowned. And it was all the theatre of it. And I thought, God, you know, Nicola, you could say anything and people would love you. Nicola Sturgeon is such a brilliant speaker, it doesn't matter what she says, she could say anything. 'Conference. Mind melt.

Sheep brains. All the boys to the yard. And they're like it's better than yours.'

And I do love Scotland, I've just been up there, Highlands, it's beautiful. Orkney, Tobermory, it's absolutely gorgeous up there. It was a five-day tour, it wasn't a proper tour, it was kind of a mini-tour. But while I was up there, the Scots rescued the Tory Party. Ruth Davidson! And in some ways it was very positive, an out lesbian becomes a very successful Conservative politician. I'm not sure that Scottish Conservatives know what a lesbian is. 'Well, I've never been to Lebanon myself, but I do hear them Arabs are fine horse people and very good with falcons, you know. She certainly looks like a practical lassie, doesn't she? Yes. A golfer no doubt.'

Brexit

Jeremy Hardy Speaks to the Nation, 2014

Farage can, occasionally, be interesting. He has regrettably spent a lot of time stereotyping Roma people as being a criminal underclass, but he's also travelled to Eastern Europe and confirms that they are victims of appalling discrimination. It's not the most enlightened message,

FARAGE: They're all thieves, but who can blame them?

But the fact that he even identifies that Roma people have reason to come here for sanctuary as well as work is more than any other party leader has done.

Sadly, he's also happy to feed paranoia about the presence of a community who might one day, like British Romanies, be citizens. It's silly to say you'd be worried about living next to a house full of Roma men, except that any exclusively male environment is dysfunctional; you end up with Boko Haram and the Bullingdon Club. And in towns where Roma have settled, people's main complaint is that they stand outside a lot. Well, if you were one of ten blokes in a small house, you'd want some fresh air. And when did standing become antisocial? They're not doing it in the cinema. They're not doing it to taunt people with bad knees. Is it the static nature of the activity that's the problem? Would it be better if they ran on the spot or bounced up and down, or is it the use of legs themselves that's so egregious?

* * *

Jack Dee's Referendum Helpdesk, 2016

We won't be 'Great Britain' if we leave the EU. Scotland will leave the union, because they'll be annoyed with England and so we won't be the 'United Kingdom'. And UKIP will just be IP, which would be quite a funny name for a party.

We will be diminished, and Scotland will be furious with us. I mean, if I lived in Scotland I'd probably vote for independence, but then if I lived in America I'd probably weigh forty stones and think the Earth is only four-thousand years old.

* * *

The News Quiz, 2016

You can make an argument that says it was a bad idea to join the EU, but it is one of those things that once you're in it's probably impossible to get out. It's like it would be a bad idea to get a pacemaker from Wickes, but an even worse idea to try and remove it yourself.

* * *

Musicport, 2016

Farage is extraordinary, he just keeps coming back. Like Dr Who but without changing heads.

* * *

MAP Comedy Night, 2017

No one is interested in Paul Nuttall. He wants to be quoted, but no one quotes Paul Nuttall. He rings the BBC up and says, 'Hello, it's Paul Nuttall here and I wondered if you'd like my opinion on anything that's happened in the news?', and the BBC say, 'Right, is your dad there?' 'Yeah. Nigel, it's for you'.

* * *

Laugh for Freedom, 2017

A lot of people find it odd that there are black and Asian people who support UKIP. But you shouldn't be that surprised because what it shows is that immigration works well: within a generation people can be so fully integrated that they become as small-minded and bigoted as the indigenous community.

I was listening to a phone-in one time, and a man rang in from Croydon and said, 'Look, I'm a UKIP activist and I'm from Bangladesh originally, and I'm telling you Britain is full. We've got to stop this, no more immigrants coming to Britain. That's it, we've got to shut the door. No one from Europe, no one from the Commonwealth, no skills, no point system, no refugees. That's it, we're full. And I'm telling you that and I'm from Bangladesh.' And I thought, look, mate, this is a harmonious multiracial country, and if you don't like that fuck off back to where you came from . . . but that's a terrible argument, isn't it?

* * *

Laugh for Freedom, 2017

You might regret your choice to trust the child with scissors, but try getting the scissors back off that child once you realise your mistake. Brexit will be a disaster and everybody will go, 'Oh yeah, we fucked that up – can we go back in?' But if you say that, you get told off by the Brexiteers, 'You're a typical remoaner. A miserable pessimist.' I thought the EU referendum was about who we are as a people, our identity, and who we are *is* miserable pessimists. If there's one thing that unites this land it's our indefatigable and chipper resignation about the absolute shitness of life. And I'm proud to say that.

* * *

I don't really suit an enthusiastic welcome, it's not really in my lexicon because I'm not used to that kind of audience. I can't come on and say, 'Whoa, Glastonbury, how are you doing?' and everyone go 'Yay!' because I know my demographic too well. I'd ask you, 'Hey, how are you doing?' and most of you would say, 'Well you know eventually you reach a stage in life where you make peace with the fact that none of your plans really came to fruition. And then you throw yourself into parenthood for a long time and you don't really address any of your own issues. And then your kids are off your hands, but then your own parents become a worry and then there you go and you're next in line. Yay!'

But for the first time in my adult life, I am feeling slightly perky and it's unsettling me, it doesn't suit me. Things are getting better. I have been a member of the Labour Party since 1980, with a short gap between 1985 and 2015. And things are looking up.

I keep trying to give up politics because my life is nearly over, you know. And I think, oh, I've been banging my head against the fucking wall for the whole of my adult life, I'd quite like to be happy. I'd like to do observational shit about smartphones and trying to find the end of the cling film – that would do me.

This all started two years ago. What happened was I was all set to give up politics and one of my friends became leader of the Labour Party. Twice. And then I thought, well, I'll have to get involved again. And then it all started to look really good. And then Brexit happened. This time last year, I woke up with a thumping hangover, text messages firing, Brexit is happening. And many of us got overly pessimistic, especially people like me, metropolitan liberals, went into a meltdown. I woke up this morning to find a skinhead literally shitting on my croissant.

But it's not going to be that bad, it won't affect us. There's always been racism. The EU is not an international agreement on cosmopolitan niceness, it's still a neoliberal cabal of capitalists. We can fix things. But people say, 'A friend of mine is a quarter Dutch, and since Brexit he's had such terrible wind.' And I think, that will be the herrings. And I'm not against the Dutch, I've got family in Holland, they're really tall. Dutch people are enormous! But it's below sea level there so at home they look normal.

But things are looking up. And I was really worried up until about three weeks ago, I was thinking, oh God, maybe this was all a mistake, maybe he should never have become leader. And lifelong Labour voters are saying, 'Well, I've always voted Labour, this time I'm voting Theresa May.' And I thought what? That's like saying, 'Well, I've always used a wet razor in the past, this time I thought I'd try setting fire to my head.'

But people were saying, 'Oh, well the thing is you see, Theresa May is doing a good job. I think Theresa May is doing a good job.' I thought, no you don't, you haven't got a clue what she's doing. Neither has she. She's just reassuringly tedious because she doesn't have a heart.

And for right-wing people they got really overexcited last year with Brexit and they loved Boris Johnson. And then they needed a period of calm because they got scared. It was all a bit too much Boris. Because he's a character in the sense it would be better if he were fictional. But people loved it. People loved him because he was a big personality. It's like when your mum goes away for a weekend when you're a kid, to look after your nan who is poorly, and leaves you at home alone with your dad and it's brilliant because it's so exciting because he's so irresponsible and he lets you eat icing sugar with a tablespoon, and watch *Confessions of a Window Cleaner*. But by Sunday afternoon you're really scared and you want your mum to come back. And that's what Theresa May was like.

And people were saying, 'Yeah, but the thing is Corbyn, the trouble is, I would vote for him but he's not electable.' If you elect him, he's electable. All you've got to do is vote for him. 'But he's not.' He is the leader, twice, and he could be Prime Minister. 'Well, the trouble is he's not prime ministerial.' If you make him Prime Minister, by default he becomes Prime Minister, that's the only time you say someone is prime ministerial is when they are Prime Minister, that's how you know. Theresa May wasn't prime ministerial before, she was just weird. She was just like an unconvincing ghost in a school play. Cameron was just a chinless pudding in flip-flops. Attlee wasn't prime ministerial, but he got a lot done. Churchill wasn't prime ministerial, he was Churchillian, that's where he got the name. You never call anybody Prime Minister unless they're Prime Minister. You don't say, 'You know Darren in the petrol garage? No, Darren, not the one with the beard, the prime ministerial one.' You never say that. And Corbyn is going to redefine what prime ministerial is. You know he's not the best speaker in the world. He does put the emphasis on the wrong syllable. He does do that. But you know it shouldn't all be about the theatre and the performance of it.

And Corbyn has struggled with the media, he has had problems. That's why he appointed as his Head of Communications somebody with even worse communication skills than himself to take some of the heat. But the media has been viscerally hateful towards him and now they realise they were so out of step. That they're just picking on Theresa May because they're embarrassed by the fact they underestimated Corbyn, so they're just acting like they never were right up her arse in the first place.

The thing about news people is they're basically just horrible people. But politics aside, most news presenters are the sort of people who did very well at university and then never really made anything of their lives. Most of their friends are sort of comedians and things like that. And so, they're all rather bitter. And I feel sorry for any politician who has to go on the *Today* programme at seven in the morning and be coherent. 'So Minister, would you stamp on a puppy's face if it mitigated the effects of climate change?' 'Well I don't think I'd quite see things in those binary terms.' 'It's a simple question! Do you want to avert climate change?' 'Well, obviously I'm against climate change.' 'So you're prepared to stamp on a puppy's face?' 'Well no, obviously animal cruelty is wrong.' 'So you're in favour of it?' I don't know, I just got up. I just want a shit and some Shreddies, leave me alone.

But my point is, when Brexit happened last year a lot of people said, 'Oh, that's Corbyn's fault. It wasn't clear where he stood.' It *was* clear where he stood, he was ambivalent. And that was an honourable position. There's an awful lot wrong with the EU – they screwed Greece over – but he weighed it up and he thought, well, let's not join in a right-wing pitchfork-wielding mob to leave the EU. We'll stay in, link up with other socialists in Europe, and try and make it better. And you might not think you're a socialist, maybe you don't. Young people are amazing, youth people are brilliant. It's young people that are turning this around. It's the yut gen. It's my young bredrin, you get me? Because I've been campaigning for Corbyn, I was spending so much time with young people, and I delude myself that there is no age gap.

But they're brilliant young activists and I'm talking about people in their early twenties and I think wow, this is amazing. And they ask me about the eighties and I tell them about the miners' strike – of course I change the ending because I don't want to upset them. 'And then we won, but everyone resigned because of climate change.' But I'm talking to them and I'm thinking this is great, there's no gap between us, they understand me and I understand them. And then I'll tell them about the lack of provisions for older people and they'll say, 'Yeah, I know what you mean like, because my great-granddad is like forty or something.' Sorry to have bothered you, my carers will be here in a minute.

But what I was saying was that Corbyn got the blame for Brexit, people said they didn't know where he stood. And people said he should have gone on a platform with Cameron, which would have been the worst thing to do, because people hate seeing all the political establishment linking up. He hated Cameron, he didn't want to be part of the Tory Remain campaign, that was as it should be. I don't want to see Labour and Tory being friends. I don't want to see them on Andrew Neil's sofa cosying up while he sits there like a man enjoying the smell of his own farts, with his hair transplant desperately trying to reject him out of pure embarrassment.

* * *

The News Quiz, 2016

I've known Corbyn for nearly thirty years, and one time I met him and he reached into his pocket and said, 'Here, Jeremy', and he passed me something. I thought, 'Oh, is it microfilm? Is it something to do with Trident?' It was five daffodil bulbs.

The Uxbridge English Dictionary

Epistle / Letter written in the snow

Eyelash / Digital whip

Eyeglass / Digital tumbler

Eyepatch / Something to stick over your bottom to help you get over computers

Falsetto / Fake ice cream

Feckless / Celibate in Ireland

Flamboyant / A fire hazard that saves you from drowning

Fundamentalist / Giving money to David Icke

Geriatric / Next time Germany starts a war

Great Western / *High Noon, My Darling Clementine, Destry Rides Again*, but certainly not the rail service out of Paddington

Jeremy by Francesca Martinez

I'd wanted to be friends with Jeremy for years so I booked him for a gig. I must have managed to hide my stalkerish adoration because, to my delight, we quickly became buddies. Cue many evenings together laughing and debating the state of the world (but mainly laughing) with my partner, Kevin, and Jeremy's lovely wife, Katie.

Jeremy was incredibly supportive of my comedy and campaigned to get me on to The News Quiz. I was invited on and found myself sitting next to him in the iconic BBC Radio Theatre. That night I saw up close what an incredible talent he had when, more than once, he launched into an entirely improvised rant that was so side-splittingly word-perfect that I could only sit back in awe. We made just three appearances together; I think the BBC feared that our combined Lefty political views would turn the show into an audio version of the Communist Manifesto with added gags.

Jeremy was not only a comedy genius, he was deeply committed to political causes, and his integrity and bravery were immense. His activism over the decades reveals a man who stood up unfailingly for those who needed it – even risking his life when he shed light on the horrors of living in Palestine. In 2015, I helped organise the JC4PM tour in support of Jeremy Corbyn, and Jeremy H was always the first comedian to agree to perform. As the months went on many acts fell by the wayside. Not Jeremy. He performed in nearly every one of the twenty-four dates, never wavering in his support. As an inexperienced political activist, I was inspired by his steely nerve. He taught me that championing a 'popular' cause was easy, but doing so when it was 'unpopular' was when our support was most vital. When the going gets tough, those of us who have a platform have to shout louder and fight even harder.

In 2013, I had booked a small tour of Ireland. When I mentioned this to Jeremy, he asked if he could tag along and open my shows. Eyebrows raised, I said, 'The venues are small, the money's shit and it will probably rain.' But, surprisingly, he was up for it so, in May, we set off on tour broken up with a holiday in Kerry. Contrary to my weather forecast, we had glorious sunshine and soaring temperatures the whole trip. From the moment we picked up our hire car in Dublin, until we returned to the airport twelve days later, we laughed. I have never laughed so much in my life. Those of us lucky enough to call Jeremy a friend, will probably agree that he was even funnier off stage than on it. My partner, Kevin (Dublin born-and-bred), is also quite a hilarious human, so being stuck in a car with both of them was quite simply the most fun I've ever had. It was the road-trip of a lifetime, helped along by many pints of Guinness served up in the friendly venues that welcomed us with open arms. It felt like we were a little comedy family and the tour remains one of my most treasured memories. We all vowed to do it again.

During one of our many long conversations hurtling along

Irish motorways, I found out that Jeremy had a deep connection to the country – he'd had worked tirelessly alongside lawyer Rosemary Nelson on the Robert Hamill campaign. She was tragically murdered in connection to the campaign. He'd also campaigned just as tirelessly for the release of Róisín McAliskey. She was pregnant at the time, and they developed a long-lasting friendship: her future daughter Loinnir would, many years later, sing a beautiful Irish folk song a capella at Jeremy's funeral. There was not a dry eye in the church.

The last time I shared a stage with Jeremy was at a benefit gig in June 2018. As always, he was the star of the show but, a few weeks later, he told me he had cancer. Like all those who loved him, I desperately hoped he'd get better.

Jeremy's life was cut short, but he spent it doing what he loved, standing up for what he believed in – no matter the personal cost – and giving joy to millions. A true example to us all. I love you, Jeremy. Thank you for making the world a more beautiful place.

4

Jeremy Hardy Speaks About . . .

Making Sense of the World

'There was a Foreign Office buff being interviewed about Kim Jong-un and he said, "Well, he's a surprisingly good-humoured chap and he always invites all the ambassadors over, which his father never did, and he's a surprisingly witty man". And you think none of this is really helping . . . It's like saying, "One of the things people don't know about Hitler is the card tricks . . ."'

Violence, War and America

Jeremy Hardy Speaks to the Nation, 1993

It can be hard to avoid the violence of others. When women are attacked, they often blame themselves, but they shouldn't take the law into their own hands; it's the job of the courts to blame them. The police offer conflicting advice on personal safety. If a lone woman is attacked somewhere, police advise all women to stay indoors for the rest of their lives. And yet, if there's a whole spate of bombings in the run-up to Christmas and hundreds of people are being injured, police urge everyone to go about their business as normal.

A bomb is a horribly random weapon which can involve dozens of innocent people being killed or injured, and several other innocent people being fitted up by the police. Fortunately, there is no longer the death sentence for murder. Nonetheless, many people in the police and prison service would like to see a return to hanging, which is why they put suicidal young offenders on remand wings and leave them to get on with it. There are only a handful of offences which the state can punish with the ultimate penalty of death, and the most notable are treason and arson in the royal dock-yards. Treason covers anything from espionage to having an illicit relationship with someone in line to the throne. And given that most of us have had sex with at least one member of the royal family at one time or another, we could all be swinging from the end of a rope – if they like that sort of thing. As for royal dockyards, you might be surprised that there are any; it's hard to picture the royals hanging around the docks. Apart from one or two of them, obviously.

* * *

Guardian, 2000

Various scientists have told us in past days that they have found no evidence of depleted uranium causing disease. We should detain them no longer with our questions; they clearly have a lot of work to do. In the meantime, let us have a serious think about this.

Perhaps we have been looking at this the wrong way. Perhaps we should begin by asking ourselves what are the chances that depleted uranium is good for us. Would we, for example, think it wise to sprinkle a little onto our breakfast cereal? Would we expect to see it next to depleted lavender in Boots' aromatherapy range? Would we give it to our kids to play with?

When I was a child, the Ministry of Defence owned the woods near our home. The Ash Ranges were ideally situated between Aldershot and Sandhurst and the whole area was effectively under military occupation. Needless to say, violent crime was rife but officially sanctioned as horseplay. In any event, the first word I was able to read was 'Danger'. It was remiss of the MoD not to display it outside pubs frequented by paratroopers, but efforts were made to warn us about the military hardware littering what served as our common land. Regrettably, a red flag meant not that soldiers had shot their officers and be proclaimed a soviet, but that the firing ranges were in use. And we were expressly and gravely warned in safety lectures about what happened to boys who collected shells and bullets for fun.

We all had fine collections of spent rounds but the real prize was a bullet in its cartridge, which could apparently be fired if you held it in your dad's vice and hit the back of it with a hammer. Unexploded mortar shells were more rare but no one tried to hide from us the fact that they could take someone's eye out. No one said that there was no proven risk that leaving unexploded bombs lying around meant kids would find them. No one said the risk from bullets was present but not significant. No one said mortar shells occur naturally in pencils or Salisbury Plain, or that we would have to hold one right next to the head to be exposed to more than a limited risk.

I'm not even sure our teachers knew the exact scientific explanation as to why being blown up or shot is dangerous; they relied largely on anecdotal evidence. And arms manu-facturers have the decency not to contest the fact that their products are basically harmful. They brag, indeed. Conversely, most things that are lethally dangerous seem to be introduced to us by our betters as a tremendously good idea. Then, after a bit, rare side-effects are acknowledged in weaklings, infants and women. Then scientists do some more work and are divided. Then ministers get jumpy and disparities appear in their public and private utterances. Then retired ministers are hired to shore up the product's image, and money is given to Children in Need as a gesture of goodwill. Then, finally, the game is up, and we all wait to see whether our offspring will live to furnish us with healthy grandchildren.

Those of us fortunate enough to have been born with eyes can see what appear to be the results of depleted uranium in Iraq. It is for this reason that the government is leaving the Gulf War out of its investigations. So much depleted uranium was used then that it might confuse the issue by proving a link. But perhaps the dreadful birth defects and mutated plants are not evidence at all, but signs and wonders portending some great event. I'm not an expert and I can't say for sure, but I think the UN weapons inspectors took a partial view of biological warfare.

Doubtless by raising the issue I risk being accused of championing Saddam, fancying Milošević and imperilling jobs in the armour-piercing-shell industry. Even to draw attention to the fact that nuclear power has more to do with armaments than providing energy and a fun day out for the whole family is to risk accusations of being ideologically opposed to employment. And I suppose I am scaremongering. Rumours spread like toxic dust on a light breeze. And doubtless the Home Office will have a harder task in rescinding its welcome to Kosovan Albanians and returning them to their bombed-out homes if they know it's not even safe to breathe there.

But perhaps I'm worrying unnecessarily. Perhaps they'll find out vCJD is nothing to do with beef but a direct result of the Iraqis stockpiling healthy brains. Perhaps tobacco companies have been right all along and fags are as good for children as cocaine and thalidomide are. Perhaps AIDS is God's curse, like menstruation. Perhaps soldiers aren't as tough as they were in my young day when the propensity to mystery illnesses was knocked out of them during basic training. Perhaps civilians have unusually thin skins. What do I know?

* * *

Jeremy Hardy Speaks to the Nation, 2001

Of course, war is now global. And America is the greatest military machine in history. It is often called the world's policeman, because it beats the crap out of anyone who doesn't do as they're told. It targets the innocent, shoots the unarmed, and puts stickers on little children at school fetes. Now, many of you will say it's easy to run down the police, but it's not as easy as it is for them to run us down. I digress. My point is that modern war, which is waged for the same strategic and commercial reasons as it always has been, is now dressed up in the garb of international justice and emergency medical procedures. A war is a 'humanitarian intervention', with a few unwanted side-effects, cluster bombs causing temporary soreness and some loss of movement in missing limbs. Even the missiles are described as surgical, perhaps because of the number of hospitals they hit.

I am sure Tony Blair does see himself as a defender of the free world. He probably thinks he's doing God's work. Hardly anyone wakes up thinking, 'How can I make the world a worse place today?' except perhaps Noel Edmonds. Blair is clearly passionately convinced by his version of truth. I imagine but for an expensive education he would be walking harmlessly down high streets clutching plastic bags and shouting the c-word at strangers. I may be wrong but I can only go on the evidence.

* * *

Jeremy Hardy Speaks to the Nation, 2001

It's true that bombing is rather random. If the programme *Ground Force* ever transfers to America, it will probably be called *Airforce* and will involve patios dropped from five thousand feet and hitting the wrong garden. But those people who thought the war would have been more moral if fought with flick-knives rather missed the point. The purpose of bombing is to destroy infrastructure and terrorise civilians. And also, to offload last season's military hardware and enable restocking. If we didn't have a war every so often we'd have to have a car boot sale to shift all our old gear.

And anyway, if you support a war, you have to accept the consequences. If you book NATO for the gig you know they're going to trash the place. It's no good saying, 'Well, I think we should intervene but I don't think we should use cluster bombs or depleted uranium.' It's like hiring a debt collector and saying, 'Now I don't want any rough stuff, okay?'

And besides, what do you mean by this word 'we'? *You're* not going to go, are you? It's like watching the football and saying, 'We beat Germany 5–1'. No you didn't, you watched it on the telly. People support a war saying, 'I for one cannot sit idly by.' Yes you can; you're a newspaper columnist, sitting idly by is all you ever do.

* * *

Jeremy Hardy Speaks to the Nation, 2003

Politicians are the worst at writing themselves into the story, making it about *them*. Sadly, people fall for it, especially after something dreadful like September 11th. Mayor Giuliani is said to have acquitted himself well before the cameras. Well how was he expected to behave? Did anyone really think he'd appear on TV wearing a 'Shit Happens' T-shirt? And George Bush was suddenly popular. What did he do that was so remarkable? He's a politician and politicians have to know how to pull the right faces. But of course, everybody wants a piece of something like September 11th. People say –

That was so weird because it could have been me in that building. I mean, I've *been* in buildings. Not the World Trade Center itself, but World of Leather. And if I'd happened to go for a career in the financial services industry with a company that transferred me to the New York office, I might have started work there just at that exact time, if I hadn't instead become part of a closed order of nuns, entirely cut off from the outside world.

And we are invited to be part of the shared experience, remembering what we were doing when we heard the news. As though somehow the fact that we were collecting earwax on a hairgrip makes the tragedy more poignant. There seems to be a fear that the established order might collapse if we don't have the same feelings about the same thing at the same time. Even if it's only for appearances' sake. What we're actually thinking about isn't important. How are we supposed to stand still in silent contemplation for a whole minute without wondering what Buffy looks like naked? We can't be expected to snap into an exact emotion at an exact time. We are not Pavlov's dogs. And yet we are supposed to salivate and indeed become sexually aroused at the thought of Kylie Minogue, but are more likely to do both while asleep next to a nun on a National Express coach.

* * *

Jeremy Hardy Speaks to the Nation, 2003

Whether or not Saddam has weapons of mass destruction we don't know. We do know that hidden underground in Iraq are large stocks of a toxic liquid that clings to the skin and suffocates victims by blocking their pores. It's called oil.

Now some people tell me that oil isn't the reason for America's interest in Iraq but that *Israel* is calling the shots and wants America to attack Iraq. Whether or not Sharon would like America to attack Iraq, why would he be able to make it happen?

Well, from time to time when I'm talking to someone and I'm being critical of Israel's treatment of the Palestinians, they'll say that the problem is America is run by Jews. And I'll say that's not the problem and it's not really true, and they'll say, 'Well, Hollywood is run by Jews,' and I say, 'So the Occupation is Mel Brooks's fault?'

I think they've got the relationship the wrong way round. Israel, like Britain, is a client state of America's. It's a strategic matter. Our special relationship with America isn't secured by a secret British Beverly Hills cabal made up of Michael Caine, Ozzy Osbourne and Catherine Zeta-Jones. But I've heard people say America is controlled by 'Jewish money'. What's Jewish money? A dollar bill with the end snipped off?

* * *

Jeremy Hardy Speaks to the Nation, 2013

I'm not being hateful towards soldiers. I want them to come home safely, and I applaud the ones who break rank to speak out against wars. They should never have been put in that position. And they should not have been recruited when they were hormonal adolescents who'd just had a dispiriting meeting with the careers advisor. Because the army might be embracing sex equality, but who is it who gets most excited by the thought of being a soldier? Not women. Not even men. Boys. Have you ever met a sixteen-year-old boy who's capable of making a sensible decision about anything? Look at their bedrooms. I don't think you should be allowed to join the army, get married, go to church or have sex with a priest until you're at least thirty.

* * *

The News Quiz, 2013

SANDI: Jeremy, who's promised to take aim on the second amendment?

JEREMY: Well, this is the American right to 'bear arms'. I quite like bear arms because you can hug people and then you can claw their back if they annoyed you.

See, I don't want to stereotype Americans as being mental because without America we would have no Willie Nelson, no Ramones, no Johnny Cash, no Bette Davis, and there are all sorts of wonderful, intelligent American people. But, there is a large rural community and as we know rural people are a little bit odd. Rural people like guns, they use guns, they're comfortable with guns. You see us urban, soppy, effeminate people, we're scared of guns because they really only have one use, which is to maim and kill.

In this country we have an unarmed police force, but they do still seem to shoot a lot of people. Weirdly. But maybe that's because they're not routinely armed.

And statistics aren't necessarily causal. I mean, Italy

has more organised crime, but it's not because it has more pasta: there are historical reasons. We have less gun crime in the UK, but we probably have more stabbings than America. And Americans will say, 'Well, you don't ban knives', and we could say, 'Well, you don't take your knife to the pub, but the bread knife has another use'. You can't ban bread knives in the home because you need them to slice bread – in America you don't need them because they don't have bread that isn't already pre-sliced and so Americans don't know how to slice real bread. If you gave real bread to an American they would shoot it into smaller pieces.

* * *

Jeremy Hardy Speaks to the Nation, 2013

There are many kinds of power. One of them is what's been called Soft Power, which is as it sounds, meaningless rubbish to sell books, so let's not waste any more time on it. But power is more complicated than it's sometimes said to be. Chairman Mao wrote, 'Political power grows out of the barrel of a gun.' He wrote lots of things like that because he was quite moody but also terribly pleased with himself. I suppose you don't lead a revolutionary war to take control of the largest country on Earth without a lot of self-belief. That's why none of his famous phrases begin 'I reckon' or 'Tell me if I'm talking out of my arse . . .'

* * *

Jeremy Hardy Feels It, 2017

People who grew up in the interwar years have a remarkable stoicism because of all they went through. The name 'interwar years' can't have helped. It doesn't bode well, does it? It does rather suggest 'unfinished business'. Imagine what it was like in the Hundred Years War – you'd know you were in for the long haul then, wouldn't you?

* * *

Jeremy Hardy Speaks to the Nation, 2010

The irrational can be very attractive. Look at the popularity of Sarah Palin in the United States. Put simply, her political philosophy is that the Deadwood stage is a-headin on over the hill. But she is driven by something much deeper than dry post-monetarist laissez-faire economic theory; she also believes that the Lord created the heaven and the earth in six days quite recently. And she is by no means alone in her belief that the dinosaurs existed on Earth at the same time as human beings, which means she thinks *The Flintstones* was a natural history programme.

* * *

Jeremy Hardy Feels It, 2017

I don't think Donald Trump has ever felt sadness. I don't think he's ever felt an appropriate emotion about anything. When someone hands him a baby, he's completely bewildered; you can see him wondering whether he's supposed to eat it, throw it or molest it.

I mean, arguably, he's a sociopath and can't help it, but that diagnosis doesn't make him any more appealing. We do tend to pathologise all human behaviour now: 'It's not my fault, I suffer from Horrible Bastard Syndrome.' But if you look up 'sociopath', it does fit quite well with Trump until you get to 'often highly intelligent' and then it all goes tits up. So, arguably, he's just a narcissist, but that's an overused term that gets bandied around and very few people realise that it refers to the Greek god of ponds, who thought he was looking at his own reflection when actually it was a tiny daffodil.

The Middle East

Jeremy Hardy Speaks to the Nation, 2003

Last year I spent time in the Occupied Territories with activists opposing that occupation; and among the most fervent and dedicated of them were Jews, from Britain, from America and from Israel itself. Some of you might have heard me last year being interviewed on the *Today* programme and on *Broadcasting House* about my experiences on the West Bank. Now that I am less of a gibbering wreck, I can explain to you more clearly what I was doing there. I was attempting to make a documentary about the International Solidarity Movement, which brings activists from around the world to take part in non-violent protests against the occupation of the West Bank and Gaza. I arrived on Good Friday. On Easter Sunday, I was fairly shaken up to see the Holy Family Maternity Hospital, which had in March been sprayed with gunfire. The main focus of the shooting had been the statue of the Virgin Mary on top of the church in the middle of the hospital grounds, but remarkably the game old girl kept her foothold. I couldn't for the life of me see how the army could claim that she had been a threat. I know her statues are reputed to move but hardly ever in a sudden way, as if to suggest she might be reaching for a concealed weapon.

The next day, I joined a march from Bethlehem to Beit Jala. And as some of you might recall, we were shot at, which I can't recommend, but doesn't half toughen you up. I now don't feel quite the level of intimidation from security personnel over here. Metropolitan Police? Royal Ulster Constabulary? I'm like, 'Oooooh. Baton-charge me, big boy. I don't get out of bed for anything less than an armoured personnel carrier now.' As we approached this Israeli APC, we all went quiet in accordance with our non-violence training. This training was given to us by a pacifist Christian group and some of it did feel a little soppy. We had to do role-play and workshops called 'tear-gas is our friend' and 'learning to embrace your bullet hole'. But it is interesting and useful. One important thing you learn is not to be provoked. Because if I'd kicked off, the army would have known about it. I don't start trouble but I know how to finish it. Another thing you do is to choose the people who, on a demonstration, will negotiate with the security forces. So us having stopped some way short of the APC, our two negotiators approached the armoured vehicle with arms outstretched in a non-threatening posture to ask that we be allowed to pass in peace. But immediately, the soldiers started shooting. But part of the training we had is that you must try to avoid running because it creates panic. So the idea is that you retreat slowly, facing the army. So I thought, I'm here as a media tart but I'm going to do my bit at this moment. Because I didn't come here as part of this move-ment, but at this moment, with this movement is where I belong. I'm going to retreat as taught, walking slowly, in a non-violent posture, non-aggressively but defiantly standing firm in solidarity with these people, not panicking or running or showing fear but making sure I'm stood behind a really big bugger.

Anyway, after a couple of days holed up in this hotel in Bethlehem, some of us were evacuated by the British consu-late. It wasn't the first evacuation of the week for me, I can tell you. Tank muzzle outside the hotel window will do that for you. But I'm happy to report that being evacuated by the British consulate is a marvellous experience and although I'm not patriotic it did give me a rare opportunity to feel glad to be British. Because there we were in Bethlehem and the army had invaded the whole town and all the various consulates sent vehicles to evacuate their nationals. The British, Italians, Japanese and Americans. And without wishing to disrespect my new American comrades, I felt very glad not to be going with them. Because they were collected in armoured limousines. Their drivers had helmets, body armour and guns. Our man had driving gloves. And travel sweets. And as we sat in the Range Rover, the Italian vehicle had to back out to let a Red Crescent ambulance through and he was having a hard time and our driver said, 'Ha, imagine that, an Italian having difficulty reversing.' I thought, 'Fantastic, it's the twenty-first century and you're doing Second World War material.' But he got us to the consulate in Jerusalem and out came the British consul and he was lovely: 'Oh come in, come in, you've had quite an ordeal.' And I thought, 'Wilfrid Hyde-White lives.' And he said, 'This is my charming wife. Darling, could you get a G&T for the young anarchists. They've had the most beastly time.'

* * *

Red Pepper, 2013

Mahmoud Ahmadinejad cannot easily attack the state of Israel because he doesn't recognise it. I don't know why he doesn't recognise Israel; it's the same shape as Palestine, give or take – mainly take, obviously.

I jest; it is Israel's right to exist that he refuses to recognise. But should people recognise it? Well, it does exist, so it's childish to pretend otherwise. But whether states have rights is another matter. Whether people have rights is a moral rather than a biological question. The right to statehood is not like a liver. People are not born with one. Saying someone has a right to something just means you reckon they should have it.

But at least such judgements apply more sensibly to human beings than they do to geopolitical entities. We'd all say a person has a right to a home, but we wouldn't say their home has rights. Let's imagine all Israel's critics recognising its right to exist – although why should they say that if they don't believe it? One can accept a fact on the ground without thinking it was historically right. But anyway, let's say everyone accepts that Israel has a right to exist. That would still not guarantee its existence, in its present form or any other.

Did Yugoslavia have a right to exist? Does the United Kingdom of Great Britain and Northern Ireland? We once laid claim to the south as well, and might not always be able to claim the north. And what if Scotland leaves the United Kingdom? Or Wales? Or England? What if we become a republic or we're sold to America as Walt Disney's Cockney World of Adventures? States come and go, and their populations change. Will Israel exist as presently constituted in thirty years' time? It seems unlikely. Israelis will still exist, but that's a different matter.

* * *

Jeremy Hardy Speaks to the Nation, 2013

To some people, revolution is still synonymous with armed struggle, even though an armed struggle can chug along for years in a symbiotic relationship with the state. Governments love an internal threat because it keeps people on their toes and saves on travel expenses.

But the AK-47 is an iconic revolutionary image despite being just a gun. It fires bullets but that's about it. It has no apps. You can brandish it. You can hold it aloft horizontally with one hand and move it up and down in a crowd scene if you're an African or Middle Eastern film extra. (Interestingly, it was Native American film extras who pioneered that gesture, usually with Winchesters. But Hollywood has long since dispensed with their services.) But basically, the Automatic Kalashnikov is a very straightforward, low-cost assault weapon. It's like *The One Show*: lightweight, unsophisticated but undeniably popular, and a quick way of getting publicity.

Migrants and Refugees

Jeremy Hardy Speaks to the Nation, 1997

I don't think we should delude ourselves that the British have a more enlightened attitude to immigration. More likely, British people have simply had to accept that if there had been no immigration into this country there'd be nothing nice to eat. Where would you go to eat in this country after half past seven in the evening? Where would you go when you're pissed and starving and it's midnight? 'Let's go to the all-night liver and onions place . . . I think the scone palace is open, we can have a cream tea.'

Perhaps the only reason the French are less tolerant of newcomers than us is that they've always had delicious food, whereas our culinary flair stretches to putting some jam in the middle of rice pudding so we can stir it in to relieve the tedium. Any government that decided to remove all non-white people from this country would have to be prepared to see the rest of us starve to death, and at the moment our Home Secretary is only prepared to see asylum seekers starve to death.

We might like to think that the stolid British temperament would never allow Nazis to take over but it could happen – quite easily if the Channel Islands are anything to go by. If anyone thinks I'm being unfair, I once did a show on Jersey and I've never met so little resistance from an audience.

* * *

Jeremy Hardy Speaks to the Nation, 1993

The human spirit has survived any amount of oppression. Many people walking around at liberty have thinking which is far more controlled and distorted than that of people behind bars. The great Russian anarchist Bakunin did much of his thinking in jail. Of course, there wasn't much point in thinking, 'I think I'll nip out for a bit,' but the fact that he remained true to his ideas was a victory over his jailors.

* * *

Guardian, 2000

All racists should be hospitalised. I say this not just on principle but because it is very hard to maintain racial prejudice while being cared for by the National Health Service.

The reason why there are so many ethnic minority nurses is partly that governments have always imported workers at times of labour shortage. Britain has imported Irish nurses, canal diggers and railway builders. And in most of our major cities, where one can walk into a pub and not hear the words, 'You'm not be from rounds these parts, be thee?', one finds a tendency for pub landlords to be Irish. The Ministry of Labour must have at some time realised that there was a major skills shortage in the licensing trade and that what was needed was an Irish publican movement.

The English are not as well suited to the task for the simple reason that, whereas the Irish are determined to give people a drink and will use any means to do so, English landlords seem mainly concerned that people in their pubs should leave as soon as possible. The stroke of 11 p.m. is merely the excuse they have been looking for all day. Conversely, if an Irish barman says, 'Come along now, people, it's nearly half eleven', it's because he's about to open up again for the lunchtime trade.

After the Second World War Britain trawled the colonies, mostly for workers to do low-paid jobs. This was in the days when a person who came to Britain to work was not abused as an 'economic migrant'. It was accepted then that people have always moved around the world for economic reasons. But now reporters search for the home villages of migrants, hoping to uncover evidence that people are not being seriously persecuted but actually come for the cynical, self-serving reason that they are destitute.

And yet, at the same time, public officials are trawling the globe for nurses, teachers and the computer-literate. Flustered immigration officers, who have spent the last few years charged with the responsibility of discounting evidence of persecution, now have new criteria: 'I'm sorry, this applica-tion is unfounded. The truth is you've been tortured; you have no IT skills whatsoever.'

At the British Embassy in Khartoum, visa applicants are being asked whether they have ever been questioned by police or security, arrested or tortured. This is not for the purpose of providing safe haven for those who answer 'Yes'; quite the reverse. The clue to the reason for the questions lies in a sign in Arabic. It translates thus: 'Some of the questions we ask you may be too personal but our aim is to ensure that you will not become a burden on the British taxpayer.' Applicants must sign a declaration that they will not apply for asylum in the UK.

If anyone doubts the claims of asylum seekers from Sudan they should read this year's Amnesty International report. And if fuel protesters knew what the oil companies do to keep the stuff pumping, they might find more important things to kick up about than the cost of diesel. Not all governments make weak-kneed concessions to guarantee fuel supplies. Some use gunships. But despite the hideous things going on in Sudan, refugees, who are forced to lie and travel using false documents, arrive in this country to face detention or dispersal. They'd do better to play down the human rights abuses and ring the Home Office direct to say, 'Let me in, I understand computers. I can even help you buy one that works.'

I do not know how many nurses, teachers, data processors, professors, poets or architects are living on vouchers in B&Bs around Britain. I don't suppose the Home Office takes the trouble to find out. Shipping them out as quickly as possible is the overriding aim. Meanwhile, nurses are brought in from Spain and teachers from Australia, and we are very grateful to them.

If the government won't offer decent wages and conditions to people already here, if it can't hold on to trained staff, people will have to be imported. Education ministers and schools inspectors are more skilled than immigration officers when it comes to driving people out. Vouchers have failed. But nothing was ever calculated to divide, demoralise and humiliate more than performance management. Lord Woodhead as refugee tsar would have them leaving in droves.

Apart from such an obvious exception, everyone living or arriving in Britain has something to offer. It's just that the government is arbitrary in recognising it. Praise is political. The government likes to put people through hoops, so it's just as well people from abroad are more athletic.

It's possible that a refugee who barely scrapes in today will be lauded in ten years' time for how he's performed, the contribution he's made, his donation to a political party. The government gives people a market value. It is not concerned with the right to decent pay, safety, freedom of movement. It treats people as goods and then gets indignant when they turn up in crates on the backs of lorries.

* * *

Jeremy Hardy Speaks to the Nation, 2001

Clearly our society has a dysfunctional attitude to children. We use children as a status symbol, but when women carrying babies go begging on the Underground, they get accused of using them as props. Where are they supposed to leave them? The beggars' crèche at Oxford Circus?

* * *

Jeremy Hardy Speaks to the Nation, 2003

Our government judges people suitable immigrants only if they have the skills we've forgotten to train ourselves in. Racist journalists ask why we should help asylum seekers 'who have done nothing for this country'. Well, give them a chance – they've only just got here. A newborn baby's never lifted a finger for anyone else but you do the spare room up for them.

* * *

Jeremy Hardy Speaks to the Nation, 2003

One thing we *can* all do is try to imagine what it's like to be someone else, put yourself in their position, walk a mile in their shoes. Don't be too quick to judge. You see a refugee woman from Eastern Europe begging with a bunch of kids in tow and you think –

DEBBIE: (SNOOTY) God, I mean look at that woman. She's got all those kids and she can't afford them. Why have them if you're not able to bring them up?

Pause and think –

DEBBIE: Oh, hang on. Those are my children. Oh, my God. It's the au pair. How embarrassing.

* * *

The News Quiz, 2016

Various young vulnerable people are being brought in from the Calais refugee camp. Had Theresa May when she was Home Secretary done this months ago, as she could and should have done with no fanfare and without photographers – taking pictures of children, in breach of press rules – no one would be making a fuss about it, but as it is it's all happened in a rush, with the demolition of the camp about to proceed, and some of the kids, it is said, look older than eighteen.

But it is very hard to gauge how old people are because different experiences will age you. If you've grown up in a war zone and you've made it from Afghanistan to northern France on foot apart from a brief sit-down on a leaky dinghy in the Aegean – that will age you, as will the fact of not having slept for about a year, that will age you. Listeners, Miles (Jupp) has five young children and, despite being under forty, looks like Margaret Rutherford in her later years. I myself am prone to stress and worry and, despite being a mere fifty-five years old, I resemble a quilt made from offcuts of Keith Richards and W. H. Auden.

* * *

MAP Comedy Night, 2017

People say we can't welcome refugees because we're a small country. But anybody who thinks Britain is small should try getting from Aberystwyth to Lowestoft on a Sunday. People say, 'Well we're full up, that's the trouble. We'd like to help people, we'd like to help the Syrians, but we're full, aren't we? Have you noticed how full Britain is? Do you know a friend of mine came back from holiday the other day and someone else fell in the sea!'

So many of my friends say, 'Oh, we don't know what to do, last of the kids are going off to uni, we don't know what to do.' I'll tell you what to do, get some refugees in their bedrooms before the little bastards try and come back. If you let your kids back in their bedrooms, you'll never get shot of them. You need refugees – people with some spirit who will build a future and move on, people with self-respect and culinary skills – not your children.

* * *

Laugh for Freedom, 2017

I was down in Dover last summer because my partner was filming a cross-Channel swim. I never understood why anyone would try and swim to France until I spent an after-noon in Dover.

People there were saying, 'There's thousands of those refu-gees over in Calais, twenty-one miles from here, and they all want to come to Dover'. And I thought, don't flatter your-selves, they want to go *through* you; you're very much a transit point. They're not coming over here to nick all your Dover sole, because we all know Northern soul is much better. And don't be a port and then be surprised that people tip up from time to time – it's what you're for. The only reason Dover exists is its proximity to continental Europe. It wasn't a palm-fringed tropical paradise until some bastard built France there.

People will come up with any reason as to why we shouldn't have refugees in this country. And they'll say, 'Oh well, what if they're terrorists?' and I think, well they're not going to be, are they? What is the likelihood that they're going to be terrorists when they're running away from terror? I'm not making light of terrorism – I live in London, we're all in danger – but the fact is most people are not terrorists. Especially not refugees. Terrorism is often home-grown, though not organic because they do use fertiliser. And people in refugee camps are much more likely to be cooks and doctors and nurses and builders. Terrorism is a fantastically unpopular career. Especially since that whole suicide element was brought into it. People look at that as an option and say, 'Well, where's the progression? I need to think about my future.'

* * *

Jeremy Hardy Feels It, 2017

Let's talk about fear in Britain today. It might be that you live in an area where you have to keep your wits about you to survive, whether because of turf wars between rival drug gangs or the risk of being crushed beneath the wheels of enormous baby buggies pushed by highly caffeinated mothers shouting to one another that they have no time to go to Pilates because they literally have to stand over the cleaner and tell her what to do because she's so useless and barely speaks English but if you want someone cheap, illegal is the only way to go.

But increasingly, in a society which in global terms is comparatively safe, people *choose* to be afraid, select from a smorgasbord of terror offered by popular culture and mass media. It might be the sickening unease elicited by horror stories or *Bargain Hunt* presenters; or the thrill of dangerous sports – you'd need to be completely unused to external threats or addicted to them to think skiing is a good idea. I take a bag of grit to the ice rink and that's flat. What's the point in paying to use a surface that's impossible to walk on and then putting on special boots that make it just about possible? It's like buying a mattress stuffed with broken glass and then sleeping in a suit of armour. I don't need to prove to myself that ice is slippery as I have many times slipped and hurt myself on a frozen pavement, and I can tell you, it's not particularly exhilarating. Although it is free.

My point is that the function of prejudice is to provide us with an *imagined* external threat, because we're looking for things to fear. And if we're not confident in our own identity, we're likely to define ourselves by what we're not. If someone has a different lifestyle from ours, we're likely to fear that they're doing it to challenge *us*, because they think they're better than us. It might be a religion, a fashion or a diet. If someone's a vegetarian people demand to know why and say, 'Hitler was a vegetarian.' Yes, but that wasn't the main thing about Hitler. No one says, 'Well, Mussolini ate pasta' or 'I'm sure Fred West was funny about olives'. We see a Muslim family calmly going about their business, not bothering anybody, and we think, 'Oh right, so the rest of us are all promiscuous, pig-eating drunks, is that what you're saying?'

Islamophobia is one of the great prejudices of the age and, as with all prejudices, the target very often gets the blame. 'Well if they're going to walk down the street with all those clothes on, they're asking for it.' The victim is seen as having a problem of their own making. People say, 'You can't help being afraid that one of them might be a terrorist.' *Yes you can*, just as you can help being afraid that a vegetarian is actually Adolf Hitler, who faked his death, had extensive plastic surgery and has been hiding out in a soya mince warehouse for seventy years.

Programme Trailers

'Later on Radio 4, Gordon Ramsay talks about his love of feline-themed pyjamas in *Gordon's Kitten Nightwear*.'

'Later on Radio 4, Evan Davis re-lives the trauma of seeing his plumber bend down to look under his sink – that's *The Bottom Line*, at half past eight.'

'Later on Radio 4, we ask whether newspapers really are tomorrow's fish and chip paper. That's *A Plaice in The Sun'*.

'Later on Channel 4, old ladies show their tattoos to Kevin McCloud in *Gran Designs*.'

'Later on BBC 1, a dramatization of Sir Arthur Conan Doyle's lost novel in which his detective hero is beaten to death. *That's Holmes Under the Hammer*, tonight at 9 o'clock.'

'Later on Channel 4, Paul Hollywood judges contestants on the amount of phlegm they can produce. That's, *The Great British Bad Cough*.'

Jeremy by Victoria Coren Mitchell

I still think of Jeremy Hardy as one of the recent arrivals on The News Quiz. *A mischievous young scamp brought in to shake things up. Even though he joined in about 1994. He's been doing the show since* before Harry Styles was born. *But my father had already been on there since I was a toddler, which was 15 years (in technical terms, nearly a whole Styles) before Jeremy turned up.*

Obviously he seemed very different to the regulars – though there were some amazing guests on that programme (Clive James, Peter Cook, people of that calibre) and it wasn't a dusty kind of show. In fact, it featured a progressive number of women – Joan Bakewell, Irma Kurtz, Claire Rayner, Ann Leslie and several more – all before comedy panel shows even really existed in their current form.

I knew Jeremy a bit already, as I'd been trying my hand at stand-up comedy at clubs in London and Edinburgh and he had been incredibly kind, encouraging and supportive. I had really fallen for the exciting, energetic, talent-filled world of 1990s stand-up so I was excited to see it start to merge with The News Quiz, *which occupied a different part of my head completely. (I have never been on that show myself, and I don't think I would ever consider myself equal to it.)*

When Jeremy started, some long-term fans of the show said he was too left-wing, that there was a sort of influx of lefty comics and the whole programme became a bit politically unbalanced. And they still say that. My view was that you can't ask people to keep their opinions out of their comedy, not if that's their natural speaking voice: the only solution is, comically, for the right to up its game. They need to find more people to express their thoughts with humour. Because you have to have funny people. My father's view was always that it's rather impolite to express one's thoughts seriously. *Anyway he adored Jeremy, thought he was brilliant and took great pleasure in the jokes.*

As a teenage comedy fan, I was dazzled. I adored almost everything that had ever been on Radio 4, but it was incredible for me at that age to go to see live comedy and encounter in Jeremy (and Mark Steel and a couple of others) this comedy with a purpose which I'd never seen. It was exhilarating, this gently angry, targeted, purposeful, comic power.

Jeremy was somebody who, in his comedy and in his politics and his work, went towards trouble. In his partner Katie Barlow, he really found a soulmate there. Such bravery and goodness. For me that was absolutely consistent with how Jeremy was personally. He was the sort of friend who, when there was trouble and difficulty, would come towards you not move away. Not everybody does that, and it's the best thing you can do as a friend.

I remember Jeremy being in touch immediately at the tough times, when my father was ill. When my dad died, Jeremy and Andy Hamilton and a couple of others came with the News Quiz *producer to see my mother at the house, like a sort of deposition from the factory come to pay their respects. It meant a huge amount, and they didn't have to come. There was a funeral, there was a memorial service, they didn't need to do that as well – but they did because they were people who weren't frightened of sadness and trouble. Or who were frightened but went towards it anyway.*

A lot of people came to my father's funeral, but Jeremy is one of those I remember most clearly. Although that may be simply because of his yarmulke *(skullcap) which he had gone specially to Golders Green to buy for the service. I don't know why he did that. Nobody else was wearing them. We were literally in a churchyard.*

It was a lovable, funny gesture that was typical of the man, and I remember the warmth of his hug that day and I miss it now.

I'm going to finish with one of my father's favourite quotes, which seems very appropriate to Jeremy Hardy. The quote is attributed to Frederick Foakes-Jackson, a theologian who was the Dean of Jesus College from about 1890 until the First World War. A new don had started at the college, and he asked for advice. Foakes-Jackson's advice was: 'It's no use trying to be clever. We are all clever here. Just try to be kind.'

5

Jeremy Hardy Speaks About . . .

Modern Life

*'It would be ludicrous for me to attempt to discuss
modern technology without mentioning computers.
Unfortunately, I can't at the moment because my printer
churned out twenty pages of asterisks and an envelope.'*

Modern Britain

Jeremy Hardy Feels It, 2017

There was a time in human history when fear was arguably our most important emotion, when our fight-or-flight response to danger was crucial to our survival. Sudden, involuntary physical changes would occur: hormones would be released to give us an energy spike, blood would flow to the muscles and our excretory organs would spontaneously release waste, so that would-be predators would think, 'You know what, I'm really not sure I fancy eating that now. I might just have a bowl of cereal when I get in.'

It makes sense that the bodily effects of fear are hard-wired by evolution; but the things we're afraid of change over time and are subject to all kinds of conditioning. People in modern Britain aren't afraid of lions, although this is not because we're unlikely to meet one but because David Attenborough has such a soothing voice. If nature programmes were voiced by Ray Winstone, we might feel differently: 'This slag of an impala is about to find out the hard way who the daddy is.' And, probably because of the film *Jaws*, which is made up, people are afraid of sharks. It wasn't even a real one, it was Danny DeVito in a costume. And anyway, sharks native to British waters don't bite and are forbidden from using leisure centres.

* * *

Jeremy Hardy Speaks to the Nation, 1993

What constitutes good manners varies around the world. In some countries belching at the dinner table is considered a great compliment to your host and profuse vomiting is a great compliment to your tour guide.

* * *

Jeremy Hardy Speaks to the Nation, 1997

Let us now move on to the next part of my guide to keeping abreast of the latest developments, How To Be Informed About Popular Music Hits Of The Day. Those of you listening on wooden hi-fidelity equipment may be hoping that I am about to answer the question 'What is Britpop?'

Put very simply, it is British popular contemporary music. Whoever coined the phrase was probably inspired by the catchy title of the BRIT Awards, which were renamed because they weren't doing too well with the name Her Majesty the Queen's National Rock & Roll Record and Tape Outstanding Achievement Gold Medal for Singing Loudly and Clearly Awards.

I often wonder what people in Northern Ireland make of an awards ceremony called the BRITs, and whether they expect categories like Best Attack on Unarmed Civilians. But, as I asked before, what is Britpop? Broadly speaking, to qualify as Britpop bands must have a one-word name with no 'the', like Oasis, Pulp, Blur, Dodgy, Sleeper, Lush,

Ash or Cast. So if you have a young niece or nephew who likes Britpop, and you want to be able to buy them a birthday present without embarrassment, simply walk into the gramophone shop, say any single word and hope that it also happens to be the name of a band.

Of course, the term Britpop was invented by journalists, and refers almost exclusively to English music. The very splendid Manic Street Preachers have until recently been stigmatised for being Welsh, a whole nation being made to pay for the crimes of Max Boyce. But in business, Britain must be packaged as a single, united country. Hence the rather optimistic new expression Cool Britannia. But the British will never be cool; the best we can hope for is to be very mild for the time of year.

Service Providers

The News Quiz

All these people know nothing, they think a Super Saver is a person who cuts the customers out of the wreckage at the end of the day. It's preposterous. The railways are being run by people who – oh, you've got a great creative sense of what you can do with mauve but no idea how to run a train. And the man comes on the tannoy, he says, 'I am your Customer Operations Leader', and you think 'What is that?' That's not a job, that's just three random words strung together. Like saying, 'I am your Farrier Crisps Pencil.'

* * *

Jeremy Hardy Speaks to the Nation, 2004

Because I'm always in during the day, I'm constantly plagued by people wanting me to change service providers. The doorbell goes and it's British Gas asking me if I want them to deliver the milk and I say, 'No, it's all right, the milk comes out of the electricity sockets.' And then Pizza Hut turn up and deliver the paper. And the reason I don't have broadband is I don't know which broadband supplier to use. If one is cheaper than another, why is that? Are they nicer people? Do they use string? Can't they form a cartel and fix a price somewhere in the middle? Why can't the council do it?

I think I preferred the days when you had to fill the bath if anything was going to be done to the house. And the street was cordoned off and the gas and electricity disconnected so your mum would make your dad's dinner in the morning and put it in a Thermos flask and spend all day making cheese and piccalilli sandwiches for six workmen with yellow fingers and the children had to go and live in Wales until it was over.

* * *

Jeremy Hardy Speaks to the Nation, 2004

Militant drivers in this country are obsessed with speed cameras being an infringement of their liberty. 'Motorists are not criminals,' they proclaim. Well, sometimes they are. Car thieves are criminals. Hit and run drivers are criminals. Getaway drivers are criminals, or very naive cabbies.

Some driving stuff is illegal, and that's not exactly authoritarian. I've read *1984* and nowhere in the canon of Newspeak do we find the phrase 'Please drive carefully through our village.' Now different countries have different rules. Abroad on the roadside you can see signs reading 'Italy welcomes dangerous lunatics,' only partly obscured by the twisted and smouldering carcasses of former tomato lorries.

* * *

Jeremy Hardy Speaks to the Nation, 2007

People keep telling me reference numbers to make a note of, which would be all right if they gave me letters and numbers, but instead they say, 'Sierra, Tango, Oscar, November' and I think, 'Oh no, how do you spell "Sierra"?' And they ask for my name, and I say, 'Jeremy' and they say, 'How do you spell Jeremy?' and I say, 'The usual way . . . J—' And they say, 'Is that Q for Quintet?' and I say 'No, J, E . . . Oh blimey, Juliet Echo Rectum Euphoria Mudlark Yeomanry.'

JULIET (STEVENSON): Imagine what it's like being called Juliet. 'How do you spell Juliet?' 'JULIET . . .' 'And how do you spell Juliet?' . . . 'JULIET' . . . 'And how do you spell Juliet . . . ?' If my husband's name was Oscar I'd be buggered.

JEREMY: I should imagine so.

* * *

The News Quiz, 2014

JEREMY: Let's just nationalise the energy companies. You know, my life's coming to an end, I haven't got time to switch energy companies. I'm not going to spend my days trying to choose between different power companies – let's just take them all back and we can choose between gas and electric and that's the end of it.

People knock on my door and say, 'Who supplies your gas?' and I think, 'Not you. Now get out of my face, I've got windows to stare out of'. They say, 'Everyone on your street has signed up to us', and I think, 'Well, then they can pitchfork me to death for not signing up. The fact that you've knocked on my door while I was on the lav means that I will never sign up. Frankly, I would rather have Imperfect Pizza deliver my gas and electricity than you.'

But they say, 'Oh, why don't you all switch?' Yeah, that's a fun game to play every day. When it comes to gas and electricity companies you're basically limited to gas and electricity companies to choose among – it's not a smorgasbord to choose from, it's not like match. com, expect to the extent that you waste all of your free time interacting with liars and mountebanks until you're so worn down by their lies and blandishments that you eventually get shafted by one of them.

SANDI: Can you imagine what it must be like if you are from an energy company and you knock on Jeremy's door?

* * *

The News Quiz, 2017

You don't want a well-spoken carpenter – you know, those people who used to work in media who go 'I'd like to do something with my hands instead'. You don't want a privately educated craftsperson in your house.

'Would you like a cup of tea?' 'Have you got any herbal tea?' . . . oh Christ . . . if they don't have two sugars they're going to be bloody useless; they're going to be trying to fix your worktops by reiki.

* * *

Jeremy Hardy Speaks to the Nation, 2013

There's a bloke on the till at the little Sainsbury's on Streatham Hill who says funny things when he's bagging, which is great because it makes you doubly glad you didn't self-checkout, and reminds you that people are funny, which makes what I do redundant. If I just stood here putting shopping in a bag, the audience would say, 'Any fool can do that', but you'd be wrong because there's a knack to it if you don't want to put the cucumber through the side and crush the rocket, and this guy manages that *and* he's funny.

And there used to be a lady in Brixton Tesco on the checkout who would say, 'How you doin', darling?', and you'd say, 'Fine, how are you?', expecting a corporate script, but she'd say, 'I'm fine because the Lord Jesus is in me life.' And that was great, that was who she was. She didn't evangelise. She didn't say, 'Have you got a divine reward card?' She just wanted to share that she was happy and I was happy for her. And I looked forward to seeing her, but then one time I went in, I made sure I got in her queue and got up to the till and said, 'How are you?' expecting the whole Jesus bit but she just nodded and looked down. She'd obviously been silenced. Someone had got to her. And I felt like saying, (URGENT SPY FILM VOICE) 'We can't speak here. Meet me in the café next to the bookshop on Kropotkin Strasse in fifteen minutes. And come alone.'

Pets

Jeremy Hardy Speaks to the Nation, 2001

Cats are rotten pets because they are self-sufficient. If you fall down the stairs and break your back, and look pleadingly towards the phone in the hope that your faithful friend will nudge it towards you, the cat will merely stare at you with a slightly annoyed expression, wondering how hungry it will have to get before it eats your face.

* * *

Jeremy Hardy Speaks to the Nation, 2013

It is forgivable to have a weird voice for talking to dogs because we don't speak their language. Talking to cows and sheep is easy because you just go Moo or Baa and they look up to acknowledge you, chew a couple of times, realise you've got no vocabulary, just very good pronunciation, and then go back to eating the grass, but barking isn't a word. Dogs don't literally say *woof*, although I did once meet a talking cat in Balham. He didn't go *miaow*, he actually spoke the word. He did. He sat on a wall and as I went past he said 'Miaow', very clearly, and I looked around to see if I was being set up by one of the many pallid and regrettable copies of *Candid Camera* that have happened since it first aired in 1948. But he did it again and his lips moved, so I think he was a man who'd been turned into a cat, but still had his own voice, but I think that's quite unusual.

However, although dogs don't speak English, they do respond to tone of voice, because they appear to be genuinely capable of understanding human emotion, in a way that's unknown among other animals and maths graduates. A dog knows when we're happy or sad or frightened, and will lick its genitals slightly differently in each one of those circumstances. Dogs also play a useful role in facilitating communication among humans. If a person is out walking a dog, you've got a ready-made conversation with them. We would never dream of going up to a random dogless pedestrian and asking what breed they are, and how old they are, and saying how gorgeous they are. We wouldn't stroke them or crinkle their ears. Certainly not if they were carrying a bag of their *own* excrement.

I always find it a bit worrying if someone's got a bag of excrement and no dog. 'Yeah, I just like the accessories.'

Fashion

Early Stand-up Set, The Cabaret Upstairs, 1985

I can't wait for the warmer weather to come now; I'm very anxious to get a bit of a tan, as well. I'm not going to give myself a head start with the lamps and the creams and so forth; it's cheating, isn't it, really? I thought I might Tipp-Ex my abdomen to make the rest of me look darker but I was wrong cos I didn't.

But I do care a bit about my appearance. I hope the people here tonight who can see me like this rather nice cardigan I'm wearing. Didn't actually cost me a penny. It was knitted in return for sexual favours. I went to Boots on my brother's behalf.

* * *

Jeremy Hardy Speaks to the Nation, 2003

Fashion companies, for whom brand loyalty is everything, are similar to religions in that they want to enslave the young as early as possible. Because capitalist production involves not diversity but uniformity, the only way of telling clothes apart is to give them names. We have lost sight of the fact that cats and dogs should have names, and trousers and underpants shouldn't. Trousers shouldn't be called 'Tommy' or 'Calvin'; they are lifeless fabric and can't hear. But people worry that they might have bought fake Calvins. How can you counterfeit knickers? If you can see them they're real. Are you going to hold them up to the light and look for a watermark?

The Nike swoosh turns kids into fashion slaves, although some earn enough to send a little bit home to their parents. And Gap is like Tate Modern, because you look around you thinking, 'A child could have done that.'

It is in the nature of capitalism that we massively over-produce celebrities, who must then either be humanely destroyed, sold cheap to pensioners, or forced onto a reluctant public. Part of the popularity of Phil Collins is that he is supposed to be an ordinary bloke. The only ordinary thing about him is that he is ever present. Now, you might protest, 'Say what you like about Phil Collins. He happens to be a very popular entertainer'. But he's not. Phil Collins is not popular. Nobody *loves* Phil Collins. Tired people find him acceptable.

Travel and Abroad

Jeremy Hardy Speaks to the Nation, 1993

An Englishman's idea of a holiday is to be flat out on a beach smothered in oil, and yet if he sees a cormorant in the same situation it's a national emergency.

* * *

Jeremy Hardy Speaks to the Nation, 2004

The things we most fear are the things that haunt our imaginations rather than things that are familiar to us. Spiders I can deal with. I've had to fly back from foreign countries to deal with spiders for other people. And abroad, they have big dangerous spiders, notably in Australia where all insects are big and dangerous. In Australia, a ladybird is the size of a car and carries a chainsaw. Our spiders are titchy, but for an arachnophobe, a spider is a miniature monster; something that has crossed into the everyday world from the world of our nightmares.

People fear things that don't even exist: demons, bad spirits, aliens. Sailors have feared sirens, sea monsters and ghost ships. Mariners do seem to have been especially neurotic in the past, before they were able to relax to Charlotte Green reading the Shipping Forecast, as the ship bucked and tossed, the salty spray . . . I'm sorry.

On the other hand, we can *develop* a fear of something, when before it didn't bother us. Now it's always entertaining to watch somebody being bothered by a wasp, the way they jerk around without a care how they look, as though they were dancing on a foreign holiday. But it's because they've been stung before and they know how painful it is. It would be impossible to believe something as puny as a wasp could cause that much pain if one hasn't experienced it. People who've never been stung by a wasp will just waft them away as though they were sultans dismissing excessive grapes.

* * *

Jeremy Hardy Speaks to the Nation, 2003

Middle-class people are the worst for this. Their holiday must always be some remarkable and fantastic adventure. 'Oh, we discovered this little village, completely off the beaten track, not on the tourist trail at all. Middle of nowhere. Tiny, tiny place. I think it only appears once every two hundred years. Lovely people. So friendly. Tiny, tiny people, no bigger than your thumb. Simple but happy. And they had this fantastic sort of ad hoc dining room carved out of volcanic lava that was still flowing. And they cooked us this wonderful meal. There were eight or nine courses, and they gave us wine and their local brandy. And they danced for us and had sex with us, and I think the whole bill came to two pounds a head.'

The point is, whether you go on holiday to visit bustling markets and beat down their already pitifully low prices, or to meet the 'real people' (as opposed to the ones everyone else sees, who aren't really there at all), you are still a tourist. Even if you had an 'amazing time' and lived really naturally (apart from the all-important mechanical bird that got you there) you are a tourist. Even if you met people who live without electricity (despite their pleas for the government to connect them so they can have fridges and less food poisoning) you are still a tourist; you're just nosier than most. And if you travelled for months and months and months, you're just a holidaymaker who takes longer breaks than everyone else. And even then, you haven't seen that much. You say you took a year off to travel round the world, but it takes a year to travel round the M25. And what does it mean to have seen something? I've seen a Rolls-Royce, but really only scratched the surface.

Emotions

Jeremy Hardy Feels It, 2017

I am very fortunate, in that I get paid reasonably well to do something I mostly enjoy. I quite like traipsing around Britain, talking to people. I could even say that I feel quite *happy* in the dressing room of a provincial arts centre, with half an hour to go. About to do the thing that I do. In the zone. Especially when the venue has made an effort with the sandwiches, and not just grabbed them from the nearest available source, understanding that a lonesome, wandering player gets simple joy from the words 'home-made' and 'Waitrose', much less so from 'petrol' and 'station'.

I mention loneliness but it's not necessarily an unbearable thing, unless it's all the time. Some people can't be alone for a day without seeking out someone to talk to: 'I don't really like my own company.' Well, why would you subject anyone else to it, then? You can't demand attention on the basis that you're repellent. What are *you* bringing to the party beyond your morbid self-absorption? There are ways of handling solitude. Use your imagination. What do you think the mind is for? It's not just for storing passwords and being weird. Try thinking; think about the world, instead of imagining it only exists when it's listening to you drivelling on.

But that's easy for me to say because I've made a whole career out of demanding that the world listens to me drivelling on. Which is quite satisfying. But, then again, there is the comedown; and, the better the gig goes, the worse the anticlimax, wide awake in a hotel at 1 a.m., watching BBC Four documentaries about the unsung heroes *behind* the success of top jazz-funk saxophone players in the period between February and April 1986, and trying to imagine that I care. Yes, that is lonely. And it's not home. So I just can't relate to people who just go to places and stay in hotels for no reason. I just think, 'You've got somewhere to live, haven't you? Why don't you just stay there?' My mortgage is a grand a month; I resent going outside. Bloody place costs me a fortune and I'm hardly ever in it. In hotels, I'm paying just to sleep, or try to, and I've already paid to do that at home. That can't be right. I think your rent or your mortgage should be transferable wherever you go.

And often on a Friday, I'll be on a train bound for a cathedral city, surrounded by old couples who are going for a weekend break. Exeter, Durham, York, Edinburgh. All lovely places – but I'm going there to work, for a reason. They're going for pleasure. I want to say to these old couples, 'Yes, it's a lovely place. You'll have a nice afternoon bimbling around York. But what are you going to do in the evening if you haven't got a gig?'

'Ooh, we thought we'd have a meal.'

'You must have had meals before, you're seventy-nine. You can't have survived entirely on Complan, even though it's supposed to be possible.'

* * *

Jeremy Hardy Feels It, 2017

Hope is one of our most positive emotions, except that it doesn't suggest certainty. If an airline pilot says he hopes you've enjoyed the flight, it's a polite acknowledgement that that's unlikely. You've been vacuum-packed and trapped in the foetal position, eating miniature food with doll's-house cutlery, fantasising about the days when air travel was special and the other passengers were mostly Grace Kelly. If the pilot says he hopes to land *on time*, he's telling you it's out of his hands but still possible if the airport can find some-where to put a plane. You know, bit of runway maybe, the kind of thing you might find lying around at an airport. If he just says he hopes *to land*, there's something he's not telling you. You don't ever really want to hear the word 'hopefully' from anyone who's in charge of a plane in flight, a fishing boat in a storm, or a camera making its way up your urethra.

* * *

Jeremy Hardy Feels It, 2017

Sadness isn't the same as feeling sorry for yourself. And sorry is an ambiguous word. It can be an expression of sympathy or regret. It can be an admission of responsibility, as in 'I'm sorry, I shouldn't have done that', or it can be Boris Johnson saying, 'I'm sorry if my words have been misinterpreted by fools whose education was free, who've chosen to be offended and who've failed to grasp that my stunning egotism and lack of emotional maturity would have made me a hero of Empire in a sadly begotten age when lesser folk revered their betters, and indeed owners.'

There's a growing list of cut-and-paste faux apologies, which you can find in self-help books. For example: 'I'm sorry for my part in it.' Which means, 'Yes, it was my flame-thrower, but your guinea pigs got in the way.'

Because regret is one of our least favourite feelings, men especially turn it into belligerence, so *we* become the wronged party: 'Oh, blame *me* for my actions, why don't you? I wouldn't have run over your foot if I hadn't been driving to Smiths to buy you a birthday card.'

The Digital Age

Computers have their uses and save an enormous amount of time, which can then be devoted to poring through manuals, crying and trying to get through to the helpline for onsite service. As a writer, I have to work on a computer; most modern radios are simply not compatible with type-written satire. I actually have two computers, a desktop and a laptop. The laptop is a sure sign of age; starting to use one corresponds with that time in life when you no longer sit up at the table to have your tea, you just have it on your lap. 'Oh, don't bother with a plate for me, dear; just tip it on my trousers and I'll eat it with my fingers.'

So being a computer owner, I occasionally have to go to computer warehouses, in the middle of vast trading estates. Out-of-town shopping, cash'n'carries and hypermarkets increasingly mean that we have no facilities in our own neighbourhoods. In the foreseeable future houses will not be built with toilets; consumers will have to drive to a trading estate and go to World of Shit.

In these giant computer outlets like PC World and Office World, I try to buy my software as quickly and discreetly as I can, but if I dither for a second computer enthusiasts approach me assuming me to be a kindred spirit: 'So what do you think of the new trackball, then?' 'Get away from me, I'm not like you.'

But what alarms me is that people who don't *need* computers have them in their homes. Many people now have computers in their places of work, they have no choice about that and that is where computers belong. They are a work thing – you wouldn't have a cement mixer in your spare room, would you? 'Great little machine, isn't it? Want to see what it can do?'

And one of the selling points of the multimedia family PC is that you can do your domestic family accounts on them. Does anybody actually do that? Keep family accounts – a record of your domestic outgoings? What's the point, you spent it, you blew it, it's gone and it's never coming back – why torture yourself? Even if you are a Catholic, let it go . . . Every month, you earn a certain amount and you spend . . . twenty to thirty thousand pounds more than that amount. Does it matter whether it was Toilet Duck or Honey Nut Loops? I don't need a machine to remind me that I'm profligate. What are you going to write on your first day of keeping domestic accounts?

'Right, that's £8.50, groceries. And £1,499 on a typewriter that can do sums. Now, how does the bastard do sums?'

And we're invited to be impressed by CD-ROM which enables us to read a book. Which we couldn't do before. And the art you can do is amazing. If you go into the artwork bit, a little brush or pencil appears on the screen and you move it around using the mouse. Say you want to do a little drawing or write in longhand, you use the mouse, then print it up and you get a sheet of paper that looks for all the world as though you wrote on it with a pencil.

And people say computers are great for the kids. They're not great for the kids. I don't want my daughter sat upstairs in front of the computer all day; I want her downstairs watching videos with me where she should be. And I know all teenagers want a computer of their own, but if they want to lock themselves in their rooms and damage their eyesight for hours on end, they don't need a computer to do it.

And they punish you, computers. You make one mistake and a message flashes up: 'You have destroyed your backup files.' No, I didn't, *you* did it, you bastard. And my computer will even tell me, 'You have performed an illegal operation.' I thought blimey, I've just carried out a backstreet abortion somewhere.

And the spellchecker. You misspell 'philately' by one letter and the suggested alternative words are pineapple, trouser-press, sodomy. We were better off when the computer was a big thing with spools which filled a whole warehouse and was operated by a treadle.

* * *

Early Stand-up Set, The Cabaret Upstairs, 1985

I like to gamble a bit. I've had quite a lucky streak on the cashpoint machines lately.

* * *

Jeremy Hardy Speaks to the Nation, 2004

I have devised a way of punishing the *Big Brother* inmates, given that they are clearly beyond rehabilitation. What we should do is audition them, get them in the house, and do everything as is, but not put it on the television. And when they come out, there's just a windswept car park, no cameras and no Davina. Just a bloke sweeping up, saying, 'They've all gone home, mate. They've all gone home.'

* * *

Jeremy Hardy Speaks to the Nation, 2007

There are about four million CCTV cameras in Britain and we are one of the most watched peoples on earth. These cameras play a vital role in providing footage for television programmes such as *Britain's Most Drunken Litter Bin Throwers*. But do they also cut crime?

Well, it's hard to say because crime and the perception of crime get confused. People are scared of teenagers. So they feel safer when teenagers are moved on. Young people are feared for wearing hooded garments, but you shouldn't fear someone in a hood, unless they're carrying a scythe. Teenagers are accused of standing around in town centres, a charge that has been levelled at asylum seekers, migrant workers and travellers. It's the use of the legs to hold the body in an upright position that's considered especially menacing.

Of course, for many people, the town centre is now a shopping precinct, a privately owned public space that can set its own rules about what we should look like. When we are shopping, one third of us don't buy anything; we're 'just looking' – but this can look suspicious to the people looking at us on CCTV, especially if they don't like the look of us. Earlier, I spoke to the manager of Brownwater Retail Marina in Ilford, Mrs Bitterly Farage:

(CCTV OPERATIONS CENTRE)

JEREMY: Mrs Farage, in front of us is an impressive array of TV screens.

BITTERLY: Yes, Jeremony. From here in the Control Room, my staff can monitor the whole spectrum of Brownwater at any given juncture.

JEREMY: What are they on the lookout for?

BITTERLY: Well, Jemenory, using retinal scans, we can immediately obtain a complete profile of whoever enters the facility. By going straight into the police National Crime Database we can see if someone's got a record of violent crime. We then approach them and ask them to work as a security guard.

JEREMY: I've heard that surveillance technology is often used to keep tabs on employees.

BITTERLY: Absolutely, Jermaloid. Before the cameras, we lost up to seven pounds a year through pilfering, refunds and double bagging. We've also had cameras installed in this room to monitor our surveillance staff, who we found were re-editing footage and submitting it to film festivals.

JEREMY: So you're concerned about the misuse of footage?

BITTERLY: Not if it's done in the proper context. A prosecution for example. We're not against the creative manipulation of images. It's all about how you frame the subject.

JEREMY: Well show me some of the hi-tech wizardry.

BITTERLY: OK, Jamiroquai, let's have some fun (PRESSING SOME BUTTONS). Look at these youths here, the one on the left is laughing as though to say, 'To heck with grown-ups and the establishment, I'm going to make petrol bombs and listen to gangsta reggae, scaring old people with my break hip dancing.'

JEREMY: Or he's heard a joke.

BITTERLY: Your utopianism is touching. But before he's able to incite the others into copycat rioting, we just press this button and . . .

FX: BLEEP

JEREMY: Wow, he's disappeared! Is that CGI trickery?

BITTERLY: No, there's a laser cannon mounted on the camera. I vaporised him.

JEREMY: Is that legal?

BITTERLY: No body, no crime.

Bitterly Farage was played by Juliet Stevenson

* * *

179

Jeremy Hardy Feels It, 2017

I'm not sure why people take selfies of their pudenda, something I've only done by keeping my phone in trouser pockets with holes in. However, if such pictures exist, they are mine and mine alone. I wouldn't want them publicised without considerable photoshopping.

* * *

Jeremy Hardy Speaks to the Nation, 2010

Most people don't lie for terrible reasons but just because they haven't got the confidence to communicate without showing off. They feel they have to prove something. But people are good. They do lots of good things – they care about the environment, they cycle, they recycle, they support good causes. And they use mass communication to do this. But they find it hard to do without showing off. I'm getting a little weary of receiving emails that read,

> Hi everyone, I'm skateboarding up Mt Everest for the British Heart Foundation.

OK, friend, let me stop you there; your doing that is not going to help them, is it? What's going to help them is my giving them money. Your contribution is to make me feel like a heartless skinflint if I don't click on the link to JustBlackmailing.com.

And how am I to know whether you carry out your stunt or not? I'm not going to study all the digital pictures you email me afterwards. 'Oh, look, there she is at the starting line in her British Heart Foundation T-shirt. Oh, and here she is at the end looking the same only pleased with herself.' Why don't you just tell everyone you know you're doing it and then not bother. Just don't answer the phone for a few days and have a DVD marathon at home. No one will know. I'm going to give you the money anyway because you've left me no choice. Even if I don't approve of the British Heart Foundation. I might favour some other organ. I might be a kidney person. I don't know where they get off putting the heart first.

I'm not being stingy. I do sponsor a child somewhere in Africa, even though she never writes, the little bugger. I don't even know if she really exists or if she's a dramatic representation of the kind of person who might be helped by my standing order. But in any case, I chose to do that so I'm not a miser and I am sponsoring her but not to do anything in particular. I'm not making her run anywhere. Apparently, she does have to walk a long way to get water, but I'm not paying her 32p a gallon. I'm not even demanding she sings in a particularly beautiful and haunting way. It's unconditional.

And one day she'll come to London and find me and say, 'Five pounds a month, is that all I was worth to you? I've had to borrow the money from people traffickers to get here,' and I'll say, 'I'm sorry. I didn't even know you were real.' But I am giving her that money and I'm not standing on one leg in a vat of custard and then telling you to give money; so I resent feeling pressurised by you making me give money to your favourite good cause, especially when it's your kids' school. Do your kids go to school in Rwanda? No, bloody Croydon, although they do have to walk 300 metres to buy Red Bull.

And I have to say that in all charitable sponsored activities there is a possible element of showing off by the sponsors as well as the sponsored. When I do go to the JustGiving website, the fact that my donation is public probably affects the amount I donate. You can't put the message, 'Go for it, Christine. We're all really proud of you', next to the sum of 40p when your name is attached to it.

* * *

The News Quiz, 2014

Sajid Javid wants there to be mobile reception available all over the country, which would involve the kind of roaming that happens when you're abroad and your phone just finds the nearest mast. But the police say that we wouldn't be able to track people properly. It turns out, there are these black spots in Cornwall where there is no mobile reception, and, of course, all the terrorists are now in Cornwall and there's a huge ISIS pasty shop there. So the police say we can't have mobile reception everywhere, and now all of these columns are appearing by fusty luddites. (POSH VOICE) 'I for one am glad that there are some corners of England that are unconnected to the world of modern technology. The other day I was at one of my homes – a cottage that nestles at the foot of Bodmin Moor and is blissfully unconnected to mobile reception or broadband – and after a morning playing the harpsichord to my falcon, I decided to go for a bracing yomp upon the moor and stumbled upon a couple in some distress (the kind of urbanites who came unstuck so deservedly in the film *Deliverance*, a magnificent celebration of rural life). The female of the species plaintively cried, "My husband is having a heart attack, please help us! Do you have a mobile phone?" She made no attempt to engage in conversation with me, she merely wanted to engage with the health and safety fanatics of the NHS. "No I do not", I retorted, "I suggest you let nature take its course. Crows and magpies will take care of his eyes and the rest of him will compost down nicely in the coming months".'

* * *

Jeremy Hardy Feels It, 2017

Being pleased with yourself is one of the least endearing forms of happiness. Because you never watch a field full of lambs joyfully hopping about in a field, and think, 'Ah, look, they're so conceited.' That's what you think when you see couples ostentatiously flaunting their physical relationship anywhere other than in their own bedroom on which you happen to be innocently spying, or in a graveyard at midnight as part of a demonic ceremony.

And our culture of self-promotion encourages attention-seeking and grandstanding. Legions of people blog and tweet and Facebook not because they've got anything interesting to say but because they can't stand not to be impinging on other people's consciousness. I agree that everyone has a right to be heard, but it's usually better if they're not. Free speech is like free jazz, mostly cobblers except to the person who's doing it.

* * *

Jeremy Hardy Feels It, 2017

The phenomenon of self-aggrandisement in order to demoralise others while purporting to be their friends is known in clinical psychology as Facebook. People's days are ruined because they wake up to one of their so-called friends proclaiming how amazing it is to be them. And what are you supposed to do with that information? Get in your 'So proud of you, babe' before everyone else, thus owning their achievement, while secretly thinking, 'Yeah, you've lost two stone, well done you; it's going to hurt a lot more when you fall over now. Which you will, being faint with hunger. You're not going to bounce off the pavement like a sumo now, you bony bastard.' And I hate competitiveness, because I know I'm better than that.

Keeping Fit and Healthy

Jeremy Hardy Speaks to the Nation, 1993

I have to admit to being slightly jaundiced about exercise, being the sort of person who gets whiplash in rocking chairs.

But one sort of exercise which is apparently very good and which I have tried is swimming.

I decided to have swimming lessons at Clapham Pool. I joined the Beginners Adults class because I thought we'd all be in the same boat . . . well, not in a boat, obviously, because there'd be no challenge, but we'd all be at the same level. But there were people at Clapham Pool Beginners Adults swimming lessons who could swim adequately, nay, well. And these people were ploughing up and down the deep end, doing butterfly, which no bastard can do. And crammed into the shallow end is me and about five hundred dinner ladies.

You could tell in the changing rooms the ones who could already swim because they had all the right swimmers' gear: they had trendy shorts and goggles and earplugs, nose clips . . . waterskis, harpoon guns. I'm in Dr. Martens and tracksuit bottoms. Obviously, their sole *raison d'être* – which is French but not a recipe for sole – is to go to lessons in things they can already do to make other people feel small. They're completely proficient in the whole syllabus of evening classes – swimming, carpentry tap, modern sequence, ballroom – but they just go along to humiliate people who can't already do it. That's like me going to a crèche and saying, 'Potato printing, bollocks, this is a fax machine, this is.'

But friends have castigated me for my inability to swim. They tell me I must learn to swim because it could save my life one day. Well, when I'm dying from a stab wound on my way back from the off-licence one night, I'll be kicking myself I never mastered the doggy-paddle.

* * *

Jeremy Hardy Speaks to the Nation, 1993

You might want to try channelling your own aggression into sports. And of course, the most aggressive of these are blood sports. When it comes to running around after animals, you really need a rural environment. If you live in a big town, the equivalent of foxhunting or hare coursing would be to go to a pet shop, buy yourself a gerbil, take it home, break its legs and kick it round the bathroom a few times.

* * *

Jeremy Hardy Speaks to the Nation, 2001

I've tried every kind of osteopath and psychopath. More recently, I consulted a chiropractor whose fingers did little tiny dances on me for a while. Then he told me to go home, get plenty of rest, drink lots of water, do plenty of very gentle stretching, walk around every so often and avoid tea, coffee and alcohol. If I could live like that, I probably wouldn't have much wrong with me anyway.

As for medical herbalism, it is frankly medieval. These people are trying to drag us back to a time when we just bloody died. 'Black Death? You want a little tarragon on that.' We need hospitals, not *bouquet garni*.

Chinese herbalism at least uses things that look scary and

come from endangered species. I decided to try it because the sign in the window claimed that it cures everything, so I went in to offer a complete package of ailments. The doctor gave me a compost heap which I boiled up as per his instructions, stinking the house out and producing gallons of this filthy brew that tasted so horrible I wanted to cry when I drank it. After two weeks, the doctor was baffled by the fact that the only change was that I was extremely depressed.

The trouble is, these days everybody takes a holistic approach and no one knows what the word 'holistic' means; it just started to appear in sentences about fifteen years ago and no one questioned it. Everyone assumed everyone else knew what it meant and was too embarrassed to ask. What it appears to mean, although it has no 'w', is an approach that encompasses the whole. Something that just encompasses the hole that has no 'W' might help with haemorrhoids but that would not be a holistic approach. To give you an example of the holistic approach, if you catch your toe in the lawnmower, they have to treat the lawnmower first, because that's the real *cause* of what's wrong. So, the lawnmower must undergo anger management to learn to deal with its aggression.

And meanwhile, as we're experimenting with all these exotic and diabolical fashions, the National Health Service is being stolen from under our noses. The greatest scandal is the private finance initiative, which involves the closure of existing city hospitals, giving the sites to builders who then open out-of-town hossies on greenfield sites miles from anywhere except warehouse stores like Land of Tiles, Kingdom of Flannels and Semi-Autonomous Peninsula of Combs.

* * *

Jeremy Hardy Speaks to the Nation, 2010

These days I worry about us, the human animal, when I go to the gym. It's all about showing off. Now, I go to make myself feel and look a bit healthier. But other people who go there seem to think going to the gym makes you a good person. They even want to communicate the virtues of going to the gym to others. While getting dressed and undressed. I think there are times when communication is inappropriate, but they stand around naked after their shower, talking about their workout, and how their times have improved, and how heavy their bench press was. They're not talking about the fact that they're naked, which seems the most striking thing about them. That's the issue begging to be discussed. That's the elephant in the changing room, if you will. People shouldn't be naked. Except in very specific circumstances. Nudism is the ultimate in showing off and an abomination in the sight of God. They should be stoned to death, nudists. German people are always naked. Or in uniform. Do you know that the only good thing the Nazis did was to ban nudism? They banned it because they were trying to build the myth of Aryan superiority, and the spectacle of random naked Germans did more to undermine that than Jesse Owens.

There's a lovely beach in Dorset, a mile of which is ruined

by nudists. It's called Studland Beach, which was perhaps an invitation. And the thing that's a dead giveaway is that when the weather turns a bit parky at the end of the summer, the nudists are donning hoodies and trainers, but still have their knackers hanging out. They're just flashers.

Anyhow, I'll get to the gym and think, 'Oh, I'm a bit achy today, maybe I'll just have a swim'. But oh no, you can't use the pool between ten and eleven because someone's giving birth in it. Or the Americans are torturing someone, or there's a class. There's water aerobics, which is code for dinner ladies stamping up and down in warm bleach. So I can't use the pool, which means I have to go to the gym. And I get on this machine, on which I simulate the experience of walking up a hill, while watching four televisions at once, with no sound, thinking, 'this is the life'. And my partner comes to check on me because she's been doing 'body balance' and wants to make sure that I'm exercising correctly. She tells me, 'You're supposed to be out of breath', and I say, 'I'm asthmatic, we've got stairs at home for that'. Pardon me if being unable to breathe is one of my least favourite experiences.

I hate the gym so much. The only thing I like is the resistance training. We blew up a bridge yesterday.

* * *

Jeremy Hardy Feels It, 2017

There's an awful lot of you out there on social media who just can't bear the idea that other people might not be thinking about you at any given moment. And for many of you, happiness seems to be about impressing others with your achievements. I don't want to hear that you're doing a 2k for Short Attention Span Awareness Minute. I'm quietly proud if I manage to post a letter, but I don't demand anyone's congratulations for it. If you want to go for a run, go for a run. I don't need to know about it.

Even a routine jog round the park is now a performance, a costume drama. People used to just put on their plimsolls and leg it out of the house. Now they dress to impress; they need branded gear, they need something hi-vis in case they have to stop and do some construction work along the way. They need a baseball cap and sunglasses, in what is surely one of the darkest countries in the world. They need to carry water because half an hour in a freezing recreation ground without hydration and they'll look like a camel carcass in the Sahara. They need props: headphones, a Kindle, a flat white, a device strapped to them that confirms to them at the end of the run that they have indeed been for a run, because reality doesn't exist until verified in digital form. I wear this nifty little gizmo on my wrist. They call it a 'watch' and what it does is it alerts me to the approach of death. But people will actually go to Currys or Argos to buy a thing that tells them how many steps they've done in a day. Does it matter? Put your shoes on a bus if you're that worried.

* * *

40 Years of The News Quiz, 2017

I've had acupuncture for my bad back because I slouch, because I'm left-wing and we always slouch in a rather gnarled way. It's called 'radical posture'. And I went to the acupuncturist and she got this long needle and went (JABBING) 'Stand up straight you little bastard!'

* * *

Glastonbury Cabaret, 2017

And let's get rid of this idea of individualism and 'personal challenges'. We've put up with it for so many years, people have given up on the idea of the collective and thought, let's all be individuals and set challenges for ourselves and then we can replace the welfare state with a Fun Run.

People say running is good because it makes you live longer. You might live longer but all the extra years will have been used up running so it will even out at the end of your life. And why should you live for a long time, you self-important prick. So you can never keep putting off the day when your kids can afford to buy their own home? And what are you going to do at the end of this long life? Look back at all the running you did and all the calories you burned? A grandchild on your knee saying, 'Oh Grandad, tell us about the running, we love that story. Tell us about that time you shat in a drain with Paula Radcliffe.'

Oh it's the endorphins, they're great, the endorphins, they're so addictive. That's not good, is it? Addiction is not good. You know people at needle exchanges say, 'How was your weekend?' 'Yeah, great actually, I went to stay with some friends because I'm homeless now. And while they were asleep I robbed them because heroin has changed my life. I literally feel amazing.'

Food and Vegetarianism

Early Stand-up Set, The Cabaret Upstairs, 1985

I have become a vegetarian. Seems quite a fashionable thing to do at the moment. I operate under the principle 'meat is murder but fish is justifiable homicide'. Fish to me are just cold-blooded unfeeling bastards. Look into the eyes of a fish. There's no love in those eyes. What story does the face of a cod tell you? '1972. Britain and Iceland fighting over me.' Not greatly bothered either way frankly. Complete indifference. But look into the eyes of a farm animal, let's say a pig, little porky pig, you look into its eyes. Doesn't it just make you want to smash your way into Dewhurst and set all the sausages free in the countryside?

* * *

Jeremy Hardy Speaks to the Nation, 1993

There is a popular cliché to the effect that health nuts look really unhealthy. This is not because self-righteousness is bad for the complexion, but because worrying about diet is symptomatic of worry generally. No one without a care in the world is going to go out of their way to buy Quorn.

But a vegetarian diet doesn't have to be dull. The reason that vegetarian food is so often boring is that it's made by vegetarians. Many vegetarians seem to believe that anything which might be regarded as a seasoning is made from crushed-up dead baby animals.

So, if you want to go out for a vegetarian meal and have more evidence that you're eating something than the fact that your jaw is going up and down, you'd do well to go for something from a culture that uses spices. Indian cooking has excellent vegetarian recipes. Unfortunately, many white English people were put off Indian food at an early age by their mother's attempts to make curry. When I go to my favourite Indian restaurant in south London, I have a wonderful delicious savoury meal full of wonderful herbs and spices like cardamom and fenugreek; but when white people's mums make curry, a great amount of fruit seems to creep into the scenario: apples, sultanas, bananas, hundreds and thousands on the top, sponge fingers on the bottom . . . jelly. Because putting some fruit in some dinner is our idea of exotic. It just transports us to a tropical paradise. This is especially true of canteen food. Whack a pineapple ring on something and you've got toad-in-the-hole Hawaiian-style.

I have to say, I'm not generally in favour of fruit in dinner. Fruit is pudding in my book, unless it's grapefruit segments with a glacé cherry on top, in which case it's a starter. But if you go recklessly mixing sweet and savoury, it's a slippery slope to monstrosities like liver meringue pie.

* * *

Jeremy Hardy Speaks to the Nation, 2001

But there's one discovery that above all others revolutionised the way we burn things: fire. We know from feverish guesswork that early man ate a great deal of salad. These were the days before nice salad could be airfreighted from warm countries with starving people, so salads had to be in season. In the winter, diners were reduced to a kind of prehistoric coleslaw made from leaves, stones and wood, much like the modern-day equivalent only without the acrid semen-like dressing. But we weren't vegetarians; the first smug pallid people didn't walk the earth for another twenty or thirty years.

* * *

Jeremy Hardy Speaks to the Nation, 2003

There was a time in this country when, if you hadn't bought bread by Saturday lunchtime on a bank holiday weekend, you would have to go without until Tuesday. So much of our precious leisure time was spent without a basic foodstuff. I once had to make do with a box of Energen Rolls, not having made it to Presto in time. All those adverts about low-cal bread being light turned out to be understated. The box was lighter than an empty box. And pushing a knife into a roll had the same effect as Buffy staking a vampire: fragmentation, then dust, then nothing.

* * *

Jeremy Hardy Speaks to the Nation, 2004

Now, people are questioning everything. It's dawning on them that private enterprise and free enterprise are not the same thing, that the world is being brought under the tight control of corporate might. People who might consider themselves Conservatives don't really like it. They like the idea of shopkeepers and farmers and food with no air miles. They remember when food was fresh and seasonal. People are against GM foods and they're not falling for the corporate line that technology will enable us to feed the world. There is already enough food to feed the world. It's just that instead of it being eaten in Kenya it's flown here, where we put it in the fridge until it goes blue and hairy and then throw it away. At least in America they have the decency to eat all of it. And one of the ways of disrupting the cultivation of GM crops has been to take direct action, ripping up the plants, a kind of militancy ideally suited to older activists because it's basically weeding.

* * *

Jeremy Hardy Speaks to the Nation, 2007

There's a fantastic self-importance to people who take a pride in being healthy. People say things like,

YUPPIE WOMAN: I like to go to the gym to work out three or four times a week because I think it's important to take care of myself.

Why? You work in marketing, who's going to miss you? It's one thing to say you don't want to orphan your children or burden the health service but please don't tell me –

YUPPIE MAN: I think it's important to exercise and eat right.

Because you cannot eat right. Right is not an adverb. You can eat well, you can eat sensibly and healthily but you can't eat right, so maybe you should master the language before worrying about your carb intake.

And health food shops are vile places staffed by the pallid smug. Everything about the merchandise appeals to complacency, from the marketing to the packaging. There should be phone numbers on the labels you can call if not completely self-satisfied. But the health industry encourages not only an obsession with longevity but also our determination to find things wrong with ourselves. People seek out problems. Before modern medicine people didn't just have adverse reactions to things, they got really ill. Someone with hay fever wasn't expected to last the night. People put straw down in the street to soften the noise of horses' hooves – not realising straw is the worst thing for someone with hay fever. I don't mean Jack Straw was put down in the street – that would gladden the heart of anyone in their final moments. Point is, an allergy wasn't something anyone aspired to. But now everyone's 'a little bit allergic'. They have an intolerance, to something which at one time would simply not have agreed with them. People simply used to say –

OLDER LADY I like cucumber, but it doesn't like me.

They understood that there was nothing special about them, they were simply unpopular among certain vegetables. Now it's considered a disorder of sufficient magnitude to warrant a whole chunk of *Woman's Hour* and funding for your theatre company. I have an intolerance, an intolerance of people with spurious allergies.

Fair enough, one in 200 million people explode if they smell a peanut. I don't mind paying the extra so that peanut butter and brittle can have warnings printed on them. If it saves one life, it's worth it. But the wheat thing I can't be doing with. How can people be intolerant to something that millions of others the world over are desperate for? And the worst thing about the myth of wheat intolerance is it's bound to turn out to be true, but until that day I shall continue to be as obdurate in my bigotry about it as I am today. And I'm just not that impressed when a healthy thirty-year-old tells me wheat makes them bloated. Try being forty-five, everything makes you bloated. I always have wind after a meal. Wind's normal. It's the price we pay for not starving to death. It's food.

MIRANDA (RICHARDSON): I know. I can't eat food.
JEREMY: Any food?

MIRANDA: Nothing. Can't even look at it. Honestly, can't touch it. I react really badly.

JEREMY: What happens?

MIRANDA: It just turns brown and falls out of my bottom.

* * *

Jeremy Hardy Speaks to the Nation, 2014

Let's take Fair Trade. We want to help people in developing countries, but don't want to have to go there and teach a man to fish. For a start we'd have to retrain to be a fishing teacher, buy the equipment, fly there, find someone who's keen to learn and then try to teach him, despite not speaking his language. He'd get hungry and irritable and say, 'Look just give me a bloody fish and at last I'll have eaten for a day, and you can get on with your marking.' So instead of all that malarkey, he grows roses and coffee and we pay him and he can buy fish in his long-established local fish market if he can get past David and Samantha Cameron and their attendant photographers.

* * *

Jeremy Hardy Speaks to the Nation, 2014

When it comes to sugar, uncultivated land of the kind lived in by early humans yielded little in the way of sweet fruit and then only some of the time. Sugar gives us a burst of energy and stimulates dopamine, making us feel briefly glad to be alive. It's fast-acting and highly addictive which is why grandparents and perverts use it to manipulate children. It also makes our bodies store fat, so we can say –

WOMAN: I love my new curves.

and

MAN: I've got more to grab hold of.

Both are pleasing euphemisms for approaching heart failure – but for our ancestors, body fat was essential for survival.

And before dairy farming, the fat they *ate* was from meat. And fire enabled them to cook it and therefore eat more; raw animal being hard to get through and hard to digest, a bit like the government's Data Retention & Investigatory Powers Bill, which would also benefit from the application of fire. Once we could cook, humans got a massive dietary boost because we could eat hi-carb tubers and high-protein and high-fat meat. But first we had to catch it, which was a haphazard affair. If you think how rubbish you are at darts and that pub walls don't run about, think what it was like for cavepeople. Which is why we had to develop meat-rage.

Today, we eat too much meat and tend to crave it in salty processed form. But dietary villains change. Salt is getting a much better press lately. Maybe Max Clifford used to represent it and now it's had to find someone more reputable. There are also now those who say the danger of eating saturated fats has been exaggerated and that people with low cholesterol and low blood pressure, like me, are not only better people, but at little risk from butter. True, dropped toast lands butter-side-down only if you use actual butter. What would be the point of Sod's Law if it led to *margarine* being contaminated and therefore improved by a filthy kitchen floor? But other than that, butter is better. Even lard isn't necessarily unhealthy. In fact, animal fats are better to fry in than almost all vegetable oils because, unlike Melanie Phillips, they don't become rancid and toxic when heated.

* * *

Jeremy Hardy Speaks to the Nation, 2014

As I became more prosperous, I became more foodie, and as London got more prosperous, *it* got more foodie, and I found myself in modern foodie situations . . .

ATMOS: DINNER PARTY (VICKI AND PAUL ARE MARRIED, JEREMY IS THE GUEST)

JEREMY: Mmm, this cheese is lovely.

VICKI: Oh, thank you, we love it. I get it from this fantastic stall in Bolivia Road Market. It's the only place in England I've ever found authentic Formaggio di Trappola Peri Topi. Yes, gotta be fresh. The chap teleports from his smallholding in Tuscany every Friday evening and I hit the market at 7 a.m. It's so fresh it's just slightly disgusting, the way it's meant to be.

JEREMY: Everything in Tuscany has that amazing disgusting freshness.

PAUL: Why do we get it so wrong in this country?

VICKI: Well, that's not entirely fair, darling. Remember we bought that lovely artisan cheese string from Julian Britpop's farm shop in Little Ponce on the Blag, but you really have to catch that village at the right time because it only appears once every hundred years.

JEREMY: He's such a breath of fresh air in the micro-cheese world. When you think what it used to be like in Britain . . .

PAUL: Oh, there was no food at all. I don't think I'd eaten anything until I was eighteen.

JEREMY: Well, you know it was Yemeni sailors who first introduced solids in the 1950s. Historians think that, before that, people here lived mainly on beer and ditch-water.

PAUL: Proper ditchwater can be amazing, but I know what you mean.

VICKI: Well, I was very lucky because my great-grandfather was a quarter Huguenot, which is where I get all my flamboyant Gallic genes, and so the house was always full of omelettes and éclairs and (BIG FRENCH ACCENT) *onvelopes* . . .

JEREMY: Oh, there's nothing like a real French *onvelope*. Ours just don't taste the same.

PAUL: They're not real manila any more, they use manila essence.

VICKI: Do you know, our *cleaner* isn't even from the Philippines.

PAUL: Isn't she?

VICKI: No. I thought they all were, but it turns out she's from Great Yarmouth.

JEREMY: Where is that?

VICKI: It is in the Far East but not that far. Straight up the A12. We were thinking of buying it actually because it's so handy for our place in Aldeburgh. Once you're in Suffolk, you can knock straight through into Norfolk if you can get the planning permission. Fantastic pub food all round there and great fish and chips, with proper vinegar, like poor people use. We're just feeling the Portugal apartment is becoming a bit of a cliché.

PAUL: Yes, we're just so over other countries.

VICKI: Mmm.

PAUL: They're all so geared up for tourists. When we go abroad, we're looking for *real* hostility.

JEREMY: It must have been so amazing when travel meant conquest and plunder, instead of good customer service.

VICKI: Yah, yah, when we said, 'We're sick of our bland food, so we're taking your bloody country.' Now, coffee, let me see what we have in the civet cat's tray.

* * *

Jeremy Hardy Speaks to the Nation, 2014

JEREMY: Perhaps we all need to be a little more grown-up about the reality of what we eat. In these times of austerity and bearing in mind the environmental cost of meat production, celebrity chefs now promote nose-to-tail eating.

VICKI (PEPPERDINE): That's how you get on in TV.

* * *

JEREMY: Let me address the manner in which we eat. There is no universally correct way of putting food in mouths. Some people use fork and knife, some use forkan chopsticks. But let us, in the following scene, study the social role of cutlery . . .

(GRAND MEAL)

POSH BIRD: What's wrong, darling? You seem nervous.

BLOKE: (TENSE WHISPER) I had no idea your family was so posh! How am I meant to use all these knives and forks?

POSH BIRD: It's very simple. You just start on the outside and work your way in.

BLOKE: All right. I'll just remember not to eat peas off my knife.

POSH BIRD: Ah no, actually, it's a vulgar misconception that you shouldn't do that. In fact, the proper way to eat peas *is* off a knife.

BLOKE: Really?

POSH BIRD: Oh, yes, yes. As long as you use a new knife for each pea. That's what all those knives are for.

BLOKE: Oh. And what about that tiny little one?

POSH BIRD: That's for peeling the peas.

BLOKE: Why would you peel a pea?

POSH BIRD: Oh, it's one of the first things Nanny teaches you, so you don't make a dreadful fool of yourself when you're eventually introduced to your parents.

BLOKE: Look, if I'm going to die of embarrassment anyway, why don't I just kill myself now?!

POSH BIRD: Oh yes, that's what the long knife on the top is for.

* * *

Jeremy Hardy Speaks to the Nation, 2014

Cutlery is not universal. In cultures in which people eat with their fingers, it is traditional to use only one's right hand, the left hand being for wiping your bottom. I advise not doing both things at the same time anyway, unless you're Elvis, and look how that ended.

* * *

Jeremy Hardy Speaks to the Nation, 2014

PAUL (BASSETT DAVIES): (EATING) I must say, Jeremy, these miniature Yorkshire puddings are delicious.

JEREMY: Those are earplugs. *The Archers* is on next. Help yourself, take a couple.

PAUL: I might have a third one.

JEREMY: Why?

PAUL: Well, I've been having problems with my high-fibre diet.

JEREMY: Fair enough.

* * *

Jeremy Hardy Speaks to the Nation, 2014

How do we bring down carbon emissions and keep transporting food all over the world? Even if you live in the luxuriant Vale of Evesham and eat seasonally, it's likely that asparagus you buy in May, even if grown a mile from your supermarket, is driven to an airfield, flown to Algeria for trimming and enhanced interrogation, then to a secret black site in a former Warsaw Pact country, where it's hosed down and subjected to a cling-film restraint technique, before being rendered back to England and driven under cover of darkness back to the area where it was picked.

Which is a good reason for eschewing supermarkets in favour of greengrocers and farmers' markets. We now have lovely farmers' markets in London. They're a sign that an area is being gentrified and the greengrocer will soon be forced out of business by high rents. But there's a new mini Sainsbury's which covers you for the six and a half days when the farmers' market reverts to being a bit of road.

* * *

Jeremy Hardy Speaks to the Nation, 2014

Another gastro-fashion to excite chefs in recent years is Local Sourcing. For someone of my generation, the issue is double-edged, because I can remember a time when I craved anything that *wasn't* local. Local was plain and ordinary. My dad sometimes had to go to London and would return with an avocado, which we didn't even know came from a hot country. The fact that it was sourced in London was exciting enough. London was forty miles away. In those days, the avocado was called an avocado *pear* to distinguish it from pears, which are pears, which the avocado isn't, and to which it bears almost no similarity.

Anyhow, Dad would place the avocado on the kitchen table, and we would stand around it in wonder. This was in the days before the avocado bathroom suite, which was a disgusting innovation because your foot went through the side of the tub and the toilet collapsed when you sat on it. Dad would bisect the avocado lengthways and remove the stone which we would plant each time so that it would grow to eight inches in height and then die. Meanwhile, Dad would eat the flesh of the avocado with a spoon, while we watched him impressed and Mum scoffed at his pretension.

Festivities

The News Quiz, 2011

It's that time of year, and I think we should remember, because two thousand and something years ago a humble Jewish carpenter called Joseph, living in Nazareth, set off to Bethlehem because he had to pay his taxes – he *had* to pay his taxes cos he didn't run a mobile phone network or a high street clothing chain . . . He went with his heavily pregnant wife; bear in mind the level of healthcare that they had then was roughly equivalent to what it'll be when Andrew Lansley's finished with the NHS . . . They got to Bethlehem and of course there's nowhere to stay because it's Christmas, and the only place available is the Premier Inn and Mary says, 'Do you know what, I'd rather sleep in the road,' because it's got as much soul as Joss Stone and there's a reason why the upstairs windows don't open in a Premier Inn.

So, they go to an inn, and the innkeeper says, 'I'm sorry, we have no accommodation,' and Joseph says (NATIVITY PLAY VOICE) 'But we have travelled such a long way and my wife is ve-ry ti-red.' And then they have to go to a number of inns in order to use up all of the kids whose parents would've gone spare if they hadn't had speaking parts, and finally they get to one where the bloke says, 'Well, I don't have a room, but there's a stable.' And so Mary says, 'Ooh, I've read about these manger births in *Grazia* magazine. They're terribly fashionable among the sort of women whose naive idea of childbirth is punished by emergency Caesarean.'

So they go, she gives birth in the stable surrounded by singing animals and wise men with coat hangers sticking out the back of their heads – this is the historical fact!

Now what we've got – the Christmas that *we* do – is kind of a mishmash: it's basically bit of Chanukah, bit of Saturnalia, bit of pagan solstice, bit of Celtic mysticism, a lot of Phil Spector. The Roman Saturnalia is all the misrule and all that; there's the lights for Chanukah, and the German stuff actually is a big thing because the Victorians really invented the modern Christmas because Prince Albert of course was German and today we see all these German markets in our towns. And in preparation for that, of course, the Germans flattened many of our town centres in the 1940s, so that a few short years later they would be forgiven and there would be sheds full of former war criminals selling pigs' guts stuffed into condoms and we'd all say, 'Hurrah for our jolly European partners, let's forget about everything they've done.' So that's Christmas. Ho. Ho ho. Ho ho ho.

* * *

40 Years of The News Quiz, 2017

Apparently, the British have started to love sprouts more than Christmas pudding, and I think it's about what you give, you get back, because I think my mother must have hated sprouts because she just wanted to boil them till they couldn't fight back. And she must have considered them to have committed some terrible ill in a previous life when they were fennel or something, and she would actually score the mark of the cross into them and that allowed greater water penetration, cos I think that was the main function of sprouts; if you boiled a sprout for a month, two months, a single sprout could contain about two gallons of water so their main function on Christmas Day was to rehydrate old people – rather like those little sponges on sticks they use in end-of-life care . . .

* * *

Jeremy Hardy's New Year Cavalcade, 2004

New Year is celebrated differently in different cultures, but it's best not to believe what we hear about the way other cultures celebrate it. Given the information available to them about how we celebrate ours, I suspect all the stuff we hear about them is absolute cobblers. Foreigners are given to believe that in Britain we celebrate something called 'Just A Few Things On Sticks So You Might Want To Eat Something Before You Come'. At British New Year, tradition has it, it seems that people eat Monster Munch – a kind of packaging material made from rice cakes and nerve gas – to symbolise renewal, and they drink petrol to symbolise drink-driving. It is traditional to buy Lottery tickets as a symbol of bad luck; and a large pig's bladder called a Pinada Colada is stuffed with a pineapple sent every year as a gift from the people of Hawaii in thanks for the airlifting of much-needed ham during the Second World War. The Pinada Colada is suspended from a kind of gibbet as a warning to others, and children beat it with long sticks made from Catholics – which the Catholics enjoy and it's more humane than shooting them. When the bladder bursts, the children are soaked in a sickly yellow liquid called Sunny Delight and whichever child catches the leaves of the pineapple is the next to marry Bill Wyman.

The Environment

Jeremy Hardy Speaks to the Nation, 1993

Nowadays many of us try to live our lives doing as little harm as possible to the environment. There are many green consumer goods on the supermarket shelves. I myself buy only biodegradable bin liners, the kind that break down naturally as you carry the rubbish down the stairs.

Instead of my old CFC-filled aerosol deodorant, I use an organic natural herbal roll-on made from coriander, which doubles as a delicious salad dressing. Indeed, some people say that they don't need to use deodorant at all, although you can usually tell that about them before they tell you.

You might also want to make sure that your make-up has not been tested on animals; after all, no one wants a lipstick with a load of dog hairs all over it. People also think much more about what they eat. Many now opt for free-range chickens which have been corn-fed and humanely strangled by vegetarians.

* * *

Jeremy Hardy Speaks to the Nation, 2010

We live in a very atomised society and people don't like to cause a fuss because they are not confident that other people will support them. Other people are busy. Those people who are prepared to take direct action for a cause nowadays are mostly under thirty. They're not immature, they just haven't had all the stuffing knocked out of them, and they haven't had their soul drained by trips to IKEA. And sometimes they're older people with a lifetime of experience and nothing left to lose. Either way they're showing great maturity because they're taking responsibility for the world they live in and are not leaving its problems for others to sort out. I'm not talking about David Cameron's Big Society. His clarion call to us all to join in the running of public services made me think of a tannoy announcement on a plane that goes –

STEWARDESS: (ON TANNOY) Could any passengers with navigational experience please make their way to the front of the aircraft.

What I'm talking about is not doing the government's job for it or letting it offload its duties to the private sector, but rather making it do the right thing. Environmental campaigners trying to stop an airport being expanded are, I contend, taking more personal responsibility than those of us who just do our bit by recycling. Especially those of us who just recycle our old material.

Now, it's good to cut our energy consumption; it is a grown-up thing to do. But direct action is even more grown up. The least grown-up thing is to say, like a sulky teenager, that nothing you do will make any difference. Environmental

Armageddon can be prevented if we all grow up and face the fact that we can't carry on as we are, using the world as a big plaything and an inexhaustible supply of treats. If we leave it to government, they will just bring in a new generation of nuclear power stations because nuclear power doesn't produce carbon dioxide. So that's the choice we'll face as a world: Would we like our environmental catastrophe to be sparkling or still?

* * *

40 Years of The News Quiz, 2017

SIMON: Who's *bagged* themselves an environmental disaster?

JEREMY: Oh bloody hell, this is one of the government's efforts to make us all care more about the environment, and I'm sorry, I mean I *do* care about the environment but pardon me for washing myself and having the occasional cup of tea; I'm not some vast chemical corporation filling our seas with filth; I'm not Balfour Beatty who the government is supporting in building a huge dam somewhere where a dam's not needed which is going to flood archaeological treasures and make people homeless; pardon me . . . I'm not NATO who's turned the Danube into a toxic soup.

And yet the government comes on the news and says, 'Are you doing *your* bit? Why aren't you having your bath in a plastic carrier bag? Why not use *both* sides of lavatory paper? And instead of using plastic bags to line your pedal bin, simply pull one over your head and then you'll breathe in and die and then you won't use up any more air because in a year you use up enough air to fill up enough balloons to fill up a whole bath the same size as the Millennium Dome. And instead of making a cup of tea why don't you just stuff all your plastic bags into your kettle and that'll cause a fire and kill your whole family who won't then eat any food or walk on the pavement and wear it out by being individuals . . .'

(PAUSE)

ANDY (HAMILTON): You're frightening me now.

* * *

Musicport, 2016

I'm not going to start haranguing you and telling you you've all got to do your bit for the environment, because we're always told we've got to do our bit as individuals. I mean, do recycle by all means; don't believe the conspiracy theorists who say, 'There's no point in recycling. None of it gets recycled, it all just gets shipped to China where former *Blue Peter* presenters force tiny children to fashion it into moonscapes to fake landings on it.' That isn't what happens. That is what happens to old computers, but not to your paper and glass.

But my point is that our efforts as individuals are piddly and only massive government invention at a global level can turn around climate change, which is why right-wing people are in denial about it. Because you cannot have a free market *and* a planet; the two things are mutually exclusive.

You get these rural people that can't abide wind farms. And I know there are all sorts of arguments about wind farms, but the principal objection seems to come from rustic *Telegraph* readers. 'Wind turbines are a terrible problem. They interfere with our beautiful British landscape.' And you think, yeah, but you don't mind any other blot on the face of the landscape. Because they're perfectly sanguine about nuclear power stations and motorways and airports and American airbases and Salisbury Plain being blown to pieces by the Royal Artillery every day. They just can't stand wind turbines because they're so tall and slim and camp. (FOTHERINGTON-TOMAS VOICE) 'Hello birds! Hello sky!' They think, 'Look at them just sporting themselves. Nothing should have that much rhythm, not something that's white.'

And you get people writing letters to the *Telegraph* saying, 'Well, so much for climate change; my roses are bang on time this year.' 'I don't know about global warming; I noticed a distinct chill in my fridge.'

People say climate change is a fraud, that it's a conspiracy among scientists. About 98% of scientists say it's true and created by us: that is not a conspiracy. Scientists don't really conspire anyway. They generally work alone for reasons associated with their social skills and personal hygiene. But if any scientist says, 'I don't know if it's *all* manmade', the right-wing press seize on him and say, 'See, we've proved it, we've found one who is on our side'. They'll always find one who is on their side. They'll do a story about zero-hours contracts, they will find one person who is happy on a zero-hours contract, because he's got low self-esteem and so poverty and exploitation keep him in his comfort zone. They'll do a thing about prostitution, and they'll find one sex worker who says she's glad she was trafficked because she'd never really been anywhere before and she gets to meet all sorts of people, some of them very important although surprisingly submissive. And you think, well, that's great for *you* – I'm happy for you – but you're being used as a propaganda tool, you're not representative and perhaps you should be quiet because you're being used. It's like being the one bondage freak in Guantanamo who finds it all very empowering.

The Uxbridge English Dictionary

Harpist / Partially sober

I Claudius / Digital emperor

Lactose / To suffer from frost bite

Midwifery / Partway through breaking wind

Module / Christmas with The Who

Morass / Buttock implants

Nandos / An old lady's afternoon nap

Orthodontist / Those very devout dentists with the
beards and the hats

Posterity / Inherited bottom size

Prolapse / In favour of having your dinner in front
of the telly

Jeremy by Sandi Toksvig

Pretending to be dead for this long is definitely Jeremy's worst extended joke so far. I've known him a lot of years. He's a genius. Well, part genius, part schoolboy and sometimes he stretches things out for too long. We did The News Quiz *together for nearly a quarter of a century, first with me on the panel and then me as the host. As the host I could always spot when Jeremy was about to go off on one of his rants. I would literally take off my glasses and sit back knowing that there was ten unbroadcastable minutes ahead of us. It was wonderful to be in the room because dear God, how often he went too far in a way none of the rest of us would dare.*

There was no news topic he didn't have the guts to poke about with. I remember there was a terrible story about a gentleman in Austria who had kept his children locked for years in some hideous basement, and quite sensibly, nobody wanted to talk about it. Jeremy however marched in giving his views on the subject of Austrian childcare and how such an appalling situation would never have occurred in this country because of planning permission. It was one of the funniest things I ever heard. Obviously it never made it to air.

Together for years, we were like a couple of doddery folk in a showbiz retirement home. Every Thursday afternoon when we were getting ready for The News Quiz, *we would sit in a tiny room reading the papers. It was supposed to be my office, but I don't think he knew that. He'd be there with some ancient Tupperware eating something healthy, me with a sausage roll. Every week he'd say the exact same thing – 'I've got nothing Sand, I've got nothing', and then he'd go out there and be absolutely brilliant. It was really annoying.*

Jeremy was never shy. In fact, sometimes he was downright rude. He referred to my attempts to found a political body to fight for equality as 'The Women's Nagging Party'. He even heckled me at my own wedding. I got married on the stage at the Royal Festival Hall on the day that same-sex marriage went through. Jeremy was sitting in the front row and at the most significant moment, when we exchanged our vows, he shouted out, 'It should have been me'.

Maybe it should have been. The last picture I have of the two of us we're in a bedroom together. I lay next to him on his sick bed and offered him the lesbian sex he had no doubt always dreamt of on condition that he just get up. We were both crying with laughter.

Anyway, that's enough now. Maybe when we've done this bloody book and all said nice things about him, he'll stop mucking about with this death lark and return pleased with his jolly jape. Alright Jeremy I'll say it out loud – you are a good guy. You've taught us all not to cut our cloth according to popular opinion. You've made us all think and, most importantly, encouraged us to dare. I love you very much. Now stop hiding and come back to play.

5

Jeremy Hardy Speaks About . . .

Identity Politics

*'Islam is no weirder than Christianity. Both are just
Judaism with the jokes taken out.'*

Religion

Jeremy Hardy Speaks to the Nation, 1994

Now perhaps we should look at the history of fatherhood and see how it has changed over the centuries. The first recorded father was of course our heavenly father, God. God is also the father of Jesus, who was the son of Mary, who, rather confusingly, is the Mother of God. There are divergent theological explanations for all this. The most popular interpretation is that God and Jesus, as well as being father and son, are the same person, which is how we know that God had long hair and a beard. Jesus is God and God is Jesus. After all, we never see them in the same room, except after the ascension when, according to Mark, Chapter 16, Verse 19,

GORDON: After the Lord had spoken unto them, he was received up into heaven and sat on the right hand of God.

The expression 'sat on the right hand of God' seems peculiar to us today and conjures up a rather bizarre image, but the meaning is made clearer by the contemporary language of the 1983 Modern Revised Contemporary Newish English Bible-Type Book. The phrase becomes –

GORDON: Jesus was a glove puppet.

There is now considerable archaeological evidence to suggest that God made a puppet which came to life. This interpretation would seem to support claims that the New Testament story is a version of a much earlier pagan myth, that of Pinocchio. Indeed, if one counts the letters in God's name and adds the number of gospels, the total is seven, almost the same number of letters as in Geppetto, Pinocchio's father.

Much of the problem with understanding the Bible is making sense of the language. For example, 'begetting', which takes place in the Old Testament, is preceded by men 'knowing' their wives – 'knowing' means sex. This gives a whole new connotation to the phrase 'nodding acquaintance'.

* * *

Jeremy Hardy Speaks to the Nation, 1994

I was brought up in the Church of England, and had always understood that 'Church of England' just meant that you believed Jesus was English, and the only reason he was crucified was that he was just too embarrassed to say anything. At that time, the C of E really just seemed like an extension of *The Archers*. However, many militants have left the church to become Catholics. It seems rather cheeky to think you can become a Catholic just because you don't like women. I'm sure there's a lot more to it than that. But anyway, the opponents of women priests say there shouldn't be women priests because Jesus was a man and a leader of men. For example, he chose only male disciples. It may be, of course, that Jesus chose male followers because he thought men were more likely to be credulous of his claims. Women are apt to have met rather a lot of men who think they're God's gift.

Belief is very important to would-be leaders, especially religious leaders. Followers must have faith and not demand proof. There'll be the odd miracle but if you miss it you're out of luck. Jesus is credited with having made the lame walk; then again, so do London Transport. On the miracle front, Moses was arguably more impressive. How many newborn babies do you know who can navigate a wicker basket through a load of bulrushes? Moreover, Jesus's miracles tend to suggest that he missed his vocation and should have been in catering.

It is also hard to be entirely clear what the Bible's message is, because of the number of discrepancies between the gospels. For example, on the cross, Jesus is initially very chipper about things, because he's British, but then he has a moment of doubt, which I think is fair enough; I think by this stage he's got grounds for wondering if possibly the whole plan isn't going hideously wrong. He's thinking, 'I'm the Messiah, I'm the son of God, I'm the King of the Jews, I'm the Prince of Peace, I'm nailed to a piece of wood.' In any event, Jesus cries out, 'My God, my God, why hast thou forsaken me?' But only according to Matthew and Mark;

according to Luke he shouts, 'Father, unto thy hands I commend my spirit', which is a totally different version of events but that's journalism for you. According to the police, he crucified himself and made a full confession . . . fell on the nails when they were putting him in the van.

* * *

Jeremy Hardy Speaks to the Nation, 1993

There are basically seven deadly sins: Pride, Gluttony, Envy, Covetousness, Sloth, Flatulence and Armed Robbery. But before something can become a sin, someone has to do it. There's no point prohibiting something if no one's likely to do it anyway. That's why there's nothing in the commandments about coveting your neighbour's CD of that bloke who's in *Lovejoy* singing.

But what *was* the original sin? Eve was tempted by the serpent to eat of the Tree of Knowledge of Good and Evil, and she liked the fruit and so tempted Adam to eat of it, even though God had warned them that to touch the tree would mean death because scrumping was taken very seriously in those days. According to Genesis – by which I mean the first book of the Old Testament not the dreadful seventies rock group, which Peter Gabriel did well to leave – once Adam and Eve had eaten of the Tree, they had the knowledge of good and evil. This made them realise for the first time that they were naked and so cover themselves with fig leaves. God doesn't actually kill them because they're the only two people he knows, but he does banish them from the Garden

of Eden which is a bind because Adam's just put a row of
tomatoes in. According to God, they must be banished lest
they eat of the Tree of Life and become immortal, although,
having said that, Adam does go on to live for nine hundred
and thirty years, which is pretty bloody immortal in my
book. However, let's recount the temptation of Adam and
Eve by the Serpent.

SERPENT: Eve?

EVE: Bugger me, a talking snake.

SERPENT: Eve, hath not the Lord thaid –

EVE: 'Hath'? What do you mean, 'hath'?

SERPENT: Don't take the pith, idth not my fault I'm a
therpent.

EVE: All right, go on.

SERPENT: Hath not the Lord thaid you may eat of every
tree in the garden?

EVE: All except that one. He says if we eat of it, we shall
surely die. Something to do with pesticides, I should
think.

SERPENT: Yeth but he'th only thaying that becauth if you
eat of it, you will have the knowledge of good and evil
and will become godth.

EVE: You've been watching too many cartoons on
Saturday morning TV.

SERPENT: No, sthtraight up.

EVE: You mean God lied to us?

SERPENT: Yep.

EVE: Bastard. Gimme some of that fruit.

(EVE PICKS AND EATS THE APPLE)

EVE: Oh, that's lovely, that is. Oi, Ad! Have some of this.

ADAM: Bugger me, a talking rib.

EVE: Shut up and try some of this. Here, I can see your bollocks.

ADAM: What bollocks?

EVE: Eat, go on.

ADAM: God says we mustn't.

EVE: So, what's he going to do? Leave one of his notes? 'Will whoever it is who's been eating my forbidden fruit please buy their own.'?

ADAM: All right.

(ADAM TAKES A BITE)

ADAM: (MOUTH FULL) Mmmm, that's lovely. 'ere, you haven't got any knickers on.

EVE: Bugger me!

ADAM: Isn't that forbidden?

EVE: Not until Leviticus.

It is at this point that their nakedness starts to make them self-conscious and they put the fig leaves on. You might wonder what the knowledge of good and evil has to do with getting hung up about nudity. Adam and Eve are only a few days old. Most of us don't start to become truly appalled by our naked bodies until we're over thirty. But how might this whole ghastly situation have been avoided? Let's listen to the same situation again, this time with Eve resisting temptation.

SERPENT: Eve?

EVE: Thanks but no thanks, serpent. I like forbidden fruit but I'm afraid it doesn't like me.

SERPENT: Oh, bye then.

EVE: Goodbye.

The serpent was played by Jeremy, Eve by Debbie Isitt and Adam by Steve Frost

* * *

Jeremy Hardy Speaks to the Nation, 1993

The rituals of new-age fads are no more bizarre than the rituals of established religions. It's just a question of what you're used to. It's very easy to sneer at things you don't understand, and I don't understand why more people don't sneer at them. But if something brings you peace and happiness, does anyone else have the right to knock it, whether it's yoga, Christianity, chocolate Hobnobs or heroin? All have been said to free the mind, apart from chocolate Hobnobs. But do they free it, or do they in relaxing it also pacify it, numb it and enslave it? Marx said that religion is the opium of the people, although the Church of England is more the paracetamol really, and Catholicism and Judaism are like the speed because just when you think you're over them, they catch up with you again. Buddhism must be the alcohol because it makes you say really stupid things over and over and over again. In many ways, religion does the opposite of freeing us: it circumscribes us – especially Judaism. Religious books are full of lists of things we're not allowed to do, most of which are highly enjoyable. But perhaps by abstention we free ourselves from the fetishism of sensual gratification and experience a higher non-secular sense of pleasure. It doesn't sound very likely, though, does it?

* * *

Guardian, 2000

I have been thinking about stem cell research. It seems that roughly two thousand years after the birth of Jesus, bishops still have a say in political affairs. You might say their role is nominal, just as it is often said that the monarchy has no real power – other than to cruise the world at our expense insulting foreigners in our name, and generally clouding our thinking with trivia about their longevity or inability to use a bath correctly.

True, churches do not have the power they once enjoyed. Women don't get burned for having a third nipple, although they do get jailed for not having a TV licence. But when society considers matters of ethics, it is deemed important for the views of 'faith communities' to be solicited. Somehow, people who believe in a deity are still attributed with more, or at least special, moral authority.

Indeed, some parents send children to religious schools on the grounds that it will 'teach them right from wrong', as though we who don't believe in God have no guiding principles whatsoever. In fact, there is little in the scriptures that is directly useful in modifying children's behaviour.

Moses does not descend from the mountain saying, 'If you can't be sensible with that Golden Calf, I'm going to put it away until you're older.'

This is not to say that religious people have nothing important to say. I'm merely suggesting that ideas about justice, kindness, humility or the right to life are not exclusive to people who believe in God. And governments are quite selective in who gets to pontificate about ethics. I don't see Robin Cook running the ethical dimension to foreign policy past the Quakers for closer inspection.

If one campaigns around human rights issues, one will inevitably find oneself campaigning alongside a number of brave, practical, good-humoured and angry people who are religious. And if a religious person is vigorously opposing racism, corporate greed and miscarriages of justice, they are hugely preferable to reactionary atheists. It can be dispiriting when they speak of prayer, but no more so than when a person says, 'What sign are you?' or 'I've got this crystal . . .'

How much their faith informs their politics is hard to say. I dare say there's the odd British Aerospace executive who has a blinding revelation and discovers from God that the arms trade is morally repugnant, but if he can't work it out for himself he is wilfully dim. On the other hand, people who have generally humane and just ideas frequently select the better bits of their chosen creed while being somewhat embarrassed about the bits that involve minor offenders being stoned to death and women being forced to menstruate outdoors.

But when people seem to be driven primarily by an acceptance of what purports to be holy law, we are usually in trouble. We hear cries of horror at the thought of a sheep grown from a single cell, from people who are quite sanguine about the idea of a woman grown from a single rib. We hear protests about the welfare of the unborn from people who wouldn't give the born the time of day.

An embryo is not a person. It is perhaps more fully developed than George Bush, but it's no more difficult to create. It is a living thing, as is a sperm. I always feel rather sorry for all those brave little tadpole-like fellows that don't get to score with the egg. I'm being flippant. An embryo can actually grow into a person, if a woman is prepared to incubate it or, in the future, if a lab technician will do so. But it is not a person.

Some people are squeamish about IVF. Admittedly, it sounds like a loyalist organisation, but it does not literally mean babies born in laboratories, except where there is a chronic bed shortage. Some people wonder where we're going with all this reproductive technology and embryo research. Jehovah's Witnesses wonder where we're going with all these blood transfusions.

If deists have something distinctive to say about abortion or the use of embryos to find medical cures, it is because of their belief in the soul. Some people have such faith in the soul that they see no value in earthly life at all, although most hedge their bets. I don't know whether the soul is supposed to be complete at conception or whether it develops with age, a 25-year-old having as much as Otis

Redding and an embryo as much as Craig David. But I do know that life isn't perfect, that an embryo is a very primitive form of it and that people's lives are more important. If God disagrees, I say, come again.

* * *

Jeremy Hardy Speaks to the Nation, 2003

I am an atheist, but, although secular, am I culturally a Christian? Well, I like hymns and home-made chutney, but I don't like raffles or Cliff Richard. And I like the fact that Jesus turns the Bible from an 18 to a PG, but I don't like the way Christianity wallows in death. The idea of people in a synagogue drinking the blood of a messiah is unthinkable. Apart from anything else, if you used kosher wine for the Communion, people would think the saviour died of diabetes. But of course, in the Jewish religion, the Messiah doesn't redeem humankind by dying. That wouldn't be thought of as a successful outcome.

I often think I should have been Jewish. I work in show-business, I prefer cheesecake to Victoria sponge, and I'm rubbish at DIY. The idea that the Jews are responsible for the crucifixion of Jesus is ridiculous. How many Jewish people could assemble something like that and have it stay up for a whole weekend? On the other hand, I'd like to have been a Catholic so I could explain why I'm tormented by self-loathing and frightened of nuns. And if I were a Buddhist, I could explain the fact that I keep saying the same things over and over again.

* * *

PAULINE (MCLYNN): So, what's your religion?

JEREMY: Diagnostic.

GORDON (KENNEDY): What does that mean?

JEREMY: It means I know there's something wrong with me but I'm not sure what it is.

PAULINE: Well, what religion were you brought up in?

JEREMY: C of E? It was founded so that when people lapse it's not too much of a wrench. You Catholics lose your faith. Anglicans just can't remember where we left it.

* * *

Jesus tried to stem the encroachment of market values, self-interest and bureaucracy. He was trying to lead people *back* to his father, not sideline him and take his whole shtick like Matthew Corbett. Jesus was upholding Judaism, the faith that seems to have introduced the idea of a single God. Until then, gods were just rather remote local bigwigs with the power to ruin your harvest, a bit like immigration officers checking work permits.

It is in the Torah, or the Old Testament, that we start to have what appears to be the word of God, written down in an unchallengeable form. God's code for living appears mostly in Leviticus, when God is instructing the Jews as they meander about in the desert taking a long time to travel quite a short distance, a lot of very short-sighted people arguing over the best way to get to Jericho avoiding the Sinai gyratory system. Jewish dietary laws were wholly appropriate to people living in those conditions, but conditions have changed which means that observant Jews should follow them only when camping, which Jewish people never do. 'We let you choose last time, Moses. From now on it's hotels.'

* * *

Jeremy Hardy Speaks to the Nation, 2007

Apparently, praying can shape world events. Tony Blair has actually prayed with the leader of the DUP, Dr Gillian Paisley, presenter of *You Are What You Eat, You Wafer-Snaffling Fenian*. It's thought that this joint praying helped swing Paisley behind power sharing. Dr Paisley has always said he would not sit down with republicans until hell freezes over. But because of global warming, hell will never freeze over, although I think it would be very pretty if it did, the way fire reflects on ice, all the demons having the day off school, sledding and lying on the ground making snow devils. In fact, the Pope recently announced that hell really *does* exist and is eternal, and begins with the words, 'Press One for technical support'.

* * *

Jeremy Hardy Speaks to the Nation, 2007

Religions have got cuter about pushing their opiates. They call themselves Faith Communities now and they call creation

Intelligent Design. Design? Who would design the Earth? Are earthquakes just knocking through? 'I love what you've done with this rift valley, there's just so much more space. All you need is some scattered boulders and you'll have added fifteen thousand pounds to the value of the tectonic plate.' If God designed me, I want to have a serious word about knees, which seemed to pack up just after the manufacturer's warranty expired.

* * *

Jeremy Hardy Speaks to the Nation, 2007

Someone once said that seeing is believing, which is not the case. I've seen Tony Blair.

And a great many people the world over believe in things they haven't seen. Although this then means that sometimes they *start* to see things. If someone says they've seen a ghost or aliens or the face of Liberace in a bagel, we are supposed to think, 'Well, that's it then, incontrovertible proof that these things truly exist,' and we might do if the person who saw them didn't also crush puppies by stroking them too hard.

If God or extraterrestrials or spirits want to be taken seriously, they need to reveal themselves to respected documentary film-makers – not disturbed people in rural communities.

* * *

Jeremy Hardy Speaks to the Nation, 2010

I'm a moderate atheist rather than a fundamentalist one. There's much to admire in most religions. And one thing that's really admirable about religious people is that they believe in something more important than themselves.

Radical movements have often been rooted in religious organisations. And you need to have faith, you need imagination to believe that things can be different from the way they are now. And you need inspiration. I would rather listen to a speech by Dr Martin Luther King than Professor Richard Flipping Dawkins.

If you don't know Dawkins, he's a secular zealot. He wrote a book about there not being a God. A whole book to say that. You'd think:

Page 1 There's no God, the End . . .

Page 2 Index: God, non-existence of: Page One.

Page 3 Acknowledgements: thank God for nothing.

but it's about 400 pages long. I don't think there's a God either, haven't done for a long time . . . over thirty-five years, I reckon, but I'm not that impressed with myself for drawing that conclusion. It was born more from despair than belief in my own fantasticness.

And I don't see religion and science as opposites. Both are practised by people, and people are flawed and limited. Scientists enquire up to a point but then they have to show their hand and we expect them to have answers. You know

235

they've got that particle accelerator, the Large Haddock Collider in Switzerland? In one of those mountains where the top slides off and a rocket comes out and the villain's stroking a cat? Well they want to see what happened at the beginning of time. They say time began with a big bang, but they don't really know. If there was an almighty explosion, what exploded? There was nothing. Time hadn't started. And given that it was all a very long time ago, isn't it time we drew a line under it and moved on? Even if there was an explosion, no one was hurt, no damage was done and no one was responsible. Or were they? Was God responsible and, if so, was God the first terrorist? Or was it an insurance job? There was no Lottery funding in those days. When you wanted a new theatre, you had to have a fire. Like in the eighties when Thatcher cut all the arts funding. Every arts centre dressing room had a sign reading, 'Before leaving, please put your towel over the electric heater.'

* * *

Jeremy Hardy Speaks to the Nation, 2004

It's not always the case that we are what we fear, but one can see the logic of it in terms of sexuality. Certainly it rather looks like that in the case of the Anglican Church, which is tearing itself to pieces over the issue of gay clergy. I have to ask: what on earth is the point in being an Anglican clergyman if you're *not* gay? It's really just for those gay men who are too plain to be airline stewards. I think that's true of all Christian clergy. Communion is just drinks and snacks. The only thing missing is the trolley. Certainly I can picture Ian Paisley handing out the sickbags.

I suspect that in all religions that are iffy about homosexuality, it's always been the case that lots of clerics are gay, everyone knows and no one says anything. That's why the confessional is a one-way process, so you won't hear the priest say, 'Oooh I know.'

* * *

Increasingly, I think religion, or rather faith, is responsible for all manner of calamity and woe. It's not the existence of words in a book we should worry about, it's the fact that people who are having a bad day will take them far too seriously.

As I watched Tony Blair's performance before the Chilcot inquiry, it became increasingly clear that he genuinely believes he is doing God's work. Unfortunately, people who believe that never ask God what needs doing. God in his wisdom would probably assign Tony Blair some light housework or just give him some felt pens and scrap paper. It's like when you leave an older relative alone in your home and they decide what would be helpful,

GRANNY: Those non-stick pans of yours were absolutely black inside, but I got them back to a nice shine.

Except it's quite a lot worse than that. And just as Tony Blair has faith that he's doing God's work, I think Osama bin Laden thinks he's doing God's work. I think Israeli settlers believe they're doing God's work, and Hamas think they're doing God's work. Clearly God is sending out some very mixed messages. He's a flipping stirrer, let's be honest. He's holding people's coats and saying, 'He called you a slag.'

Race, Ethnicity and Racism

Jeremy Hardy Speaks to the Nation, 1993

If money gives you freedom, how do you get money? Some people believe that, no matter how we start, talent, grit and sheer hard work can overcome any obstacle to our becoming rich. A black guy from Notting Hill can end up driving a Rolls. Of course, there'd be no point because he'd be stopped by the police every four or five feet, but in theory he could do it.

* * *

Jeremy Hardy Speaks to the Nation, 2004

Political parties on the make, especially those of the extreme right, always have lists of people we should be afraid of. And the people at the top of the list today are Muslims. Because

Islam is a religion rather than a race, devotees of Islamophobia can say they are not racist; but the fact that Muslims are generally not white makes it all the more fun for fascists. It's always handy if scapegoats are colour-coded because that way BNP activists only need to be shown pictures.

* * *

Jeremy Hardy Speaks to the Nation, 2007

Of course, it's easier to be prejudiced against people who look different. They might be of a different race, they might wear something different: a cross, a turban, a yarmulke or a veil.

In the current climate, some politicians consider it appropriate to throw their weight around when it comes to what women wear on their heads. Jack Straw kicked this off saying, 'I always ask the ladies to remove their veil when they come to constituency surgery.' I bet you do. 'Hello, my dear, you look awfully hot in that thing. Wouldn't you like to slip into these leather hotpants I've made for you.' And then other MPs pitched in, saying, 'Well, I'd never given it any thought, but now Jack's raised it I realise it's a vital subject of national debate.' Mind your own business! So you can't see the nose and mouth of someone in a veil. You can see their eyes, the windows of the soul, you don't need to see the catflap. If your mum rings for a chat, you don't say, 'Get in a cab, woman, if I can't see your nose and mouth, I'm not interested.'

But other people followed MPs and started saying that

they also found it off-putting to see a woman in a veil. College lecturers have refused to teach young women in veils, because they can't see them yawn. People speak of banning veils altogether and pretend that they're doing it to liberate women. I'm sorry, but if women want to wear something, whether it's hotpants or a burka, that is surely their right. You can't force people to dress as you say and then claim to be liberating them. For many young women, dressing in an Islamic way is an act of defiance against government policy, and a sign of solidarity with Muslims facing oppression and occupation. Women are saying, 'I am gonna hijab up, because yes I am a Muslim and if you don't like it I'll put the whole tarpaulin on to wind you up, you bugger.' By the way, I am entitled to speak for Muslim women because I am a community leader.

And if you think Muslim dress is unliberated, well can you tell me where in the world is this mythical land in which women dress in a way that's completely untainted by conditioning and patriarchy? Women the world over wear unpractical, uncomfortable and undignified things because that's the received wisdom about what they should look like. In most of the world women remove varying amounts of body hair because it is perceived as unfeminine even though all women have it. Women in the Middle East remove all of it which is a bit weird but I suppose it is quite sandy there. And even in the West women take off quite a bit of body hair, including from what is known as the bikini area, not an atoll with French nuclear tests on it, but the crotch.

And the main reason they depilate there is that they can't find a swimming costume that covers what God gave them. How insane is that? You have to have hot wax smeared on your groin and ripped off again because in our glorious free democratic consumers' paradise, you can't get women's swimming trunks that cover your twinkle properly. And we bomb people so they can learn our way of life.

And the amount of hair allowed seems to diminish every year. Quite normal now is the tiny strip known as a Brazilian. I don't know why it's called that; it looks more like Chile.

But all right, let's not avoid the issue of Islamic women's clothing. Customs can seem strange to people who aren't used to them and the burka, the total covering with even the eyes obscured, might be seen as alienating. But if it were just a fashion trend I doubt it would bother anyone. Weirder things have been worn. It's because it's Islamic that people are especially troubled by it. But let's say you find it sets up a barrier between you and the person wearing the burka. Well, think laterally. Maybe you should put one on yourself. And the gap is bridged. And other gaps would be bridged if we all put one on.

You wouldn't be able to tell a person's religion or sex or age or colour. And if you think about it, it's a very practical garment. Especially for women, who spend ages trying to work out what to wear. Just have a burka. You'd never be late for work. If you oversleep you can quickly pull it on over your nightclothes and rush straight into work. No one would know you've got your pyjamas on underneath. How cool would that be? You're in an important meeting being completely in control and no one knows that underneath your burka you're wearing jim-jams and slippers and holding a teddy. And if it's freezing in the office you can keep your coat on under your burka and still look smart and professional. If it's boiling in the summer and the air conditioning has packed up, you can go commando. Completely naked under your burka and no one knows. You always look smart, you're always on time. Just throw your burka on. Set your alarm for five minutes before you have to leave the house, burka on, out the door, never late. Don't feel like going in? Send a couple of the kids one on top of the other.

* * *

Jeremy Hardy Speaks to the Nation, 2007

If there are schools where someone insists the blackboard is called a chalkboard, don't get all D. W. Griffiths about it. Just explain to them that cultural awareness and anti-racism are about the feelings and opportunities of human beings; blackboards don't mind what they're called and aren't under-represented in the judiciary. It is a board and it is black. It's not being likened to a black person and black isn't being used in any negative way. The point of avoiding language such as 'black-hearted' or 'whiter than white' is that the association of whiteness with virtue and blackness with evil has impacted on the way people see race. If you talk about black and white coffee, there's no implication that one is better than the other. The term 'black coffee' is

242

no more offensive to black people than 'espresso' is to train drivers. It's not racist to call coffee black. If someone called black people 'people without milk' that would be racist, albeit in a rather feeble way that the French would find both amusing and acceptable.

* * *

Jeremy Hardy Speaks to the Nation, 2010

Commissioning editors have decided that the white working class – as though that's one thing – have all been left behind because the rest of us have spent too much time being nice to black people. And it's fashionable to be a bit edgy about race. Attempts have even been made to rehabilitate Enoch Powell, probably the most repellent man in mainstream politics in the last half century. A man so extreme, he had to leave the Tories, go to Northern Ireland and join the Ulster Unionists, to be among people equally bigoted, a man who famously made sure that every speech he made was on a full bladder, in order to achieve that pained expression and whining voice so familiar from his Rivers of Piss speech. Perhaps he was right, even a prophet, people say. After all, he predicted rivers of blood in 1968 and then, hey presto, there were some riots in the early eighties and then another one in Bradford in 2001. It all fits. *No it doesn't.* What is not mentioned is the fact that riots have been part of a history of public anger with authority; and that white British people fought the police during the Vietnam War, the miners' strike of 1984–5, during the campaigns to bring down the

Poll Tax, and the Criminal Justice Act of 1994. White people have a long and noble history of rioting. Perhaps not that rhythmically but we've done our best.

* * *

Jeremy Hardy Feels It, 2017

Let's move forward from the dawn of history, to the coffee break of history. Why did human speech develop far more complexity and nuance than was required for purely practical purposes? There's a theory that someone who used language to control social information gained status. In other words, complex language evolved so that we could gossip.

PAULINE: (OVER-THE-GARDEN-FENCE-TYPE GOSSIP) Her in the cave next door is no better than she should be. Flaunting herself like a woolly mammoth on heat. And she's not a natural blonde; oh no, you can tell she dyes her beard.

PAUL: (SIMILAR) And him on the other side, the new fella – he's only gone and put curtains up!

PAULINE: Curtains? What's his game?

PAUL: It's obvious, isn't it? He's one of . . . them.

PAULINE: One of what?

PAUL: (WHISPERING) Homo . . . sapiens!

Now at a risk of explaining what you've just heard in a way that sucks all mirth from life, as Nicholas Parsons does in *Just A Minute*, what you just heard was a joke that derives from the Latin prefix meaning 'man' being the same as the Greek prefix meaning 'the same'. Some people might conclude that because of an implied reference to gay men, it is *hostile* to gay men. I would never countenance such a thing because I'm trying to blag comps for *A Chorus Line*. And because, in addition to the fact that gay people would find it offensive, *I* would find it offensive.

We can and should be offended by things without necessarily being the target of the offence. But if, for example, someone says something antisemitic, and I object, people will say 'Why, are you Jewish?' Why do I need to be? If I sign a petition against torture, it's not because I've got a low pain threshold. And by the way, the number of petitions I'm signing online, this world is going to be a really good place pretty soon.

But take, for example, the n-word, which is very commonly used by black hip hop artists, reflecting the fact that quite a lot of African-American people use it among themselves. Last year, I went to a debate about the positive and negative aspects of hip hop. Now, Radio 4 listeners will have difficulty picturing me at such an event because you probably have me pigeonholed as more of a dubstep man. But I was interested in the discussion and it was obviously very much about language and there was a focus on words that are homophobic and misogynistic and, of course, racist, especially the n-word. And there was this discussion about whether white people can ever use it. And I thought, 'Why would I want to use it? It offends *me*. As a human.' I'm offended by the N-word because I'm not a c-word. And I'm sorry if you're offended by my use of part of the female body as an insult, and I agree with you in principle, but we lost that battle in the nineties and now I think the word has more value pejoratively than anatomically. You don't hear doctors use it except about Andrew Lansley. That's why he was replaced with Jeremy Hunt, who can imagine it's a verbal slip. Thank you Jim Naughtie, you spoke *for* the nation. But I digress. And I'm being undermined by my own intellectual inconsistency. So let's try to focus for a minute on the n-word.

Now I'm not saying it's a straightforward issue and there is the argument that there is language that stays in the group. Obviously, the fact that people talk about themselves in a certain way doesn't give you the right to join in. I mean, that's a principle we apply to the whole of life. When someone says,

WOMAN: God, I look terrible.

I've learned that there are things to say and things not to say. One of the things not to say is,

MAN: Thank you. Finally. I was beginning to think it was just me who thought that.

And if a word is supposed to be some sort of private-circulation expression for use only within a community, I'm not sure that putting it in the lyrics of popular songs of the day is the best way to keep it there.

But there is also the argument that a fixation with words ignores hidden prejudice and I take the point, I just think you ought to be able to do two things at once. Not if you're a man obviously; we'll have to leave women to tackle terminology and intent simultaneously while we get on with taking our Christmas tree lights out of the loft.

Sex and Sexuality

Jeremy Hardy Speaks to the Nation, 1993

A video can't teach you to have sex, except with yourself. But learning some degree of sexual technique can be beneficial; if someone says, 'Was *what* all right for me?' you may be on the wrong track.

But there are extremes. One reads of the painstaking efforts of couples in their attempts to prolong and to heighten the intensity of their ecstasy – just before the moment of climax the man has to withdraw and hit himself in the testicles with a hammer. Women's magazines, not the knitting ones but the fashionable ones for independent go-ahead confident women, revolve entirely around men. They have headlines like, 'Is your man a real man?' What's a woman supposed to think? 'Well, he can't be a hologram because he can catch peanuts in his mouth.' And they have lots of articles about orgasms: Orgasms & Tax, Orgasms for the Self-Employed, Orgasms & Starting Your Own Business. And I even read one about the male orgasm which said that men can have multiple orgasms too. Now the word 'too' seems to presuppose that people other than men have multiple orgasms, by which I assume they meant women. Now, I'm not an expert on female sexuality but from what I can gather a multiple orgasm is like a good stereo: something you see in magazines and other people have. You may have thought you had one but it was probably hiccups. And by multiple orgasm, I should explain that I don't mean several over a period of years. And it's foolhardy to tell men there's more to be gleaned from sex because men *always* want more from sex. Now men will ask their partners why they can't have a multiple orgasm and their partners will say, 'Oh, we've been through this, the flat's too small, it would make too much mess.'

And couples who've just achieved simultaneous orgasm after years of practice now have to have eight or nine orgasms each, all at the same time, so they have to have the same number and if one of them has one too many, the whole evening's been a total disaster. It's no wonder human beings can't face sex until last thing at night. Which is a shame. We should really be able to just make love when we feel like it – public transport permitting. But sex is relegated, shoved up the wrong end of the day, so it becomes this last grisly chore we have to struggle through before we can sleep. Our attitude to sex is 'Well, we're lying down anyway, might as well give it a try.' And you can have an early night but that's over by about five past ten and you've got to get up and watch the telly, make it down the pub for last orders.

Of course according to popular fiction, we make love all night. A note of caution here – making love all night is possible and often desired in a new relationship. In the early days of a burgeoning romance you may well find that you make love all night but there are harmful side-effects and what you may not realise is that you're *using up your goes*.

* * *

Jeremy Hardy Speaks to the Nation, 1993

Our society is quite tolerant of homosexuals who don't force their sexuality on others by going outside or saying 'I'm gay' in a residential area. If you do your best to keep your sexuality a secret, you will be forgiven if you get caught. It will be said that you are basically a heterosexual who, owing to pressure of work or overexuberance in a crowded changing room, suffered a momentary loss of concentration and started having it off with someone of the same sex, and so long as you didn't enjoy it no harm's been done.

Pressure upon gay people to return to the closet has built up because of the HIV virus. Some people believe that AIDS was sent by God to punish people for being homosexual – which begs the question, 'What was the plague for, to punish people for wearing period costume?'

But hysteria is rife. When I recently applied for some life insurance, I was asked if I'd ever had homosexual relations. I said that there was a cousin we used to wonder about but I couldn't swear to it. Aside from HIV, the justification given for the oppression of gay people is that homosexuality is unnatural, although the person saying that is always dressed from head to toe in polyester, anyway. Frankly, I don't care whether a thing's unnatural anyway, I mean babies' incubators aren't natural, dialysis machines aren't natural. I'll tell you what natural is, natural is earthquakes, wasps, stinging nettles, shit, pain and death.

Much of the oppression of gay people is justified by religious zealots. The Bible is invoked because Leviticus, Chapter 18, Verse 22, says that homosexuality is an abomination. Well, Leviticus says all manner of inane things. For example, Leviticus says that if a woman having a period sits on your sofa, you've got to burn it, and it says that if a man has sex with your donkey, you must put your donkey to death. So, how did it lead him on, I want to know. Was it wearing a provocatively short saddle, or do donkeys sometimes say 'hee-haw' when they mean 'Yes'.

* * *

Jeremy Hardy Speaks to the Nation, 1993

There is evidence to suggest that there was more free love in previous millennia than there has been in the post-war period, including the supposedly permissive 1960s. I for one don't remember the sixties as being that permissive; apart from being allowed to stay up for *High Chaparral* on a Monday night, that was about it.

But it was during the sixties and seventies that it became apparent just how sexually uninhibited previous civilisations were. The availability of cheap package holidays brought a sudden influx of postcards featuring statues of naked ancient Greek men in a state of arousal. For most of us, this was the first time that unclothed erections had popped through the letter box with the morning mail. Unless we had an overzealous postman. Before this, we'd only seen pictures of statues with erect phalluses in school library books, and then only because we'd drawn them on. The urge to draw genitals on pictures is irresistible to teenage boys and provides even more entertainment than crossing out the 'not' on signs saying 'Do not lean out of the window', and asking a maths teacher if it would be possible to have a maths debate. Therefore the revelation that there are works of art which already have excited genitalia on them left a whole generation of schoolboys feeling quite redundant.

The time we generally think of as being the height of repressed sexuality is the nineteenth century. For the Victorians, sexual intercourse would seem to have consisted of a married couple lying fully clothed in separate rooms and remaining completely still while doctors poured boiling water over their private parts and recited 'The Charge of the Light Brigade'. The only publicly recognised reason for having sex was so that a woman could conceive, and preferably die in childbirth. Of course, on the quiet, the

Victorians were up to all sorts of things. A Victorian gentleman would spend the day lamenting the moral laxity of the poor and planning missionary expeditions to force the Maasai to wear underpants, and at night would go cruising round the slums hiring chimney sweeps to dress him up as a shepherdess and sodomise him with a bust of Palmerston.

Men, Women and Gender

Jeremy Hardy Speaks to the Nation, 1997

When men say they are trying to get in touch with their female side, they mean they want to be able to show emotion, to cry for example. Actually, if you do want to learn to cry, the best way is to wait for a bank holiday when all the shops are shut and you have no food in the house but the arse end of a loaf of not very fresh bread. Toast it, butter it, preferably using real butter, but a substitute called something like 'Heavens To Betsy Are You Sure This Is A Butter Substitute?' or even 'Bugger Me, This Is Marge' will do. Having toasted and buttered your only slice of bread, and having first checked that your kitchen floor is really filthy, start to walk out of the kitchen with your plate slightly tilted so that the toast slides off and lands face down on the floor. You will then weep like never before.

When men talk about their female side, it shows they've fallen for the old idea of what a real man is, someone who can map-read and grip branches with his feet. The secret fact is that all men have a hard time keeping up the front of being proper men – but none of us are prepared to admit it to each other. Secretly, we are all sick of having to know all this obligatory bloke-shit about drill bits and war. None of us really care about any of it but we have to feign interest and knowledge because we're men. I'm sure that the appeal of things like camp and drag is that they are ways of escaping that.

But what men do achieve by cross-dressing is to opt out of their traditional image as men. Not many men do cross-dress, but all men feel the lure of camp in some way. If a man ever finds himself in momentary possession of a curly blond wig he is unable to resist the temptation of holding it to his head and asking his mates how he looks. Any man who does what he considers to be an imitation of a gay man will assume a camp voice immediately, in a way which is oddly natural to him considering he says he can't do accents. The point is that whether openly or subconsciously, all men seek remission from their traditional role. Gay men should not have a monopoly on camp. Even for one day, a man should have the right to sit in front of a Jean-Claude van Damme video, saying, 'What's she like?'

Incidentally, I notice that emergency vehicles have become very camp. Fire engines, for example, used to be very boysy,

(FORTIES NEWSREEL VOICE) Dingaling, the plucky chaps
of the London Fire Brigade do their best to douse the
flames as Hitler's bombs rain down on plucky London.

Then they went through an infantile playground phase:

NER-NER, NER-NER.

And now we have the screamingly camp new sirens. Fire
engines scream past the house going:

OOOOOOOH-OOOH . . . look at the fire on that. Mind
you, with those curtains it's a blessing.

* * *

Jeremy Hardy Speaks to the Nation, 1994

In these days of post-feminism, which is what I think we
used to call sexism, women are constantly accused of winding
men up by 'giving them the wrong signals'. But it's hard to
avoid giving men the wrong signals; half the men in the
world think their luck's in if an elderly lesbian nun stops to
ask them the time. Men constantly delude themselves. When
a man's just got married, he says, 'Do you know, since I've
been a married man, other women find me so much more
attractive.' And it's only because his wife's bought him some
decent clothes and made him sort his dandruff out. And
when a man hears that Jodie Foster's a lesbian, he says
'Oh' . . . as if it makes any material difference to his chances.

* * *

I'm Sorry I Haven't A Clue, 2001

HUMPH: Jeremy, here's a question for you. How can I tell whether the aubergine in my larder is male or female?

JEREMY: If the aubergine is female, it says, 'We should really knock this larder through and have a fridge-freezer in here.' And then a couple of years later it says, 'You know, things kept much better when we had the old larder before we got the fridge-freezer.' Then you have to get a new kitchen cos the old one doesn't go with the napkin rings.

* * *

Jeremy Hardy Speaks to the Nation, 2003

I have never thought I'm a proper bloke. I have no interest in cars, tools, sport or mountain bikes. The one thing that does activate my X chromosomes is a barbecue.

Men, it has been discovered, have a fire-starting gene. This kicks in not only during the balmy smoke-filled days of summer but also during the bonfire season of autumn and winter. The period around 5 November is very important for us. It puts us in touch with our primordial selves to build a big pile of leaves, torch it, and develop a slightly sicky feeling as it all gets horribly out of hand. That's why the patio season is safer. We can give vent to our burning tendencies in a secure, controlled environment, with the fire safely contained in metal. But we still get to hold the sharp things. Not the effete, short-handled kitchen sharp things Mother uses the rest of the year: peelers, corers and zesters. Big, nasty, outside, garden pointy things. We stand firm with our barbecue tools like a warrior chieftain. We are Conan the Suburbian.

But apart from fire I have no great interest in most of the things men are supposed to like. Sometimes I wonder whether lots of other men secretly feel the same way as me. To be a proper man, you have to like football, preferably to the point of hysteria. A man stands on a freezing football terrace shouting the c-word as though the ability to pronounce it were about to be taken from him; affecting an acute insight into the game while unable to grasp the one key fact that foreigners are better at it; and commenting on the fitness of men who can run around for forty-five minutes without stopping, when he himself can't raise a knee past waist height without breaking wind. Is he truly passionate about football? Does he really love it? Or would it just destroy his sense of himself if he admitted he'd rather be watching *West Side Story*?

* * *

Jeremy Hardy Speaks to the Nation, 2003

JEREMY: Gordon, what men's cosmetic products have you tried out?

GORDON: Well they're basically girls' things with butch names. For example, this deep-cleansing milk is called Facial Swarf, the exfoliant is called Sanding Lotion, the moisturiser is called All Weather Sealant.

JEREMY: What's this – 'Mouth Bastard'?
GORDON: Lip gloss.

* * *

I'm Sorry I Haven't A Clue, 2007

Rejected Mr Men first lines:
Mr Big was the envy of the other Mr Men . . .

* * *

Jeremy Hardy Speaks to the Nation, 2007

Of course, men aren't under the same pressure as women when it comes to appearance but there are still preconceived ideas about what we should look like. And women are happy enough to undermine our confidence if we don't conform to the advertising hoarding image of muscled manliness.

You'll say, 'Why don't you have big muscles on your arms?' And I think, 'Because my job doesn't involve arm muscles. I don't pose without a shirt and I don't spend all day shinning up ladders holding building materials. My job involves sitting for long periods in badly ventilated rooms, staring at a computer, sitting for long periods of time on badly ventilated trains staring at England, and sitting for long periods of time in completely unventilated dressing rooms, staring at a blank sheet of paper on which I've written the word "Sheffield".'

I'd have big muscles if my job involved manual labour or it was so mind-numbingly pointless that I had to expiate my self-loathing by spending all weekend in the gym. But everything about *my* profession is geared towards my committing suicide in a hotel room, so no, I don't have big arm muscles. You might as well ask why my cheeks don't expand like Dizzy Gillespie's.

* * *

I'm Sorry I Haven't a Clue, 2011

JACK: Okay, the teams are going to bring this show a more contemporary flavour now with a look at the 1930s . . . I've brought with me a selection of genuine advice for young husbands taken from a 1930s etiquette book, certain parts of which have been removed; your job is to fill in the missing section.

'It is very lowering to her dignity to have to ask you for money, every time she wants to . . .'

JEREMY: ' . . . but that won't stop her.'

JACK: 'Do realise that a little persuasion will attain far better results than . . .'

JEREMY: ' . . . waterboarding.'

JACK: 'Don't squeeze the tube of toothpaste from the top instead of from the bottom; this is one of the small things of life that . . .'

JEREMY: ' . . . shouldn't be in your bottom.'

JACK: 'Do be careful not to criticise the imperfections of other people – remember the saying: When my friends are blind of one eye, I . . .'

JEREMY: ' . . . have fun moving the cornflakes around the breakfast table'.

JACK: 'In matters of dress, don't wear a white waistcoat with a dinner jacket; this experiment has been tried and . . .'

JEREMY: ' . . . you get mounted by a king penguin.'

* * *

Jeremy Hardy Speaks to the Nation, 2013

How *do* you 'be' a woman? Well the obvious way is to put on a frock and a funny voice which is what *actors* mean when they talk about acting. Historically, male actors have often played women. In Shakespeare's time, males acted all the female roles. And Shakespeare plays around with that convention in *Twelfth Night* and *As You Like It* because he's got male actors playing females who are playing males who make females played by males fall in love with them, so you've got these multiple layers of ambiguity about gender which was probably quite edgy in those days. I mean, it's not *Some Like It Hot*, but to be fair to Shakespeare, he was pretty useless at comedy. Actors try to spice it up by grabbing their genitals to point up the double entendres, but it's very thin stuff and only funny if you're on a school trip and you've never seen an adult touch themselves, which hopefully you haven't. But in terms of sexuality and gender, they're quite radical plays. *The Taming of The Shrew*, not so much. Kate isn't the most positive representation of a woman's role in a relationship, but bear in mind it was written four hundred years ago and more importantly, Shakespeare was from the West Midlands.

WILLIAM : (HEAVY BRUM ACCENT) She is a bloody night-mare that one, she wants putting in her place.

But, of course, modern, progressive men from the south of England don't think like that. We just think: 'Oh well, what can you do?' I do wonder if Shakespeare's wife Anne was upset by the play.

ANNE: I hope you don't think *I'm* like that, William.
WILLIAM: Course not, you're not from Verona. You
    know what they're like, the Eye-ties, hot-blooded.
    You're just a simple home-loving Warwickshire lass.
ANNE: Oh William, am I the Dark Lady?
WILLIAM: . . . er, yeah.
ANNE: Who you texting?
WILLIAM: Nobody, just deleting old messages.

Women in Shakespeare's plays are always important roles, often driving the whole plot. They make things happen – often bad things. One thinks of Lady Macbeth, the ultimate Jacobean villainess, suppressing her own womanly compassion and nagging her big dumb, loveable husband till he's killed half of Scotland so she can have a new kitchen. But most of Shakespeare's women are not the main character. In movies today, it's more common for a woman to be playing the title role, like the Queen or Margaret Thatcher who are both real-life people, unbelievably, or a literary heroine such as Tess of the Doobie Brothers or Anne of Green Gables, by far the most skittish of Henry VIII's seven wives, and one from whom he had an amicable separation followed by a lasting friendship. As you can tell, I know as much about the sixteenth century as David Starkey knows about this one.

William was played by Gordon Kennedy
and Anne by Sara Pascoe

* * *

Jeremy Hardy Speaks to the Nation, 2013

Throughout history, some trans people have been convincing enough in their adopted gender that people accepted it and treated them accordingly. Women sometimes cross-dressed in order to have opportunities not open to them as women. There are historical cases of doctors, musicians, even pirates. Women posed as men in order to serve as soldiers, often receiving high praise for their valour. One famous example was Frances Clayton. She enlisted as 'Jack Williams' in the American Civil War in order to fight alongside her husband Elmer. It's reported that when Elmer was killed at the Battle of Stones River, Frances, without pausing, stepped over his body and bravely continued to fight, which I think says more about marriage than it does about women's courage.

FRANCES: Do you have to lie there, right where I'm fighting? I'm trying to wage war here. I wish *I* had time to fall down dead, but some of us have got bayoneting to do.

261

What is less well known is that, at the start of the war, Elmer and Frances were in the middle of an argument, which she was able to put on hold and continue at his graveside when the war was over.

Some of these women lived as men for years and were only discovered in hospital. The jazz musician Billy Tipton, born Dorothy, was found out on his deathbed. And who's to say he was not a man? If all the world believes you are something, and you maintain that role all your life, does the fact that you weren't born that thing mean much? It might be that at post-mortem it is discovered that Michael Gove is actually human, but until then to all intents and purposes he's one of the mutant fish people.

* * *

Jeremy Hardy Speaks to the Nation, 2013

It is often said that there aren't enough women in the board-room. But in reality there are thousands of women in boardrooms. It's just that they're the women who have to clean boardrooms at four thirty in the morning and then be home in time to get their kids off to school before going to their other job while hoping their asylum claim isn't turned down because they haven't got enough documents to prove they were sufficiently tortured to satisfy a civil servant in Croydon.

* * *

Men and women have different but complementary skills. Men have much less understanding, but women compensate for this by being impossible to understand anyway. However, the brain changes according to how it is stimulated. And adults behave completely differently towards boys and girls. We use gender-specific baby talk. The whole tone of voice is different. We give them different toys. Girls are given My Weird Pink Horse, with a huge array of plastic haircare equipment to style its nylon mane, whereas boys get the Captain Vengeance Ninja Attack Helicopter, with detachable hooded prisoner. Without meaning to, we're still raising boys to be dominant and girls to be subordinate. Society is still preparing girls for a time when women had no aspiration to independence. If you were poor, you faced a life of drudgery, and if you were well-to-do, it was hoped that you would marry a much older man, learn three notes on the piano, and die in childbirth. In fact, that melodramatic spirit lives on in today's teenage girls –

TEENAGE GIRL: Oh mercy, I have lost a nail; I shall not last the night.

After the period of witch trials crushed independent womanhood, women who attained status independently were exceptional and stood out as *strong* women. And because of the odds women have faced, people often admire a strong or successful woman, regardless of any other aspects of her personality. The thing that unites such twentieth-century female icons as Wallis Simpson, Coco Chanel and Leni Riefenstahl is that they hold a fascination for people who like to pretend they weren't Nazis. In the case of Riefenstahl, one can argue that she was a talented film-maker who achieved much in a male-dominated society, but if the male dominating your society is Adolf Hitler and you're pals with him and one of the things you're best at is propaganda films, that old glass ceiling shouldn't be too much of a problem. The Nazis were keen on breaking glass, after all. And, if they'd won the war, she'd never have had to say she wasn't one any more. If Hitler had conquered Europe, I doubt she'd have said,

LENI: (A BIT LIKE A FEMALE SCHWARZENEGGER) All right, Adolf, you've got what you wanted – now it's time for a few home truths.

Coco Chanel was also talented, and she didn't actually make little black uniforms for the SS – unlike Hugo Boss, who was an active Nazi even before they reached power so at least can't be accused of jumping on the bandwagon, Wallis Simpson didn't contribute anything to the world, other than causing an abdication that spared Britain the embarrassment of having a Nazi King; although if he hadn't stood down, I think the fact that, when war broke out, a reigning monarch would have had to be interned might have set a useful precedent. Nonetheless, despite the fact that

Simpson didn't do much, her life has been dramatised many times, most recently by Madonna in her film *W.E.* If you haven't seen it, try to imagine Martin Scorsese in a conical bra, then think of Madonna directing a film.

The Teenage Girl and Leni were played by Sara Pascoe

* * *

Jeremy Hardy Speaks to the Nation, 2013

We really haven't progressed much when it comes to the objectification of women. Women acting in films are generally expected to get their kit off on camera at some point before they're forty-five. Highly respected women from film and theatre will even pose sexily and scantily clad in magazines, sometimes in the broadsheet supplements, whose readers I presume are expected to react,

MAN: My goodness, darling, we should certainly investigate who retails that nightie. Those nipples are on a woman who's done three years with the Royal Shakespeare Company.

The only progress is that occasionally you'll see the headline 'Still sexy at fifty-five' attached to a photo of a woman who's just started to get acting work again now she's old enough to play the overbearing and/or alcoholic mother or quirky younger gran stroke homeless eccentric. You might, if you're a woman, think:

WOMAN: I think it's positive that physical beauty is now celebrated in the over-fifties.

JEREMY: Or you might think:

WOMAN: Oh God, does it never end? Do I have to be cremated before I stop being judged by my cleavage?

JEREMY: I mean, do you really want the priest at your funeral to be going –

PRIEST: Ashes to ashes, dust to dust . . . and I certainly would, wouldn't you, eh, lads?

JEREMY: Or the humanist celebrant to say –

HUMANIST: And now I'd like us all just to take a moment to think about Teresa and just quietly pleasure ourselves.

* * *

Red Pepper, 2014

The Everyday Sexism Project is an excellent initiative by Laura Bates, and she is a brilliant, brave and determined activist who suffers horrifying threats that more than make her point for her. But knowing that, and reading the accounts that pour in from women inspired to tell the world of the abuse they suffer, I don't think 'sexism' is a strong enough word. It's fine for the instances of people mistaking presidents for tea ladies, but what we're looking at is deep and aggressive misogyny.

Women can be 'sexist' to men: assuming we don't know how to look after children, expecting us to have a facility with shelving and objectifying David Beckham when he poses in his pants. There is all sorts of stereotyping of both sexes, backed up by cod-science and faux irony. The innovation of the term 'man up' is demeaning to both sexes, and is as deliberate a piece of sexism as the appropriation of 'gay' to mean all things crap is a piece of homophobia.

But 'sexism' is an expression like 'racial tension', meaning something that can cut both ways. And even though it is usually reported with women being the recipients, it doesn't come near to describing what we're dealing with. I'm not saying we shouldn't be concerned about women in the cabinet. And I'm certainly not saying we should ignore women being whistled at and think about Boko Haram. I'm saying women being whistled at and Boko Haram are on the same spectrum of contempt and inhumanity.

Perhaps some men think women like men to shout, 'Hello, darling!' from a van. Doubtless some think being enslaved by a militia is every woman's dream. Wolf whistles are the mild end of something that gets very ugly very quickly. We're talking about hatred.

* * *

Jeremy Hardy Speaks to the Nation, 2013

Sean Bean gave a rather beautiful performance as a transvestite as part of that TV drama series *Accused*. Now, some people are bound to say it was unrepresentative and transvestites aren't really like that, to which the author can legitimately say, 'This one is. I made him up and that's what he's like.' And that's fair enough. People don't go and see *Hamlet* and say, 'That's so unrepresentative. Danish people are nothing like that. Most Danes are incredibly decisive in matters of retribution and family honour. I don't know any Danes like Hamlet.'

Probably don't know any Danes. I only know one, and she's a lesbian and therefore not completely representative. I did meet one other Danish person and she was black, which I'm guessing is even *less* representative. I haven't been there but I imagine Danes are some of the whitest people on Earth. Certainly, if you see Sandi dance, that would tend to support me.

* * *

Jeremy Hardy Speaks to the Nation, 2013

A minority of transgender people are born with ambiguous genitalia, which must be very distressing or a lot of fun depending on how philosophical you are. But most are people clearly born male or female, but who find they are unable to identify with that gender. I think quite a lot of people find the antics of their own sex quite alienating. I would urge any man considering gender reassignment to bear in mind that there are other men who've tried going to football matches but had to run straight home and read some Sylvia Plath. In fact, I once spent an evening at Wimbledon dog track and would quite happily have resigned not only from my gender but also from my race.

But there must be more than this level of alienation involved when people decide to undergo surgery. Many people in Thailand, for example, say they were trapped in a man's body, having been convinced it was a woman when they left the nightclub. But are ladyboys men, or are they women? In Thailand, ladyboys, or *kathoey*, represent a third gender, apparently female, legally male and accepted as neither, but playing a useful role in humiliating sex tourists. Because to my mind, if someone's prepared to use another human being's body as an item to be bought and sold, they forfeit all consumer rights; it's buyer beware in those circumstances. But then you have to suspect that a man who winds up in bed with a transsexual in a country so famous for them is – subconsciously at least – wanting to. That doesn't mean he's gay. More likely, he just doesn't like women. A lot of men fancy women but don't actually like them. Their ideal woman would be one who's been hollowed out and stuffed with a man. But now I'm sounding like a serial killer, and of course *kathoey* don't just look female, they *feel* female, emotionally. I mean, I have no inside knowledge. Let's move on.

Males who become like females, in clothing and increasingly by medical treatment, exist in large numbers all over Asia and have done for centuries. Some people think of Eastern cultures as being backward, but Norfolk has made a lot of progress in recent years, and fewer people are now born with the feet of aquatic birds.

The First Words of Famous People . . .

Oedipus / I'll be back.

Sting / Da Doo Doo Doo Da Da Da Da.

Philip Larkin / Oh, thanks for nothing.

Updated sayings . . .

An Englishman's home is . . . unaffordable.

Love thy neighbour as . . . someone has to feed the cat when you're away.

Don't cut off your nose to . . . make it easier to put your jumper on, just get a cardie.

Familiarity breeds . . . in East Anglia.

Jeremy by Andy Hamilton

One of the great sadnesses of writing these reflections about Jeremy is that I won't get to hear him complain about them.

Jeremy didn't have much time for memorial tributes or eulogies, and I have a distinct memory of him telling a News Quiz *audience that, when he died, he wanted his ashes to be scattered over the mourners. Jeremy didn't gush. Gushing was one of the things he moaned about.*

Usually, people who moan are a bit of a drain, aren't they. They can be quite exhausting. But when Jeremy complained, somehow it was invigorating. You buckled up your seatbelt, sat back in delight, and got ready to be taken on a wonderful, life-affirming ride. You would hear that excitement and anticipation in audiences whenever they realised that he was about to go off on one of his trademark rants. They even lapped it up when he was laying into them. Often, during recordings of The News Quiz, *he would berate the studio audience and tell them that they were a bunch of geriatric, middle-class freeloaders, and the more he did it, the more they would laugh.*

Not many performers could risk characterising their audience like that, but Jeremy could, because they loved him, unreservedly. You would feel the wave of affection that greeted him the moment he was introduced onto the stage. They understood how good he was, and they were looking forward to spending a couple of hours in his company.

From a professional perspective, I was always a little bit in awe of Jeremy, because he had brilliant technique and a perfect all-round game. There was nothing he couldn't do. He could summon up comic invective, surrealist fantasy, brilliant one-liners, pin-sharp mimicry and, along with Linda Smith, he was the most inspired and instant ad-libber that I've ever worked with. And all of these talents sprang from the instinctive playfulness at the heart of Jeremy's personality.

He hated unfairness: this informed his whole life and gave his material such drive and direction. But it was his playfulness that gave it colour. This extraordinary mix of purpose, precision, and imagination enabled him to develop arguments with total conviction, and yet be joyfully funny at every point along the way. He was a unique comic voice. And they are always greatly missed, because they are irreplaceable.

I find myself thinking about Jeremy every time that I do a radio show now. I miss the conversations we would have on stage, in the green room, or in the pub, when we would laugh at how ridiculous everything is. I miss the gossip, the accents, and the impressions of Wilfrid Hyde-White. Most of all, I miss his giggle. He had a wonderfully mischievous giggle, that, for some reason, always reminded me of Muttley the dog in Wacky Races.

This piece has, I realise, started to teeter on the edge of 'gush' and Jeremy would take the piss out of me for doing that. And I wish I could hear him do it.

7

Jeremy Hardy Speaks About . . .

Being a Comedian

*'Don't clap, that means you agree
but it's not very funny.'*

Good evening, my name's Jeremy Hardy . . .

Aspects of the Fringe, 1985

Well, you're probably thinking I'm being a bit gloomy for a compère. I'm not really jollying you up that much, but I have been a little bit depressed, because I've seen a lot of comics on the Fringe and I've found that some people have been nicking my material. And that hurts, frankly. I believe that sometimes there are innocent accidents, whereby somebody has coincidentally stumbled upon the same idea; they've developed it in parallel to me, they've never seen me before and the whole thing's been a ghastly embarrassing coincidence, no plagiarism intended, I mean I can believe that. But when I see another comedian get on stage and say 'Hello, my name's Jeremy Hardy', I smell a rat . . .

* * *

Early Stand-up Set, The Cabaret Upstairs, 1985

Performing's in my blood. My grandfather actually was a seal.

* * *

Jeremy Hardy Speaks to the Nation, 1993

You know what people who listen to the radio are like. They all sit there naked with balaclavas on, waiting for something to phone in and complain about.

* * *

Jeremy Hardy Speaks to the Nation, 2010

When I started to research my family tree in order to research my bestselling but largely unread book, my dad advised that I should 'get on the programme'. I thought he meant rehab, but he was referring to the television programme in which all the research is done for you and all you have to do is to say 'Gosh' to affect surprise that an ancestor's name was written down somewhere.

Now I'm not enough of a celebrity to be on that show. If I were to be asked, it would be because some people in TV imagine that every comedian is necessarily someone that people have heard of. And I would hate to be on a programme called *Who Do You Think You Are?* with most viewers thinking, 'Well Who Is He?' I'm in that infuriating category described by my friend Mark Steel as 'slightly successful'. This means that quite a lot of people recognise me, but don't know why. If you are properly famous, like Nelson Mandela or Antony Worrall Thompson, people know exactly who you are. They presumably say things like –

This is such a great honour, Mr Mandela, and such a coincidence because I just happen to be rereading *Long Walk to Freedom* at the moment – I don't suppose you could please sign it for me?

and

Oi, Thompson, you fat weirdo, make my dinner!

But to me, people say things like –

Are you a comedian?

Not when I'm on stage, mercifully . . . well sometimes, but in the street. Far worse is –

Are you on telly?

I haven't yet been rude enough to say, 'No, I'm really here.' I just sullenly reply, 'Sometimes.' Then they ask -

So what have you been on?

And I think, I don't know, why is it my responsibility?

But I say, 'Well, I was on a *QI*', and they say –

No it wasn't that.

So I say, maybe it was *Grumpy Old Men* and they say –

No it wasn't that.

And I want to say, 'Look, why does it even matter? I obviously made very little impression on you. You can't remember my name or the name of the programme. All you can remember is that a television was in some way involved. So why do you care? Lots of people are on TV. *You* could get on. You could, you could get on *Jeremy Kyle* if you lost some teeth and slept with your mother's stepbrother.'

Let me give you an example of the status of semi-success. I once did a one-man show for the BBC, recorded at the famous Theatre Royal, Stratford, in east London. On the day of the recording, a car was sent for me, a black taxi driven by an old East End Jewish cabbie. The conversation went as follows –

CABBIE: It's Jeremy, isn't it?

ME: That's right.

CABBIE: Sorry, I don't know the name.

ME: That's okay.

CABBIE: I hope you're not offended.

ME: No.

CABBIE: Only sometimes people get offended.

ME: It's fine, honestly.

CABBIE: They say, 'Don't you know who I am?' and I say, 'I'm a cab driver. All day I'm in a cab. I get home, I have my dinner, I sit down in front of the TV and I'm asleep before I find out who anyone is.' You might be the biggest star in the West End, Jeremy. The fact that I don't know who you are means nothing. You might be top of the bill at the Palladium and meet the Queen, I still won't have heard of you, so I hope you're not offended.

ME: No.

CABBIE: Because a lot of people are.

ME: I'm not, really.

CABBIE: Good. Because I wouldn't want you to be offended.

ME: No.

CABBIE: Only . . . how are you going to sell tickets for tonight when no one knows who you are?

* * *

Jeremy Hardy Feels It, 2017

I do get feedback from audience members, not all of it wholly reassuring. It's no help when people offer compliments such as, 'How do you remember all that?' Is that it? Is that your only comment? Because it's my job, that's how. The same reason bus drivers don't say, 'Am I supposed to be stopping from time to time? I seem to have covered a lot of ground very quickly today . . . where's everybody else?'

Or sometimes people plainly haven't enjoyed a show but are trying to be polite: 'Well, that was informative. Course, you're not really trying to be laugh-out-loud funny, are you?' Oh God *no*, perish the thought, not at all. I hate that. I much prefer the mirthless, silent chuckle of the academic who gets a physics joke at a TED Talk. I can't *bear* to see people wiping tears from their eyes, except when I've lobbed gas canisters into the audience to bring them under control because they were enjoying themselves too much.

* * *

MAP Comedy Night, Feb 2017

Some comedy fans just want the stuff about how hard it is to find the end of the cling film. I'd rather be doing that, to be honest. But sadly I've been cast a bum steer in life because I'm a political comedian. And it's a miserable time to be a political comedian. I keep trying to give up, I keep getting dragged back. People say, 'Oh it must be good for you. Trump must be good for you comics.' But you know what, I think an untrammelled expanding Israeli state is a high price to pay for some fake tan gags really.

* * *

Jeremy Hardy Feels It, 2017

So, is stand-up frightening? Yes, inasmuch as there is always the possibility of failure. Humiliation. Because the rejection is not just a rejection of your labours, but you personally. You can't 'make good'. You can't knock a few quid off so the customer is satisfied. If the audience sits in stony silence, you can't say, 'Yeah well, they were like that when I found them', or 'They were a lot more work than I was expecting'. You can't say your progress was held up by the discovery of ancient skeletons just below where you were working, unless you're onstage in Eastbourne.

The Uxbridge English Dictionary

Rambling / Sheep jewellery

Shambolic / False testicle

Soya Milk / Looked in your fridge

Tissues / Important matters in Yorkshire

Toils / What Brummies have on their roofs

Trump / Noisy, noxious emission from an arse

Uganda / Go and have a look

Unfettered / A Greek salad with the cheese taken out

Urethra / A soul singer who takes the piss

Ventricle / Diagram explaining bladder weakness.

Jeremy by Hugo Rifkind

I worked with Jeremy for a little bit over a decade on The News Quiz. *We did six or seven shows together a year, maybe more, and afterwards we'd usually go to the Yorkshire Grey for a pint or two. That's a lot of shows, and a lot of pints.*

He was very good to me when I started out. A mentor, really. The first time I went on stage with him I was nervous and terrified, right up until the point I told a story about nearly being killed by a giraffe and he laughed. 'My God', I thought, 'I can make Jeremy Hardy laugh. It's all going to be okay'. For a time, I basically considered myself to be the disappointing and frankly inexplicable radio lovechild of him and Sandi Toksvig. Which would make both of them feel very squeamish. And maybe you, too. And, indeed, also me.

For me, Jeremy, wasn't quite a comedian with a political edge. Rather, he was a political activist who was also an absolutely peerless and professional stand-up – as in, his humour was political, but the joke always came first. Some political comedians will, in a friendly room, go for the clap rather than the laugh. Jeremy would never have done that. When other people did it, he despised it. He once said to me 'If you don't have a joke, shut the fuck up. No one came here to find out what you think'.

When we weren't on stage, pretty much all we talked about

was politics. We'd talk about politics in the pub. We'd talk about politics on the phone. He'd send me those long emails that I'd imagine he sent to everyone, where you'd think, 'mate, use a paragraph break once in a while, it wouldn't kill you'. And I'd reply, and we'd fix the world, and the next time we were in the pub we'd unpick it again. We came from very different places politically; he was off in what I thought of as the further bits of the Left, and fervently pro-Palestine. I was meandering around nearer the middle, and forever fretting about great aunts in Tel Aviv. Somehow, though, we never actually argued. Although that doesn't quite capture the magic of it. More accurately, once we'd spoken for about 60 seconds or so, we hardly ever seemed to disagree.

Jeremy used to joke that he had been a supporter of the Labour party all his life, with a brief hiatus between 1983 and 2015. When he told me in 2015 that he'd rejoined the Labour party to vote in the leadership election for Jeremy Corbyn, I told him that I had, too, but to vote against him. And Jeremy being Jeremy, he approved of that, utterly. A little bit after that he was barred from the Labour party as an entryist, and I wasn't, and perhaps he didn't approve of that quite so much.

He got his own back very shortly afterwards by going on the Today *programme and contrasting my situation to his own, which of course involved him announcing, on air, that I'd joined the Labour party. Or, as I put it at the time, 'outing me to my dad'. A little bit after that we met up the Labour Party Conference. I guess they'd let him in by then. I took him to various centrist media parties, where he was very well* behaved and only mentioned Iraq a little. And then, once they'd all ended, he took me to the Momentum party. Arriving with him was like turning up at the Brit Awards with Mick Jagger. We drank Red Stripe and he knew almost everybody. I suppose I was a little worried he might be ashamed of me: a wibbly centrist who wrote for The Times and the Spectator, whose dad had been a Tory MP. But of course, that wasn't him at all.

I know this might sound strange but since Jeremy died, I've tried to keep him alive. I've done this by trying to recreate the political friendship I had with Jeremy, with other people with whom I might think I'd disagree. Because, thinking back, he wasn't just the funniest person I've ever met. He was an antidote to the kind of political times we find ourselves in now. Where if you don't agree with somebody straightaway – if you don't agree on the headline, or on a Twitter summary, or a slogan, even – then that's it, it's over, you're enemies. He didn't do that. And since then, when I write, even when I tweet, I sometimes feel him standing over my shoulder, telling me not to behave like that. I don't always manage it. Frankly, I sometimes wish he could just help with the jokes instead. But he's there, and he always will be, and how lucky I am that he is.

8

Jeremy Hardy Speaks About . . .

Getting Older

'Well. How do we live life to the full?
At the age of forty-three, I have decided to
live each day as though it were my last,
so I lie in bed all day, slipping in
and out of consciousness.'

Reaching Middle-Age

Jeremy Hardy Speaks to the Nation, 1994

As we've seen, fashion goes round and round. And the same criticisms about the younger generation have been voiced for generations. But for the first time in history, these criticisms are actually true. Their music is synthetic rubbish, their clothes look ridiculous and I pay taxes.

In some ways, however, one feels sorry for the young. Again, this is partly because of being older. I want to go up to fifteen-year-olds standing around every Saturday by the fountains in shopping precincts and say, 'I've done that, and believe me, nothing happens.' But nothing alienates the young more than attempts by their elders to understand them – isn't that right, kids? When I was a young slip of a tearaway, your mum saying 'I like your trousers, they're very snazzy' was enough to make you burn them.

And the old are the last people who should be trying to steer the young onto the right path. Which is why government campaigns about drugs and smoking have no effect. It doesn't work saying to a sixteen-year-old crack addict, 'You don't want to go messing about with that gut-rot – why don't you go and build yourself a treehouse?' If you want to put a teenager off doing something it's best to tell them to do it or make it part of the national curriculum. Then you'll find kids trying to get off drugs by forgetting their kit.

But a recent suppressed Home Office document did recommend that cannabis be decriminalised and raves be licensed by local authorities. Here is an extract from the report:

REPORTER (FIFTIES VOICE): These rave-style discotheques are very much the happening thing with the up-to-the-minute crowd, and look set to take the place of skiffle and coffee bars. One must not diss the ravers by driving their activities underground, and if a puff of weed helps the kids to get down to the hardcore hit parade then we say, 'It's only rock and roll.'

What the civil servants missed was that raves are riddled not with cannabis but with ecstasy, a drug that can lead to soft drinks.

There are other things about the youth culture which are worrying. There has been much controversy about the dispensing of condoms to the under-sixteens. Part of me says, 'If it takes the risks out of underage sex, it's a good thing.' While part of me says, 'The lucky little bastards, when I was under sixteen, sex with a condom was sex with a condom – nobody else was involved.'

* * *

Jeremy Hardy Speaks to the Nation, 2003

Although we buy fewer *clothes* in shops as we get older, we still manage to spend the whole weekend shopping. Sundays we used to relax. Bit of worship maybe, sacrifice a leg of lamb, and then watch *The Cruel Sea*. Now we go to Homebase and B&Q. And there's an important point of principle here, which is that you shouldn't do DIY at all because it's scabbing. That's skilled, two-sugars-please, City & Guilds trades-persons work, and you're scabbing. If you truly, absolutely have to do something yourself, there are shops open Monday to Saturday. Real builders' merchants and hardware stores are never open on a Sunday. And they are magic kingdoms where wise and helpful people will seek out anything you need and there's smoke coming out the back and a faint whiff of opium and if I need a Rawlplug that enables me to screw an elephant to a Ryvita, they will find you one or, failing that, suggest an ostensibly competing store, saying, 'Ask for Tony', in a way that suggests a fraternity bordering on organised crime. In fact, it's time the brotherhood closed down the big DIY stores completely. By making them an offer they can't assemble.

* * *

Jeremy Hardy Speaks to the Nation, 2003

Shopping isn't actually very relaxing. Especially once we are at an age when people aren't sure whether we're shopping for ourselves or our children. I actually like Topshop, but if I buy stuff for myself people assume I'm shopping for a fat teenager and if I buy stuff for my daughter they assume I'm a skateboarding transvestite who's too old to read the sizes on the label.

* * *

Jeremy Hardy Speaks to the Nation, 2003

What steps can we actually take to hold on to our looks? An issue that confronts men such as Sir Elton John is what to do about hair loss. Obviously, some people are slightly sensitive about this unsightly and ridiculous disfigurement but there's really no way of confronting it with any dignity. Elton John is one of the richest people in the country, able to pay for treatment that is more complex, intricate and labour-intensive than the Bayeux Tapestry. Whole orders of nuns have been murdered to supply the hair. But it still looks like a nylon joke shop imitation of the hairstyle of a six-year-old whose very old mother cuts it while he fails to sit still on a kitchen stool.

* * *

Jeremy Hardy Feels It, 2017

I try to be proactive in arresting decrepitude. That's why I exercise. But the staff and the punters at the gym don't realise that people like me aren't trying to build a body, just maintain one. Trying to postpone the day when we have to go and live in a place where a nice man brings us owls to look at twice a year.

I don't feel part of the changing room brotherhood. I

don't want to chat. Certainly not with a man who's using a hairdryer on his pubes. And don't tell me you've been 'training'. You're not *training*, you're picking heavy things up and putting them down again. If you were training, you would have learned something by now. And you might have made your body look like a balloon animal but that's got nothing to do with strength. A fat builder with a beer gut and sausage fingers could snap your head off with one pudgy hand.

There's a guy at the gym who hangs around in the changing room a lot, striking up conversations. Straight away he alienated me by calling me 'Buddy', which annoyed me because he's not American, it's not the 1930s, and I must be older than his dad. If you're twenty, you call me Mister or Wise One. As I've said, I don't like the generation gap; that's why I want it bridged with deference and wonder.

Anyway, he always asks me how my workout was, and it was only after our third encounter that he produced a business card, revealing that he's a personal trainer. That's why he lurks in changing rooms, trying to groom old unhealthy men; luring us into his web of kettle-bells. And I want to say, 'Look, Tyrone, I'm not working out. I'm just trying to salvage enough remaining fragments of cartilage to keep managing the stairs at home. At my age, cardio isn't a fat-burning regime, it's a department.'

* * *

Jeremy Hardy Speaks to the Nation, 2013

It takes confidence to seek power, or keep it, or to challenge it. So confidence *is* power. Believing you can change the world doesn't mean you will, but if you don't believe you can, you won't, unless by accident. And then it's most likely you'll change it for the worse, because you're a clumsy lab technician at Porton Down or a White House cleaner with a fascination for what buttons do.

But let's say you actively want to change the world for the better. It's common for older people to say things like,

OLD FART: When I was young I thought I could change the world like these climate warming activists. But as you get older and wiser, you realise you can't change the world.

One thing I'm certain of is that as we get older, we don't get wiser, we get knackered. Or we get complacent. The reason activists are often young is not naivety. They're at their intellectual peak; and what makes them so active is that they've got so much more energy, so much more passion and so much more time. Their lives are less full of rubbish. They don't spend their weekends in Pelmet Warehouse or World of Grouting. You might watch the news and see people marching, and say,

PERSON: What's the point? It's not going to make any difference.

But how did you spend *your* Saturday? What difference did you make? Choose your new cupboard handles, did you? Think your new kitchen will make you happy? Yes, well done, you've really opened it out. It's made *such* a difference, all your guests will say so. Now you'll be able to chat to them while you cook, so the poor starvelings have to wait till ten o'clock to eat because you can't be arsed to have it ready for them when they arrive. They have to sit there for three hours admiring your units. Well done you. It's a great kitchen. But you're still going to die in pain or on morphine. And your legacy – your legacy will be granite-effect worktops for future generations. You sacrificed your youthful radicalism so that they don't have to.

Healthcare

Jeremy Hardy Speaks to the Nation, 2001

JEREMY: People told me it's great being over forty. And what could I say? I couldn't ask, 'Well, how come you look like shite then? Didn't you prefer your old face, the one without the pleats, the one topped with hair?' It is sometimes said that men get better-looking as they get older. This is untrue but is said a lot by women. Women feel an urgent calling to make men feel better about falling apart. For example, Debbie, you've known me since I had a 29-inch waist and thick floppy hair. How would you say I compare today?

DEBBIE: (KINDLY) Well, you've got a 29-inch forehead and thick floppy waist, but those things don't matter. Lots of women find receding hair sexy. And fatness. And prostate trouble.

JEREMY: My brothers, do not listen to her! Baldness is not sexy; it is the absence of hair, hair that was there before and should be there still. Baldness is a disfigurement, a disability warranting medical retirement. It means bits of you are falling off. If you found an ear in your comb you'd mess your pants. Ears, of course, are the only genuine love handles, unlike the folds of fat around the midriff, which a person might grip only to avoid a slapping noise. And Debbie, a few streaks of grey hair are . . . ?

DEBBIE: Errr, distinguished.

JEREMY: Distinguished on the head, perhaps, but it makes the penis look like a badger.

* * *

Jeremy Hardy Feels It, 2017

It's our increased longevity that's putting some of the greatest pressure on public services. Older people accept austerity, saying, 'We need to live within our means', and I think, 'Yeah, you could help by dying within yours'. Not that I want them to. I'm glad people are living longer, but it is expensive. And medical advances mean the NHS has to do more and more things. Every innovation requires new buildings, new equipment, more training for more staff. There'd be no crisis in A&E if no one had invented bandages. They'd just say, 'I'm sorry, there's nothing more we can do. All your blood's falling out. If you could just take this mop and wait by the mortuary, someone will see you in a few minutes.'

* * *

Jeremy Hardy Speaks to the Nation, 2014

Now, I'd like everyone in the audience and all those listening to take part in a mental exercise. Don't be scared; it'll be fun.

Think of a number between one and ten. Any number, doesn't matter what it is. Don't tell anyone else, just hold that number in your head. Now double it. Now add four. Now double it again. Now multiply by the number you first thought of and add six zeroes. That's how the government comes up with figures for benefit fraud and health tourism.

* * *

Musicport, 2016

The human contact level in the NHS is going. If you treat the NHS as a business, then humanity has no role in it. But we need to have time with medical personnel, not only because of their skills and their knowledge, but because of their compassion. You can have a web diagnosis, but if there is anything more dispiriting than showing your arse to a person, it's mooning at a laptop. At least if there's a screen around you, you feel that it's in some way a procedure.

I haven't got a doctor any more; I go to a group practice. When I was a kid the family doctor was an incredibly revered figure, the pillar of a community. Our doctor was Dr Turner and he had this swivel chair that was leather with big wings and metal studs in the back. Dr Turner would sit there with a fag on the go all day. And a glass of scotch. And he'd be shooting up heroin. 'Medical grade, dear boy, help yourself.' Dr Turner was brilliant because he knew four generations of my family. He cared, he thought, he asked questions. You could go back and see him again. He would make time in his schedule and he would have thought about what you said. You could talk about emotional things. You could talk about puberty. You could show him something and say, 'Is this normal?' and he'd say, 'It's repugnant, but sadly normal and will only get worse'. My mum had a bad back – there were no chiropractors and sociopaths in those days – and so he read a book about spine manipulation and he manipulated her spine. Not in a cynical scheming way, he just adjusted her back around a little bit and that helped and it was holistic before anyone had even made up that word.

And now I just rock up at the group practice. I had to have my prostate checked, because if you're a man over fifty you get a choice: you can either have a flu jab or a prostate check. I'm terrified of needles and can't see what goes on behind me, so I thought I'll go in for the prostate check and think of England. Who knows, they might find my keys. So, I went. The doctor was a young woman in her late twenties. She said, 'Would you prefer a male doctor?' and I said 'Frankly, I'm past caring'. Now that wasn't the answer she was hoping for. I didn't get the hint that she wanted to be let off the hook.

Women, you've got to spell things out to men because we are balls-achingly slow creatures. If you are in a relationship with a man and you want it to in any way work, tell us what it is we're supposed to be doing, rather than waiting for us to disappoint you. Don't speak in riddles. 'My first in is in bin juice, but not in Christmas tree lights.' Is this, 'We don't talk any more'?

So, this doctor should have signalled to me what I was supposed to say:

DOCTOR: (WHISPERS) Say 'yes' to this now, Jeremy.
(LOUDER) Would you prefer a male doctor?
JEREMY: Oh, can I have a male doctor please?
DOCTOR: (WHISPERS) Oh thanks, I just had my nails done.

And then she said, 'Would you like a chaperone?' Not unless we're going for a stroll in an Edwardian garden, and I haven't got the bonnet for that.

Getting Older

Jeremy Hardy Speaks to the Nation, 1993

The fact of being an adult can come as quite a shock. I realised that it had started to happen to me when I was watching *Top of the Pops* this year and found myself saying, 'Well, it all sounds the same, doesn't it? There's nothing you can tap your feet to. In the old days we had the Pistols and the Buzzcocks, something with a bit of a tune. But this rap – that's not music, you can't hear the words.'

* * *

Jeremy Hardy Speaks to the Nation, 1997

The important thing to remember is that it's never too late to learn, it just becomes increasingly pointless as you start to forget everything a few minutes after learning it. I used to have a photographic memory; I still do but all the heads are missing now.

These days I spend much of my time confined to one room of my house, not because I can't afford to heat the others but because I can't remember what I've gone into them for.

Why is it that as we get older, we can remember with startling clarity things that happened in our childhood but the only thing we can remember about the present is that we've forgotten something? For example, we can remember vividly that William Hartnell was the first Doctor Who, but we have absolutely no idea who the present one is. It could be anyone from Alan Rickman to Ant and Dec. What happens to the memory, and who are you anyway? The answer to that question is written on the back of a till receipt in the pocket of my other trousers.

* * *

Jeremy Hardy Speaks to the Nation, 2003

Unfortunately, the government is not content with the fact that the British work the longest hours in Europe. It looks as though most of us are going to have to keep working well past sixty-five. We'll finally have time to relax when we have just enough strength to dissolve a Werther's Original if we keep our mouths closed and the heating up full.

* * *

Jeremy Hardy Feels It, 2017

It's true to say that as we get older we are likely to become fearful of change. It's natural to look backwards. We get to an age when we imagine that the world was a much better place when we were young. But it wasn't. It was we who were better, because we weren't about to die, and we could make it to the lavatory on time.

Perhaps that's why Take Back Control was such a powerful slogan. People thought they might be able to master their bladder weakness if only they could get foreign fishing vessels out of their waters. And the rate of change of all kinds has accelerated dramatically in the last century. So, the elderly are often cast as intolerant and easily offended, and some people claim to want to shield older people from things that might offend them.

This is Nigel Farage's get-out when it comes to his own illiberalism. Asked for his views on homosexuality, he says it makes older people uncomfortable. Well, perhaps they're doing it too much. But this has become a stock response from him. When asked for his views on women breastfeeding in public, he said it could make older people awkward and embarrassed. I just think, what's your problem with old people, Nigel? Why do you attribute mimsy shockability and reactionary views to a generation that survived the Great Depression and the Second World War and out of those ashes built a socialised medical system and a welfare state?

My late mother was born in 1924. My dad was born in 1926. Both their fathers were in the First World War, and both traumatised as a result. Dad's dad was made to be a sniper, creeping out into no-man's-land with a Lee–Enfield to kill Germans. After the war he was an alcoholic and gambling addict. Mum's dad was a pacifist so he joined the Medical Corps as a nurse. His horse-drawn ambulance was shelled, and Grandpa was buried alive and left permanently deaf. In the 1930s both men lost their jobs and the families were plunged into poverty. By the late thirties they're back on their feet and it's the Second World War. Both families were bombed out. My mum, at the age of seventeen, became an Air Raid Patrol Warden in London during the Blitz. Her brother was a pilot who was shot down and killed. After the war, she met my father and they were so skint that their first home together was a tiny caravan on a farm. Then they got a prefab. Then they got their first council house. And my mother bore five children in eight years, all in social housing, all of us breastfed. She wouldn't have been shocked by a gang of Hells Angels pleasuring each other in a National Trust tea-room, let alone a woman naturally feeding her own baby!

And when Mum was too old to be cared for by us, who looked after her then? Immigrants, that's who, Nigel. Bloody immigrants coming over here, looking after our old people. Makes you sick, doesn't it? People of every nationality, race, colour and creed. People of all ages and different sexual persuasions. I worried for the new gay, Chinese male nurse when he started, because it's quite a conservative area, but do you know what? The old ladies in that home loved him, because he loved them. 'Hello, darling, I come to change your pad!' What's not to like about that?

And would my father have been shocked by the sight of a stranger feeding her baby? Well, not long after she died, he also had to go in somewhere, where he was cared for by a similar array of humankind, and in his last months he suffered with good grace the indignity of being helped in and out of his clothes by young women a quarter of his age, and if any one of them had popped a tit out for any reason he'd have been delighted.

* * *

Laugh for Freedom, June 2017

Many of my friends are leaving London to move to somewhere like Bishop's Stortford and they say, 'Oh, it's only 40 minutes from London', and I think, London is *no* minutes from London, you idiot!

* * *

The News Quiz, 2018

People don't *know* stuff any more. Do you remember, we used to all know what leaves go with what trees? I mean not that you'd try and put them back on. I mean, my late father would be appalled by my inability to identify British bird life by its plumage.

I was walking on a beach in Orkney earlier this year, and there was this big weird duck in the sea, and there was this dogwalker – I assume she was a dogwalker, she had a small bag of shit – strangely, no dog – but anyway – I didn't ask; it wasn't my business . . . I assure you, it wasn't my business. Anyway – I said, 'Excuse me, do you know the name of that?' and she said, 'That's an eider.' And do you know, I'd never put it together that an eider was a kind of bird, and that the 'eiderdown' we used to sleep under was stuffed with its down – and, apparently, a 'duvet' is a kind of grebe. I did know the difference between a cormorant and a shag cos you can get into a lot of trouble if you get that wrong.

* * *

Jeremy Hardy Feels It, 2017

Of course, even if our basic needs are comfortably met, it's unlikely there's nothing else we'll hope for materially. I'd *like* a bigger home, with a proper garden. And my own office, with a turntable and all my records in it. And some career memorabilia that wouldn't be vain because it would only be me that goes in there. And a guest room. With the rest of my career memorabilia in it so it doesn't look too spartan. And I'd take a year off to learn languages and travel. And once I upscale from the Co-op and Sainsbury's to Waitrose and the farmers' market, there's no limit to what I could get through. I could probably do a grand a week on cheese.

And I can't be completely pessimistic about the possibility of being considerably richer because I do the Euromillions. Which demonstrates hope. But knowing my luck, the day *I* win the Euromillions will be the draw immediately after someone's won a hundred million pounds and the jackpot drops right back down to 15 million. What use is 15 million quid? And the bloke who wins a hundred million says he plans to give half of it away to a slug sanctuary, extend his conservatory, go on the trip of a lifetime to Durham Cathedral and put the rest away for a rainy day. Rainy day? He could roof the bloody country and still have enough left over to keep a fridge full of Veuve Clicquot in every room, but what does *he* do with champagne? He sprays it over the front lawn for the local paper to photograph because he once saw Emerson Fittipaldi do that on *Grandstand* and always liked the idea. And he'd never bought a Lottery ticket before. It was his first time. In fact, he only bought this one by mistake. He actually asked the man in the shop for 'A lot of Tic Tacs' but was misheard. The stupid, mumbling, undeserving bastard.

Now you might say you don't think I'm actually *hoping* to win the Euromillions, because hope suggests some degree of likelihood and the odds are such that buying tickets with the aim of winning the Euromillions could hardly be considered financial planning. But when I tell you that that is my *only* financial plan, you'll have some idea of the level on which my mind operates. And so far, I've disproved the idea that, if you really, really want something to happen, it will happen, because I really, really do want it to happen. Ah, but, I have to *believe* it's going to happen. Of course I don't believe it's going to happen. I might be doing a grand a week on tickets but I'm not an idiot.

* * *

Jeremy Hardy Feels It, 2017

I'm a natural pessimist. I'm a little ray of sleet. I'm a glass half-full of someone else's sick type of person. But it's not that I expect bad things to happen to me personally. They will or they won't; I'm quite philosophical about that.

One thing you learn with age is that a lot of what happens is out of our control, although there are exercises that help. Even if you're young, don't believe motivational TED Talkers who tell you that you can be anything and do anything *if you have a dream.* You can't be anything. I'd like to be a kestrel but there are laws of nature – the kind of red tape we won't have to put up with after Brexit. And I do have a dream but it's the one about suddenly realising I'm naked on public transport so what's that got to do with anything?

Inspirational speakers and fridge magnets are obsessed with the individual pursuing their path, with no emphasis on community and solidarity. It's all very well saying, 'Be the change you want to see' but personally I've never found it possible to be a nationalised railway system or a fully funded NHS, even in the most elaborate of role-play exercises.

And the realities of life mean you can't just do anything you want to do. You can't buy a fridge part online without registering and creating a password, of between six and fourteen characters with a mixture of letters and numbers and at least one Viking rune, ideally a password you've never used before and will never remember again. You can't get men's walking boots in a size six, so your choices are to go hiking in pink and purple ladies' boots, start a business specialising in small men's shoes, and then turn it into a feelgood film and successful stage musical, all of which will require crowdfunding that puts your friendships under enormous pressure, or just forget hiking and simply have a brisk twenty-minute walk remembering to swing your arms.

* * *

Jeremy Hardy Speaks to the Nation, 2013

The thing is, my mum had dementia and of course, when someone dies, you have all kinds of regrets. Things you didn't do, things you didn't say. I regret that I never got into a confrontation with a man who said,

AGGRESSIVE MAN: By the time I've finished with you, your own mother won't recognise you.

So I could have said, 'I'm afraid you've rather missed the boat there, dear boy', before starting to run.

* * *

The News Quiz, 2005

Accidents in the home – they filed a report of all the things that cause accidents, but they didn't tell us *how*. Tea-cosies, loofahs, all these things that cause accidents, and it just makes you wonder, because if you ever spend an evening with three or four nurses – I mean, in your dreams – but I mean in a social situation, they will start telling you these apocryphal stories about people who came in to Casualty. And it's like that game where you go, 'My auntie went shopping and she bought a hat' and the next person says, 'My auntie went shopping and she bought a hat and a coat,' and the nurses will say, 'Someone was brought in to Casualty, and we removed from him a billiard cue,' then the next one says, 'Someone was brought in to Casualty, and we removed from him a billiard cue and a light bulb.' And then, 'Someone was brought in to Casualty, and we removed from him a billiard cue, a light bulb and a bust of Napoleon.' On it goes . . . Sometimes it's Beethoven; same sort of head size . . .

But they don't tell you how these loofah accidents happen – 'I fell on my loofah as I was getting out of the bath . . . Sebastian.'

* * *

Jeremy Hardy Feels It, 2017

It's been suggested that older people who voted Leave were messing up the future because they don't have one. But that's unfair. Many of them care passionately about the future of their descendants. And they're fearful for that future. And regrettably, immigration was a key issue for many, because in the last twenty years it has been cast overwhelmingly as a threat. Of course, the movement of people can bring pressures with it, but so can pretty much any change, however welcome. The end of child labour put pressure on school places. Of course it did. If the leaving age was six there would be an abundance of school places. And cheap trainers. And increased life expectancy puts pressure on the NHS. Old people say, 'I don't want to be a burden,' but they're bound to be a burden because all people are at some point. We're a burden when we're young, we're a burden when we're sick, we're a burden when we're old. When old people say 'I don't want to be a burden', what they mean is 'Could you say, "You're not a burden"?' Because you'd never say it unprompted, would you? 'Right, Dad, I've unblocked your toilet; just remember it's not for the cat litter. I've ironed all your pyjamas, because I know you like them like that. Your lunch is in the Tupperware next to the microwave. I'll drop your prescription off on the way to work, pop in at lunchtime to put the washing in the tumble-dryer, and then I'll stop in on my way back from work to put out any fires you've started. I'll see you later. You're not a burden.'

* * *

Jeremy Hardy Feels It, 2017

We need to make space. And if we can accept that, there's more hope that we can enjoy life than there is if we're in a blind flap about trying to pack everything in before it's too late. The number one thing everyone must do before they die is to stop making lists of things they must do before they die, because the great thing about dying is you don't have to do anything. 'Oh, thank God. I'm dead so I don't ever have to stay in the Ice Hotel. It might be one of the Top Ten Things to Do in Sweden, but it sounds bloody stupid. I've lived in places that were freezing and there was nothing romantic about it.'

And if you stop thinking of the world as a playground, you might hope to be part of making it a better place for yourself and other people. I'm not being pious and I'm not saying you should neglect your own happiness, just asking, realistically, what will make you happier: ticking off the hundred best locations for 'wild swimming' – which is what we used to call 'swimming' in the days before someone apparently invented it – or just spreading a little joy?

I prefer to be discreet about the amount I give to charity because it's pathetically small. But most of us care about other people and do altruistic things. And it makes us feel better. More hopeful. I know that people who are *totally* selfless are at risk of being exploited. It gets taken for granted and you get lumbered. As the Bible tells us, when asked by his disciples, 'Lord, how shall we be redeemed?' Jesus says, 'Don't worry, Muggins'll do it.'

On Funerals and Death

Jeremy Hardy Speaks to the Nation, 1993

The purpose of the funeral is not to remember people as they were but to try to remember them in the best possible light and hope that, if there is a heaven, that's where they'll be. We all like to think that the dead have gone to heaven. Children are told that their gran has gone to live with the angels. 'Why do angels live at the crematorium?', the children ask.

We simply can't accept that there is no positive interpretation of death. We have to think of something cheerful to say: it was a lovely service, wasn't it nice so many people came, the flowers were beautiful, the hearse started first time.

At the wake, we all sip sweet sherry and speak of the departed. Our memories of them conflict so wildly with each other that we begin to wonder if we've cremated the same person. Then we start to talk about their passing in such a positive way, you start to wonder why she didn't fall downstairs and break her hip years ago. We lessen the tragedy of mortality by saying what a full life they had. But how does having a full life justify your death? I don't think people should die because they've committed murder, let alone because they had a lot of hobbies.

All this studied cheer only makes death more ghastly. Funerals are depressing, there's no way round it. Even if we held them in the evening and then went on to a club, we all have to face the fact that the death of one more person we know seems to drag each of us one step nearer to the grave. But to be serious for a moment . . . Old people, however, are usually completely philosophical about dying. They tell us not to make any fuss and just leave them round the back for the dustmen. Mind you, they'd be pissed off if we held them to it.

Of course, the funeral is not for the dead but for the living. So maybe we should each put more thought and planning into the kind of funeral we are going to have. Sometimes a person says that they want their funeral not to be an occasion for sadness, but a joyous celebration of their life, with music and laughter and where all their friends can think of the good times and be happy. Personally, I want people's lives torn apart when I go. It's down in my will that I'm to be embalmed and brought out when we have guests. Propped up in the trolley and wheeled round Texas Homecare on the weekend.

* * *

Jeremy Hardy Speaks to the Nation, 2007

JEREMY: Pauline, while I've got you, what's the Irish Catholic attitude to death?

PAULINE: Oh we live for death. Very big on the whole thing. Wakes, open coffins.

JEREMY: What's that about, the open coffin thing?

PAULINE: Keeps the flies off the sausage rolls. Plus, we don't shy away from death like you Protestants.

JEREMY: What's a Protestant funeral like in Ireland?

PAULINE: Miserable. You wouldn't get a sandwich. *We* know how to commemorate people. My granny's funeral was fantastic. The whole town turned out. Everyone came to the house. Shots were fired over the coffin.

JEREMY: Was she in the IRA?

PAULINE: No, a vulture had escaped from Dublin Zoo.

* * *

Jeremy Hardy Feels It, 2017

Let's just run through some advice for those inexperienced in offering condolences. A sad face emoji is inappropriate, as is, 'You OK hun? Awww.'

But traditional expressions aren't much better: 'He had a good innings.' So? We don't reward top cricketers by burying them. And I don't think my parents have gone to a 'better place'. Aldershot Crematorium has nice flower beds, and an okay chapel, but it wouldn't be my choice for a wedding.

Bizarrely, it's next to the lido which is handy for the staff after a hot day's burning.

But I still worry about descending ash. When I was a kid, it was like paddling under a volcano. I haven't been there for fifty years, it must look like Pompeii. People forever frozen in agonised diving poses.

I'm not very good at condolences myself. I'll ask, 'Had your mum been ill for some time?' What difference does it make? If they say yes, I'm hardly going to follow up with, 'Well, that's all right then. That's a win-win isn't it?' But at least I do try not to offer my philosophy of life. Some people are too forthcoming with their beliefs. 'Well, one thing I do know is: this can't be all there is.' Firstly, it doesn't speak well of you that you only know one thing, and, secondly why can't this be all there is? There's loads of it, have you been outside? Assuming you're saying there's a Creator, try telling him you're not satisfied with all there is, and see how he reacts. 'How much do you bloody want? I only had six days. Shut it Darwin, you try fixing the wings on a mosquito; and then all anybody does is complain about it. All there is! Jesus Christ. Sorry son, sorry. I should never have named you after an expletive. Imagine how your sister, Bollocks, feels.'

* * *

Jeremy Hardy Feels It, 2017

We scattered my parents last year. We did cremate them first. We didn't just dismember them and leave them in carrier bags in service station lavatories. We're not weird. They died four years apart but wished to be scattered together, so we had to hold on to Mum until Dad was . . . ready.

The spot they'd chosen was the top of a hill in Hampshire. The trouble is that scattering ashes there is discouraged by the National Trust because of the delicate chemical balance of the soil which sustains a rare wild orchid. But it was my parents' dying wish to endanger a rare wild orchid, so what were we to do? So, my sister transferred our parents into two cardboard tubes of the kind that house bottles of single malt whisky sold in airports, but covered them in brown paper, making them look much more suspicious than if they just said Talisker or Laphroaig. And we walked around this Site of Special Scientific Interest, dodging the National Trust Rangers, in their peculiar, green, paramilitary, Cats Protection League-style uniforms, looking like the SWAT team from a garden centre. And we had to drop handfuls of ash surreptitiously, a bit at a time, and work it into the ground with our feet. It was like *The Great Escape*.

* * *

Jeremy Hardy Speaks to the Nation, 2007

Children are expected to be able to deal with everything that's thrown at them. 'Children are amazingly resilient', we say, because it's easier than imagining what they might be going through. Whose idea was it to make children write and read poems at funerals? Aside from the fact that children's poems are dreadful and they have no idea how to perform them, the poor lad's already got a lot on his plate. Grandma's dead. Isn't that enough? And it's only six months ago the lad lost his hamster, who by the way got a much-sought-after plot in the back garden, unlike Grandma who was roasted and ground like a winceyette-clad coffee bean at the municipal dump for the dead. The boy's had two bereavements in six months, he's lost two important figures in his life and at least one of them gave him toffees, so spend some time with him, and make sure he's okay, don't make him perform doggerel beneath the stern gaze of the souls of the elders.

* * *

Glastonbury Cabaret, 2017

Despite me cheering on the young, a lot of people blamed Brexit on the old, which was unfair. People said, 'Old people are bastards, they don't care about the future because they haven't got one. They thought they'd shite it up because they hate their grandchildren.' I don't think that's what this was. I think Brexit was a confusing mixture of stuff. Young people are afraid of the old, and so they stereotype the old as being xenophobic and homophobic and generally phobic, when it's really *they* – the young people – who are afraid of the old. The prejudice against older people is because old people look like what we're going to look like – young people see an old person as their future. So, it's not quite a vicious cycle, but certainly an aggressively driven mobility scooter.

So I think it's just change that gets difficult as you get older. It's not prejudice, so much, just change. Everything is going too fast. The shop keeps moving the things to different aisles and you get confused and you just want things to slow down. You become nostalgic and that was part of the appeal of Brexit.

I think my parents' generation was a heroic generation. They are gone now, the people who grew up in the twenties and the thirties, but they were heroes. A lot of old people worry about things like immigration because it's always sold as a problem. It puts pressure on hospitals. The immigrants in hospitals are putting pressure on the wounds to stop the bleeding. Cluttering up the place with their stethoscopes. But actually, it is our ageing population that puts the most burden on public spending, not immigration. It's the fact that we're all living too long. It is a thing to be celebrated but it is also the biggest crisis. That's why Theresa May wanted to cap winter fuel payment: she wanted the winter to be her ally in reducing the ageing population.

My parents are both gone now. It's weird, people don't know what to say when you've had a bereavement. We're not very good at addressing death in my white Anglo-Saxon culture. We deal with it very badly. A condolences card says 'with deepest sympathy' and I think, all right, what shall I put inside? 'Lots of love from Katie and Jeremy'? And my partner says, 'You can't put lots of love, it's not Christmas. You could put "thinking of you"? Well, obviously I'm thinking of them, aren't I? I'm obviously thinking of them, or I wouldn't be sending them a card. But I don't know what to say because I haven't got the words. So, you think 'Oh, words cannot express' – if we haven't got the words we're screwed aren't we? What else have we got but words? Semaphore, contemporary dance. You're going to go around somebody's house to offer your condolences. 'I wanted to pay my respects on your father's passing and I've prepared this short piece. I hope that's of some comfort.'

When famous people die, though, everybody directs all the emotion that they're not normally able to channel into grief for somebody they *didn't* know. What's the point in grieving the death of someone famous if you haven't got any of their records? I was so relieved when Lou Reed died I had both *Transformer* and the first Velvet Underground album on vinyl. Conversely, I've got an embarrassingly small number of David Bowie records, but I like to think one Greatest Hits album is the equivalent of everything everybody ever did. It's terrible in south London now, because four years ago we had this mural put up on the side of Morleys Department Store, where Bowie was born, but had we known he was going to die a couple of years later, we would have got someone decent to do it. And now it's become a shrine. People fly in from Tokyo with flowers to come to see this, and it looks like we've got Year 6 to decorate the wall of an adventure playground.

I suppose the thing about death is, if you believe that there is something after, it's going to be comforting. Because nobody thinks that they're going to go to hell. Even people who believe in an afterlife don't think they'll go to hell. Because I suppose there's always the possibility of last-minute repentance. Like one of those left-it-too-late insurance policies they advertise on daytime TV, where there's no medical because it would be pointless. They could do those adverts for repentance: 'Oh, remember when Charlie used to play darts with us? I can't believe he was three years younger than me and now he roasts in the eternal fires of damnation.' 'Well, we all need to think about being cleansed of our transgressions at our time of life.' 'I could never expect absolution, not with my history of venal depravity and extreme violence.' 'That's where you're wrong, British Sinners guarantee forgiveness. There's no retribution and no obligation to make up for all the harm that you've done.' 'Really?' 'Yes, they accepted me and I'm an arms dealer, give them a call.'

* * *

Jeremy Hardy Speaks to the Nation

Death, as Hamlet describes it in *Macbeth Prince of Thieves*, is 'That undiscovered country from whose Bournemouth no traveller returns.'

* * *

Generally, most of us don't want to die. Even if we say we do. 'I wish I was dead' is a terrible thing to say – because it's 'I wish I *were* dead' – conditional tense. I'm sorry but someone's got to uphold these standards.

* * *

I'd rather die with a sword in my hand because I'll be thinking, 'Blimey, bloody thing weighs a ton. I can't wait till this is over.'

* * *

Having said that, I don't especially want to die heroically; but I would quite like to die in a way that causes maximum inconvenience to others. On an escalator or having my blood pressure taken. Or at somebody else's funeral.

* * *

But who knows how to plan their own memorial? I suppose if you work in public relations you've got the skills to design the perfect funeral for yourself, but then no one will go to it anyway.

* * *

I'd rather my funeral were moderated by a vicar than have my corpse exploited by the humanists. However irrational religion might be, I prefer the diffident mumbling of a cleric to the outpourings of people so unrelentingly pleased with themselves. I'm serious about that.

* * *

Early Stand-up Set, The Cabaret Upstairs, 1987

Ultimately in this biz – this biz as we call the biz in showbiz – I'll either fail or die . . . or both. To fail *and* die is very humiliating actually. Because the nice thing people say in showbiz tributes about people who've passed on is, 'Well, of course, the marvellous thing about him was that he was just as funny offstage as he was onstage' – great when you've paid to go and see someone isn't it? You could have just watched them get out of their car.

The Best Joke Ever

Jeremy Hardy Feels It, 2017

Some retired people are fortunate to have had a rewarding career and feel satisfied at the end of it. It must be great to feel you've completed your life's work.

I suppose all comedians dream of one day thinking up the best joke ever. The joke to end all jokes. One night onstage, they crack a joke so good that the whole audience just can't stop laughing. They laugh for hours. And the venue staff are laughing too but it's gone midnight and they need to clear the building, so the police are called, and people are being dragged out and loaded into vans, and a police officer asks what it's all about, and someone tells him the joke, and he can't stop laughing, and he gets on his radio and it goes all around the station and the press get hold of it and the joke goes viral and gets translated into every language and even children who don't really get it know there's something brilliant about it and they laugh and the whole world stops what they were doing and laughs for a week, and then experiences that emptiness and post-euphoric despair you feel when you've laughed so much that you can't laugh any more. And the comic thinks, 'My work here is done.'

But what can he do then? Hide from the world, because every time he goes outside, word gets around that he's the joke guy and people come up and say, 'Tell us another joke, like the one that made us laugh for a week, before the despair set in', and he just can't come up with one as good, and people feel betrayed, and he offers instead to make a documentary series, travelling around the developing world in a hat being impressed by the dignity and manual skills of poor people and how happy they seem, and no one wants him to do those programmes because they're craving a joke; a joke that's as good as his other one; a joke that can never be. That's why, even though I have jokes of that quality, I know that, like nuclear weapons, they can never be used.

Afterword by Katie Barlow

By agreeing to edit this book, it felt like I was accepting that Jeremy has gone and I will never accept that. I will never accept what happened to Jeremy. I'd rather have him here than have to be searching for the right words to say. Jeremy didn't want to die, and this book only exists because he did.

It felt too soon for me to be going through this process, but in the end it kept him close. I found myself laughing out loud one minute and then being moved to tears the next, as his words brought Jeremy to life in such a visceral way. And working on this book afforded me the opportunity to explore Jeremy's work in a way that I hadn't before, re-enforcing and renewing my appreciation of just how brilliant he was. Because he was, he was a comic genius. And the breadth of his work was so vast that I found myself discovering material for the very first time. It made me feel proud. I just wish I could tell him.

This will never be the 'perfect' book. How could it be? It often felt impossible to decide what should be included and what should stay out due to the sheer volume of incredible material to choose from. Jeremy was so many things to so many people and many books could be written about him and all the different facets to his life. So, we decided very early on to make this book a book of Jeremy's work, a sort of anthology if you like. And that way, we could not go wrong.

There were concerns that some of the work I wanted in the book was not funny enough. But the fact was, some of the issues Jeremy chose to write about were simply not funny – though his satirical tone ran throughout everything he wrote – and it was important to me that the whole Jeremy was presented here. The *Guardian* famously sacked Jeremy, accusing him of not being funny enough and using his column as a platform for the socialist alliance. Did Jeremy care? No. He was even funny about that. And in his departing column for the paper wrote:

> The increasingly humorous tone of the news media is not an illuminating, penetrating, invigorating or even uplifting trend, but a whimsical levity calculated to reassure us that nothing really matters any more. A little chuckle and everything's alright again in our postmodern consensual culture. In fact, much of satire, and even much of investigative journalism, has become part of a self-cleaning establishment, a purgative tonic for the belly of the beast. Frankly, I do not see my job as keeping our rulers on their toes; I'd rather see them hanging by their feet.

And it was true of Jeremy to champion causes as and when he felt fit, despite the consequences. The issues were more important to him than his reputation or career. It is said that this is what cost him his fame and fortune, but Jeremy was famous and we were not poor. So, he survived putting his neck on the line for the things he felt passionate about. Years later a critic from the *Guardian* wrote, 'In an ideal world, Jeremy Hardy would be extremely famous, but an ideal world would leave him without most of his best material'. Jeremy would have settled for an ideal world any day and that was something that he strived for tirelessly.

Most people know Jeremy for his comedy. I met him through his activism. We liked to say we met in Bethlehem, but it was in fact at Heathrow airport, on our way to make a film that changed the course of our lives. I didn't know *who he was* when I met him, and he loved that. (Not that he thought he was famous enough for me to have known who he was; he was always self-deprecating and played down his popularity, hilariously pointing out to me he didn't want to go on the programme *Who Do You Think You Are?* with people saying, 'who *is* he?!'). We fell in love under siege and Palestine became an issue that bonded us. The plight of refugees remained a constant in our lives and a constant point of reference in both our work.

But first and foremost, Jeremy was a stand-up comedian and he loved performing. He was devastated once it became clear he would never tour again. He didn't publicise the cancellation of his last tour. He didn't want the press to write about his illness, but one paper put two-and-two together and this is what Jeremy had to say about it:

> I should be flattered that my tour being cancelled was big enough news to make the *Pocklington Post*. I've had a look at the paper

online, and it does seem to struggle for news, so I suppose 'Thing Not Happening After All' is a reasonable headline. And if anything, I'm slightly disappointed by the fact that my whole tour is cancelled and I've pulled out of *The News Quiz* has gone pretty much unnoticed. It doesn't bode well for my forthcoming death.

The truth is, we all noticed and we are all devastated. Jeremy knew he was loved and respected, but he didn't know to what extent. When Jeremy died, the public outpouring of love for him was overwhelming as were the hundreds of letters that blocked our doorway from friends and fans. He'd become Saint Jeremy. I'd been living with a saint. Albeit, one that said c**t a lot. Comedian Arnold Brown referred to Jeremy as a 'mensch', an old Yiddish word meaning a person of the highest integrity and honour.

Jeremy was a committed and loyal friend. He loved people (not everyone) and was truly loved. BBC broadcaster Steve Lamacq said at his memorial, 'Jeremy was a collector of people'. And his memorial attested to this with hundreds of people from the world of comedy, theatre, film, music, politics, activism and academia. Even our fertility consultant attended!

One of the most memorable moments was when Afghan brothers, Ahmad and Jawad, took to the stage. They talked lovingly of Jeremy and how he had become family to them, and how after all his support with their asylum claim, he had died the day it was finally granted. Nine-year-old Ahmad went on to say that he would never forget when describing how he had wanted to 'fly free like a bird' when he was trapped in the

Calais refugee camp, Jeremy had responded with, 'You don't want to be a bird, they shit everywhere!' Ahmad had found this the most hilarious thing and it had tickled him ever since.

People often asked me: what's it like living with a comedian? Are they funny all the time? The truth is, Jeremy *was* funny most of the time – he made light of some of the most inappropriate things and brought playfulness to many awkward family gatherings. I often found myself referenced in jokes on the absurdities of domestic life – but, more often than not, I didn't mind. Living with Jeremy meant you were never allowed to take yourself too seriously. And, of course, I had to share him with his many fans and with the causes he felt most passionate about and for whom he'd frequently do benefits, but he was a brilliant husband and a wonderful father too.

Jeremy claimed that I was his harshest critic, but I saw it as love. In his final diaries he said, 'She's always right!', though of course I wasn't. But the fact that he trusted his work to me after his death left me feeling hugely overwhelmed, re-affirming to me that we had been a great team after all and that he trusted me with his legacy. I feel flattered, humbled, privileged and heartbroken all in one. Only Jeremy could make me feel like that.

And so I hope we have done him proud and that this book encapsulates some of the very best of Jeremy and goes some way towards filling the void that so many of us feel by putting him centre stage again.

I miss you Jeremy, I love you, we all loved you, I loved you more.

Appendix 1: 'Ask Mr Hardy'

Jeremy Hardy Feels It, 2017

So I'm hoping that in the last couple of minutes, we can together create some joy with a question and answer session that I like to call 'Ask Mr Hardy'. Q&A is the sort of thing a Radio 4 demographic absolutely *loves*. Come on, you've all been to book festivals, you love Q&A. It's karaoke for the middle classes. Your chance to shine. Okay, so we have one there. Yeah, go on.

AUDIENCE MEMBER: Out of all the people that you have worked with who has made you laugh the most or was the happiest?

Now you've made me sad. Linda Smith. Thanks for that. But yeah, Linda, bless her. And if she were looking down now she'd be thinking, 'Oh shut it. Stop trying to milk my memory to make yourself look nicer . . . just because you loved me. It wasn't reciprocated, you little berk.' That's what she would think.

* * *

Jeremy Hardy Feels It, 2017

AUDIENCE MEMBER: Can you ask anything?

JEREMY: Well, try and keep it broadly about . . . I mean I don't know much about what kind of plants grow in shade in loamy soils . . .

* * *

Jeremy Hardy Speaks to the Nation, 2003

JEREMY: . . . There's a man in a mauve shirt there . . . is that mauve? Or is it more purple. I'd say mauve. Split the difference. Hideous.

AUDIENCE MEMBER: There was a report out that said that Ryvita was very very bad for you and then there was another report out today that says that Ryvita is actually going to help you from getting cancer. Do you ever take any notice of health scares?

JEREMY: I don't ever really remember being put on a course of Ryvita. I mean, you might use it to make a raft if you're on a desert island. I suppose it would so sap your will to live that you didn't have the enthusiasm for any of the other things that are bad for you. You'd go to reach for a cigarette and you'd just . . . (APATHETIC) oooohhhh. And once you've eaten Ryvita you've got so many holes in your throat you're hardly going to be able to inhale, are you? But I didn't know that. There was just a bizarre accident in the seventies when we got diet-conscious and started eating packing material by mistake.

* * *

AUDIENCE MEMBER: Well, you said you haven't travelled much. So what's the saddest place you've been?

JEREMY: Well, in all honesty, the saddest place I've been is the West Bank in Palestine, which is incredibly – well, the people are so broken, so down. I was there in January. There's a real sense of demoralisation and it's going to be even worse now that people think they're never going to get a state, there's never going to be peace, they're never going to be recognised as a people. But the thing about sadness is that within it there is always hope. That's the great thing about human beings – resilience – and the Palestinians have it in spades.

And they are incredibly hospitable people as well. It is a cliché . . . everywhere in the world we go, 'Oh everyone was very hospitable'; we haven't noticed there's a pattern to this. Hospitality's a really quite normal human phenomenon and it's really only in England where you are lucky to get a biscuit. Palestinians are the most *insanely* hospitable people because even though they've got nothing and their situation is really rubbish, you have to eat a meal every time you go into a Palestinian home. I was there with this charity called Medical Aid for Palestinians and every home we went into we had to eat something. And it was becoming a problem because we were trying to make short films about medical projects and everyone we spoke to made us a meal and you had to eat it, because it was rude not to, and it was delicious but we were stuffed. It was wonderful and terrible at the same time. I've seen lifelong vegans leave a Palestinian home with a whole sheep inside them looking completely traumatised – and yet strangely happy for the first time in so many years.

You did ask.

* * *

Jeremy Hardy Feels It, 2017

AUDIENCE MEMBER: What was your happiest memory as a child?

JEREMY: My happiest moment as a child was driving a combine harvester while Theresa May was running through a field of wheat. Nearly got her as well.

* * *

Jeremy Hardy Feels It, 2018

AUDIENCE MEMBER: Do you ever hope to release your songs on CD?

JEREMY: Do you know what, I don't think a recording can ever really capture the magic of a live singing performance. I could do my singing as a download, but that always sounds rude to me. I'm old school. When people talk about downloading from their laptops I think that just sounds disgusting. But no, for those people who have never heard me sing I have a beautiful singing voice.

* * *

Jeremy Hardy Feels It, 2017

AUDIENCE MEMBER: Have you thought where you would like your ashes scattered?

JEREMY: What I want is to cause massive inconvenience. I don't even want to be cremated. I just want my body tipped out of a moving car on the M6. And then someone's going to feel really guilty even though it wasn't their fault.

* * *

Jeremy Hardy Feels It, 2018

JEREMY: I have had some complaints from listeners that I haven't been answering their questions. That's because I can't hear you at home. Now I know Radio 4 listeners tend to believe that if you speak clearly you should be audible, but there is a matter of being present. So this is a moment for the studio audience because listeners won't be able to see, but we've got about twenty thousand people in here in the O_2 tonight. So if you would like to raise your hand . . .

* * *

Jeremy Hardy Feels It, 2018

JEREMY: Any other questions? There's a hand up there. Either that, or it's a Nazi. Might be that my alt-right fanbase have turned up. Yes, carry on . . .

AUDIENCE MEMBER: Just wanted to ask you what your hopes are for 2018?

JEREMY: Do you know what? I'm not very hopeful for 2018. I give it about a year.

* * *

Jeremy Hardy Feels It, 2018

AUDIENCE MEMBER: Is there any hope?

JEREMY: No, sorry.

AUDIENCE MEMBER: My darling man sitting next to me, we've been together for fifteen years. He's French.

JEREMY: Does he understand what we're saying? No, he doesn't? Okay, good, you can let rip then.

AUDIENCE MEMBER: Should we get married next week? Is there any hope?

JEREMY: You've been together fifteen years and you're not married? Well, just keep at it. I've been with my partner for fifteen years and we're not married. And do you know what? We never go to Ikea. I've still got all my old friends . . . I mean, marriage is like the witness protection scheme: you're living in the suburbs some-where you don't want to be, wearing clothes you don't like, you're not allowed to see anyone you know ever again.

* * *

AUDIENCE MEMBER: As you get older, is there more to fear, or less to fear?

JEREMY: Well, there's less at stake. I mean, yeah, you've got less to lose. There's a time when you worry about things like your guttering and now you see a crack in the plaster and you think 'it will last longer than me'. So, yeah, you stop worrying about all that. But then it's the big one, isn't it? When it all turns out to be true and there is a God and we have to face Him and we just have to hope that He's flawed. Probably is fairly flawed. The coast of Norway is a mess, isn't it? I mean, anyone who's designed that is clearly a shoddy builder.

So, has anyone here seen God? People do. My grandmother claimed to have had a divine revelation once and I said, 'When was it?' and she said, 'Oh, darling, I was just coming out of surgery', and I said, 'Was morphine involved at all?' 'Oh yes, yes, we loved morphine in the thirties'.

So no one's met God? He's about average height, broad shoulders, wiry hair, Jewish looking. You might have just thought it was a publisher, but it was probably God.

Appendix 2: Listeners' Letters
(as written by J. Hardy esq.)

Dear BBC,

I was interested to see advertised free tickets for recordings of *Jeremy Hardy Speaks to the Nation*. I wrote off to the address and the so-called free tickets arrived. Not so free when you consider that my return train ticket from Cardiff Central cost £38.90.

* * *

Dear *Jeremy Hardy Speaks to the Nation*,

Half-hour radio programme this may be, tense psychological thriller it most certainly is not. In vain I waited for the kaleidoscopic montage of flashbacks relating to an actual or imagined slaying and the final and disturbing hypnosis sequence in which the psychiatrist exposes the dwarf Spanish nun in the red dufflecoat as the actual killer.

* * *

Dear BBC,

British Broadcasting Corporation? More like Unbritish Pro-IRA Politically Correct Jewish Conspiracy Corporation. I was disgusted by *Speaks to the Nation*. If people have to use humour to get a laugh, then God help us all.

* * *

Dear BBC,

What is happening to Radio 4? 6.30 on a weekday evening is the time that my family and I sit down to our evening meal and tune in to your broadcasts to hear news of how the war is going. So we were appalled to hear the schoolboy filth and tenth-rate, lavatorial, lowest-common-denominator negro humour of Mr Jeremy Hardy. This kind of junk is bad enough at any time of day but all the more so at a specific time. Doubtless you will think me a meddlesome crank with nothing better to do than write belligerent letters in weird handwriting, but if it's demented to dress as William of Orange and sit in a sandpit all day, then demented I may be.

* * *

Dear BBC,

I am writing to say how disgusted I am. Not about anything in particular, just in general. It's come to something when I can't even turn on my radio without being disgusted. And have you thought about your younger listeners? They disgust me too, with their little bodies and small clothes; what kind of example are they setting their parents?

Major General Sir Agnes Moorehead in Guildford

Acknowledgements

We would like to thank the following people for their contributions to the compilation and production of this book.

Thanks to Lisa Highton, Kate Craigie, Kat Burdon, Amanda Jones, Rosie Gailer and Emma Petfield at Two Roads Books and to Jeremy's agent, Nick Ranceford-Hadley.

Thanks to Paul Bassett Davies and Alice Nutter.

Thank you to everyone at BBC Radio 4 – Julia McKenzie, Richard Morris and Jon Naismith and Megan Landon of Random Entertainment for the News Quiz and Clue clips

Thanks to Joe Norris and Amy Dillon at Off The Kerb and to Jeremy's publicist Amanda Emery.

Thanks to Pozzitive Television, *Guardian*, Musicport, Freedom from Torture and Medical Aid for Palestinians for the use of the extracts. Thanks also to Charlotte Lang, Frank Spencer and Haggis McLeod at The Cabaret Tent, Glastonbury Festival. Thanks, too, to *Red Pepper*, for whom Jeremy was a columnist from 2010 to 2016. The *Red Pepper* extracts from pages 73, 81, 101, 134 and 262 are taken from issues 175, 178, 195, 189 and 198 respectively, and are available at www.redpepper.org.uk/by/jeremyhardy.

And thanks to Jack Dee, Mark Steel, Rory Bremner, Paul

Bassett Davies, Jon Naismith, Graeme Garden, Francesca Martinez, Sandi Toksvig, Victoria Coren Mitchell, Andy Hamilton and Hugo Rifkind for their wonderful reflections.

Thanks also to everybody else in Jeremy's three radio families – Gordon Kennedy, Debbie Isitt, Steve Frost from *Speaks To The Nation*, and Barry Cryer, Tim Brooke-Taylor, Colin Sell and Miles Jupp from *Clue* and *The News Quiz*.

Katie would also like to thank: Warren Lakin, Libby Asher, Debbie Toksvig, Juliet Stevenson, Michaela Loebner, Tim O'Dell, Simon Clarke and Diane Chandler, Joy Hardy, The Hardy Family, Kathryn Williams, Steve, Jennifer and Elizabeth Lamacq, Leila Sansour, Deborah Burton, Fenella Greenfield, Tom Dale, Kim Noble, Jan Rowley, The Barlow family, Catherine Seymour, Olivia Gideon Thomson, Ken Loach, Laura and Jeremy Corbyn, Cynthia and John McDonnell, Clare Gumley, Ariela Cravitz, Stephanie Aungier, Sally Bunkham, Tricia Taylor, Kristina Forrester, Kevin Hely, Kate Higginbottom, Penny Quinton and Ewa Jasiewicz.

And finally, thanks to Idrees Holder Barlow, for giving me a reason to get up in the morning and to Betty Hardy-Sparrow, for making your Dad so proud.

Jeremy by Alice Nutter

I met Jeremy twenty-something years ago when I was still in 'Chumbawamba' and interviewed him for a magazine the band was putting together. He ended up doing some vocals (really well) on a song about Harry Stanley – who was accidentally shot by the police. Jeremy was involved in the campaign to get justice. When I say 'involved' I mean he was the person regularly heading to the post office and doing the shit work. Like the Birmingham Six and Guildford Four, campaigns that Jeremy was part of weren't the most popular of causes, but Jeremy grumpily stuck at stuff because it was the right thing to do. One of the reasons Jeremy Corbyn loved Jeremy so much and vice versa, was that for over thirty years their paths crossed at benefits and campaigns. When Thatcherism attacked the left with a vengeance from the 80s onwards, demonising and discrediting anybody who fought the cruelty of the swing to the right, both Jeremys stayed on the right side of history.

Despite the reputation for being left wing, Jeremy's comedy wasn't 'right on'; he said outrageous things that he got away with because he was so funny. But when it came to arguing for the rights of others, be it present-day austerity, Palestinian Rights or getting the troops out of Ireland, Jeremy was never afraid to be serious and he was in it for the long haul.

He had the same attitude to friendship, once you were Jeremy's friend, you could piss him off and he could piss you off but there was no losing touch, he put the effort in and demanded the same back. And Jeremy could be very demanding when he felt like it but also extraordinarily thoughtful and kind. He never missed a birthday and if I had a play opening he always came, when my Mum and my sister died he trekked up to Leeds each time to be with me. The same when I had a serious illness. And when his Dad died I came down to London to be with him and he gave me a bollocking for not putting enough effort in.

Jeremy claimed to never read anything and I believed him but he somehow had extensive knowledge of more or less everything political, while denying having any. He was naturally smart, he could moan for Britain but he also listened. When his partner, Katie, or one of his friends achieved something he'd proudly tell you about it, or if a friend did something kind for him, he'd relay it, touched. He valued people. I don't think Jeremy was ever interested in politics in an abstract big ideas way, he talked in terms of what injustice and ideologies did to people's lives. He was always on the side of the person getting a raw deal. You can hear it in his comedy: he never punched downwards, never made fun of the powerless or the marginalised, though he frequently complained about how many bloody benefit gigs he'd had to play for them. Holding a torch for what is right can be a drag at times but Jeremy never stopped, I don't think he ever realised that just by keeping on keeping on he was setting an example for the rest of us. His hatred of cruelty, his refusal to believe other people were worthless and his basic democratic attitude to everybody he met, are the raw materials of a new better world. And this old world is so much poorer for not having him in it.